IDA B. WELLS

Born into slavery in 1862, Ida B. Wells went on to become an influential reformer and leader in the African American community. A Southern black woman living in a time when little social power was available to people of her race or gender, Ida B. Wells made an extraordinary impact on American society through her journalism and activism. Best-known for her anti-lynching crusade, which publicly exposed the extralegal killings of African Americans, Wells was also an outspoken advocate for social justice in issues including women's suffrage, education, housing, the legal system, and poor relief.

In this concise biography, Kristina DuRocher introduces students to Wells's life and the historical issues of race, gender, and social reform in the late nineteenth- and early twentieth-century U.S. Supplemented by primary documents including letters, speeches, and newspaper articles by and about Wells, and supported by a robust companion website, this book enables students to understand this fascinating figure and a contested period in American history.

Kristina DuRocher is an Associate Professor of History at Morehead State University, Kentucky.

T0406023

ROUTLEDGE HISTORICAL AMERICANS

SERIES EDITOR: PAUL FINKELMAN

Routledge Historical Americans is a series of short, vibrant biographies that illuminate the lives of Americans who have had an impact on the world. Each book includes a short overview of the person's life and puts that person into historical context through essential primary documents, written both by the subjects and about them. A series website supports the books, containing extra images and documents, links to further research, and where possible, multi-media sources on the subjects. Perfect for including in any course on American History, the books in the Routledge Historical Americans series show the impact everyday people can have on the course of history.

Woody Guthrie: Writing America's Songs
Ronald D. Cohen

Frederick Douglass: Reformer and Statesman
L. Diane Barnes

*Thurgood Marshall: Race, Rights, and the Struggle
for a More Perfect Union*
Charles L. Zelden

Harry S. Truman: The Coming of the Cold War
Nicole L. Anslover

John Winthrop: Founding the City upon a Hill
Michael Parker

John F. Kennedy: The Spirit of Cold War Liberalism
Jason K. Duncan

Bill Clinton: Building a Bridge to the New Millennium
David H. Bennett

Ronald Reagan: Champion of Conservative America
James H. Broussard

Laura Ingalls Wilder: American Writer on the Prairie
Sallie Ketcham

Benjamin Franklin: American Founder, Atlantic Citizen
Nathan R. Kozuskanich

IDA B. WELLS
SOCIAL REFORMER AND ACTIVIST

KRISTINA DUROCHER

Routledge
Taylor & Francis Group

NEW YORK AND LONDON

http://www.routledge.com/cw/historicalamericans

First published 2017
by Routledge
711 Third Avenue, New York, NY 10017

and by Routledge
2 Park Square, Milton Park, Abingdon, Oxon, OX14 4RN

Routledge is an imprint of the Taylor & Francis Group, an informa business

© 2017 Taylor & Francis

The right of Kristina DuRocher to be identified as author of this work has been asserted by her in accordance with sections 77 and 78 of the Copyright, Designs and Patents Act 1988.

Library of Congress Cataloging-in-Publication Data
Names: DuRocher, Kristina.
Title: Ida B. Wells: social reformer and activist / Kristina DuRocher.
Description: New York, NY: Routledge, [2016] | Includes bibliographical
    references.
Identifiers: LCCN 2016005150 | ISBN 9781138786875 (hardback) | ISBN
    9781138786882 (pbk.) | ISBN 9781315767024 (ebook)
Subjects: LCSH: Wells-Barnett, Ida B., 1862–1931. | African American
    women—Biography. | African American women civil rights
    workers—Biography. | African American women social reformers—Biography. |
    African American women journalists—Biography. | Lynching—United
    States—History. | Civil rights workers—United States—Biography. |
    Social reformers—United States—Biography.
Classification: LCC E185.97.W55 D87 2016 | DDC 323.092—dc23
LC record available at http://lccn.loc.gov/2016005150

ISBN: 978-1-138-78687-5 (hbk)
ISBN: 978-1-138-78688-2 (pbk)
ISBN: 978-1-315-76702-4 (ebk)

Typeset in Minion and Scala Sans
by Apex CoVantage, LLC

To my daughter Katie

CONTENTS

ILLUSTRATIONS

ACKNOWLEDGMENTS

I would like to thank the many people who supported my work on this book, especially Scott Davison and Scott McBride, as well as extend a special thank you to my research fellow Chelise Conn. My colleagues, among having many other good qualities, remain essential springboards for ideas, and I appreciate Tom Kiffmeyer, Alana Scott, and Kelly Collinsworth for always lending a listening ear. I am grateful to my husband for his encouragement and understanding. I hope the words of Wells inspire new generations to fight for social justice and speak up against inequality.

PART I

IDA B. WELLS

INTRODUCTION

"The way to Right Wrongs is to turn the Light of Truth upon Them." Ida B. Wells[1]

In 1883, Ida B. Wells, a twenty-one year-old black woman, boarded a train in Memphis, Tennessee to commute to her rural teaching job. On September 15, as on countless other days, she purchased her thirty-eight cent ticket and boarded the first-class car. A little under five feet tall, Wells wore a full-length dress covered by a linen duster with a hat and gloves. She carried a satchel, a newspaper, and a parasol, all trappings of a middle-class traveler.[2] She later recalled in her autobiography that when the train was underway, the conductor, instead of collecting her ticket, "handed it back to me." She remembered thinking to herself, "If he didn't want the ticket I wouldn't bother about it" and resumed reading her newspaper.[3] The conductor continued gathering the remaining passengers' tickets and then returned to her side, informing her that she had to transfer to the other train car. Surprised, Wells reminded the conductor that "the forward car was a smoker."[4]

The smoker car, located directly behind the locomotive, was so-named for the debris and fumes that floated in from the coal-powered engine, making it a dirty, noisy space occupied primarily by male passengers of both races who could ride unencumbered by restrictions on smoking, drinking, or using coarse language. In contrast, the first-class car required passengers to observe a code of behavior in order to protect its respectable female passengers, leading to its common name, the "ladies" car. Wells, who had purchased a first-class ticket, refused to leave her seat and relocate to the smoker car, an inappropriate place for any reputable woman. While the exchange started out as a polite request, the encounter quickly escalated after she informed the conductor, "as I was in the ladies' car, I proposed to stay," prompting him to seize her baggage and proceed to the smoker car in an effort to compel her to follow.[5] When she remained seated, he returned and grabbed her arm, endeavoring to drag her out of the car. Wells reacted by biting him on the back of his hand. When he drew back, she locked her feet under the seat in front of her to brace against any further efforts to remove her. As "he had already been badly bitten," the conductor retreated. He soon returned, accompanied by a baggage worker, and both men seized Wells. At this point, one may wonder about the other train-car inhabitants. What did they think of the employees manhandling a well-dressed teacher? In response to her struggle, the white women and men in the car repositioned themselves in order to gain a better view. "Some of them," Wells recalled, "even stood on the seats" and applauded the men for their efforts.[6]

After the employees bodily removed her from the first-class compartment, Wells declared that she would rather "get off the train" than ride in the smoker car. To the two Chesapeake, Ohio, Southwestern Railroad Company attendants, this was an acceptable option. When the train paused, Wells disembarked. Although she had not been physically hurt during the confrontation, the men's rough handling had torn her clothing.[7] On the side of the tracks, still clutching her train ticket in her hand, she determined to fight her treatment. After returning to Memphis, she contacted an African American lawyer who attended her church, Thomas Cassells, and initiated a lawsuit using an 1881 Tennessee state law requiring separate first-class accommodations for each race as the basis for her case.[8]

Wells's legal complaint was just the beginning of her lifelong dedication to determinedly and vocally fight for social justice in every place she encountered inequality. Wells's lawsuit introduced her to the world of newspaper publishing, where she shared her perspective on the myriad issues facing African Americans and women, and as her point of view gained widespread recognition she earned the designation of "Princess of the Press." An experience with racial violence led her to confront the emerging system of white supremacy in the South, and she single-handedly launched an international campaign that revealed the motives behind the increasingly widespread practice of lynching. Despite threats of deadly violence, she continued to spread her message by publishing her findings and publically lecturing across the nation and in England.

Her reform work gained her allies in Frederick Douglass, Jane Addams, and William Edward Burghardt Du Bois, while she publically opposed Booker T. Washington and temperance leader Frances Willard. She founded and participated in numerous organizations to combat social disparity and organize for political power. She created the Alpha Suffrage Club to advocate for black women's right to vote and participated in the national women's suffrage movement. She established the Negro Fellowship League to educate and support urban black men and fight issues of poverty in Chicago, and was among the founders of the National Association for the Advancement of Colored People (NAACP). She started the first black kindergarten, fought several legal battles for the fair treatment of African Americans within the judicial system, and became the first black female probation officer in Chicago, applying her salary to support these efforts.

Wells returned to her journalistic roots in the early twentieth century, investigating and publishing tracts on race riots in Missouri, Illinois, and Arkansas. Her protests against the government's treatment of black soldiers during World War I earned her a visit from the Secret Service and the label of a "subversive."[9] Undaunted, Wells enlisted black women to participate in politics during the 1920s, when Prohibition, corruption, and mobsters made such attempts a precarious enterprise. In 1930, she ran for an Illinois State Senate and lost, but this defeat only increased her resolve. Unfortunately, she died from kidney failure the following year. During her life, Wells, as a black middle-class woman, participated in almost every major social reform movement from 1880 to 1930 at the local, regional, or national level.

Wells lived in a rapidly evolving world, and the racial, gendered, sexual, and political mores shifted greatly during her lifetime. Her story is of a woman in the front lines of a society facing the challenges of a modern world, one that contained massive inequalities she fought to correct. Wells recognized, however, that her battles were part of a larger war. She began the last chapter of her unfinished autobiography with the words, "Eternal vigilance is the price of liberty," quoting Wendell Phillips's 1852 speech to the Massachusetts Anti-Slavery Society. Phillips, an abolitionist, told his audience, "Eternal vigilance is the price of liberty; power is ever stealing from the many to the few." To prevent an unequal balance of power, the orator continued, required "continued oversight" and "unintermitted [sic] agitation" lest "liberty be smothered."[10] Using his words, Wells connected her attempts to Phillips, and her efforts for social equality as a fight for liberty. She believed that social change required agitation and that every right gained needed protection, lest those in power usurp it. Wells committed herself to these pursuits, and with these words, reminded her readers of the need to be ever vigilant in ensuring that civil liberties apply equally to all in order to end social injustice.[11]

NOTES

1   "Miss Ida B. Wells, A Lecture," *Washington Bee*, October 22, 1892.
2   Paula Giddings, *Ida: A Sword among Lions, Ida B. Wells and the Campaign against Lynching* (New York: HarperCollins Publishers, 2008), 61; James West Davidson, *"They Say": Ida B. Wells and the Reconstruction of Race* (New York: Oxford University Press, 2007), 69.

3   Ida B. Wells, *Crusade for Justice: The Autobiography of Ida B. Wells*, ed. Alfreda M. Duster (Chicago: The University Press of Chicago, 1970), 18.

4   Wells, *Crusade for Justice*, 18.

5   Davidson, 70.

6   Wells, *Crusade for Justice*, 19.

7   Giddings, *Ida: A Sword among Lions*, 63; Wells, *Crusade for Justice*, 19.

8   Giddings, *Ida: A Sword among Lions*, 62–63; some accounts spell his name as "Cassels." Patricia A. Schechter, *Ida B. Wells-Barnett and American Reform, 1880–1930* (Chapel Hill: The University of North Carolina Press, 2001), 43.

9   Linda O. McMurry, *To Keep the Waters Troubled: The Life of Ida B. Wells* (New York: Oxford University Press, 1998), 317.

10 Wendell Phillips, *Speeches, Lectures, and Letters* (Ann Arbor: University of Michigan Library, 2005), 52.

11 Wells, *Crusade for Justice*, 415.

CHAPTER 1

ESTABLISHING CITIZENSHIP, 1862–87

Ida Bell Wells was born into slavery in the midst of the Civil War on July 16, 1862. Her mother, Lizzie (Elizabeth), and father, Jim (James), lived in Holly Springs, Mississippi. Two weeks prior to her birth, the Union and Confederacy fought near the town, which changed hands between the two armies at least fifty-seven times.[1] Later that fall, Union General Ulysses S. Grant made Holly Springs his headquarters as he prepared for the Vicksburg Campaign. On January 1, 1863, President Abraham Lincoln's Emancipation Proclamation went into effect, freeing all slaves residing in the rebelling states, and although many African Americans sought liberation by escaping to the Union lines, Lizzie and Jim did not. With a young baby, they were perhaps unable or unwilling to leave Mississippi.[2]

Holly Springs, the seat of Marshall County, grew rapidly during the antebellum period due to its ideal location for growing cotton.[3] In 1840, the census for Holly Springs recorded 9,276 white residents, a number that more than tripled by 1860 to approximately 29,000. The slave population also grew rapidly between 1840 and 1860 from 8,260 to 17,439.[4] Correspondingly, vast plantations spread across the countryside and, in 1860, just before the Civil War, Marshall County produced 49,348 bales of cotton, the most of any county in the nation.[5] One of the slaves among this increasing populace was Ida's father Jim, born near Holly Springs, the child of his African American mother, Peggy, and Morgan Wells, the white master of the plantation. Jim, a mulatto, or person of mixed race, inherited his mother's slave status. As Morgan and his wife Polly were childless, Jim, the only son of his white planter father, received a measure of protection from the harshest aspects of slavery.[6] His father took him to Holly Springs to apprentice as a carpenter under wealthy builder Spires Bolling and Jim soon met and married another of Bolling's slaves, a cook named Lizzie.[7] Born in 1844, Lizzie's master in Virginia separated her and three of her sisters from their family, selling each of them to different buyers. Lizzie later told her children of the violent beatings she suffered from several of her masters, and the scars upon her back served as a lifelong reminder of her slave experiences. After the Civil War, Ida recalled her mother searching for her family, locating only one of her nine siblings, her sister, Belle. Like Jim, society defined Lizzie as a mulatto, with her heritage reflected in the light skin color she inherited from her Native American grandfather.[8]

After the Confederacy's surrender at Appomattox, the nation attempted to reunite and rebuild. This era of Reconstruction began with the extension of citizenship to four million newly freed slaves. Like thousands of newly emancipated people across the South after the Civil War, Lizzie and Jim remarried in order to enjoy the legal rights now granted to African Americans. During the Civil War when escaping slaves reached Union lines they sought officers, missionaries, or clergymen to officiate their marriages, demonstrating how the institution of marriage was tied to freedom. Marriage symbolized a permanence denied to their relationships under slavery.[9] While they could be married with their master's permission, since slaves were not legally permitted to enter into contracts, the union was not lawfully binding. After the Civil War, as married citizens, both Lizzie and Jim enjoyed the legal recognition of their relationship, remained in Holly Springs, and continued to work for Bolling as paid employees. They also grew their family over the next decade, having seven children in addition to Ida: Eugenia, James, George, Eddie, Annie, Lily, and Stanley.[10]

After the Civil War, African American men made inroads to gaining political power due to the three Reconstruction amendments. The Thirteenth Amendment ended slavery and the Fourteenth Amendment offered equal protection before the law. The final of these, the Fifteenth Amendment, stated that the "right of citizens of the United States to vote shall not be denied or abridged by the United States or by any state on account of race, color, or previous condition of servitude."[11] Following the Civil War, the composition of voters reflected the population statistics, with African Americans the majority of constituents in many areas of the South. During Reconstruction in Mississippi, black voters elected forty African Americans to state and federal offices, including Hiram Revels, a minister and free black who fought for the Union during the Civil War.[12] Revels became the first black senator in Congress, winning the seat of Confederate President Jefferson Davis.[13] A former slave from Holly Springs, James Hill, served as secretary of state and Mississippian Blanche K. Bruce became the first former slave to preside over the Senate.[14]

In addition to establishing voting rights for African American men, in 1865, Congress created the Bureau of Refugees, Freedmen, and Abandoned Lands, or Freedmen's Bureau. Described in its charter as "responsible alone to the President," its mission was "to take charge of the abandoned and forfeited lands of the rebels, settle them with freedmen" and to "guard the interests of these latter, aid in adjusting wages, in enforcing contracts, and in protecting these unfortunate people from injustice, and securing them their liberty."[15] African Americans supported the Freedmen's Bureau, but many white southerners opposed giving land to former slaves or instituting a free labor market. One South Carolina politician referred to the Bureau's representatives as "a horde of barbarians."[16] Ruth Watkins, an early Mississippi historian, noted that many southern whites believed that while "probably right in theory," the Bureau would make "negroes idle and vicious by giving them a place of refuge where food was provided."[17] This view of the organization prevailed when President Andrew Johnson vetoed the renewal of the Freedmen's Bureau, weakening it until it dissolved in 1872. Despite its limited authority, the Bureau's relief and educational work had an enduring impact.[18] Holly Springs served as a regional headquarters of the Freedmen's Bureau, resulting in the founding of Shaw University in 1866, an institution for African Americans, which in 1882 would change its name to Rust College.[19]

A world where blacks could gain an education and vote shaped Ida's early life, and the Wells family became one of many African American families who made social gains during the early years of Reconstruction.[20] Jim was involved in the local community; he sat on the board of trustees for Shaw University and joined the black fraternal order of Freemasons, gaining the rank of Master Mason.[21] Although he never ran for any electoral office, Jim strongly believed in African American men utilizing their new political power and became active in Lincoln's Legal Loyal League, an organization formed during the Civil War to help abolish slavery. During Reconstruction, the group dedicated itself to educating black men on political issues and mobilizing them to vote. The Lincoln's Legal Loyal League, which would later go by the shortened name the Union League, spread throughout the South after the Civil War.[22]

In 1867, black males voted in their first election. Like most freed people, the Wells considered themselves Republicans, loyal to Lincoln and the political party that had won the Civil War. Unsurprisingly, most southern whites identified as Democrats, unhappy with the extension of citizenship to former slaves. As the election neared, Spires Bolling ordered his employee Jim Wells to vote for the Democratic ticket. Voting transpired differently from today's private affair, as each party created a brightly colored ballot for the election to aid the less literate, and men voted in a public community space. With different colored ballots, the election judges and any observers could see from a distance the party that each voter chose. Bolling's demand did not intimidate Jim Wells, and he proceeded to vote Republican. News of his choice spread quickly and when Jim returned to work, he found the carpentry shop locked with all of his tools inside. Bolling, as punishment for Jim's refusal to follow his order, attempted to deprive him of his livelihood and evicted the Wells from their rental home, which he also owned. The Civil War damage to Holly Springs had created a demand for carpenters, and Jim's savings prevented Bolling's retaliatory behavior from leaving the family homeless. Ida recalled that they simply moved across the street to a new house and her father bought new tools to reopen his business.[23]

Many former slaves did not have the resources of the Wells family, for the end of slavery severely disrupted the economy of the South. Whites still owned large plantations but no longer controlled the considerable number of laborers needed to maintain their land or harvest their crops. In addition, Confederate currency was useless, leaving many white southerners without cash and unable to pay freed blacks to work their land for wages. Former slaves also needed an income and lacked property or savings. These economic conditions resulted in the creation of a system of sharecropping across the South. Blacks worked on the land of white owners, but instead of paying them in cash wages, they received a share of the crop they produced. Since white landowners could only pay their workers after they sold the crop, sharecroppers financed their first year out of pocket. Without money for equipment and living expenses, many former slaves applied for loans, offered by white bankers to African Americans at interest rates of seventy percent or higher.[24] Such high rates ensured a level of debt that prevented African Americans from seeking other work opportunities. Adding to the economic struggle, the total value of farm products declined dramatically after the Civil War. In 1860, Marshall County boasted a value of $779,723, while in 1870 farm product profits were only $225,568, a drop of more than two-thirds.[25]

In addition to debt and the devaluation of crops, former slaves struggled against Black Codes targeting the rights of African Americans. These included vagrancy laws, where authorities could arrest, jail, and fine an African American up to $500 if they could not produce proof that they worked for a white.[26] Tax laws offered whites a similar method to control black labor, levying a heavy fine on African Americans who worked in any profession other than as a farmer.[27] Black Codes became a way of instituting a "state of servitude but little better than slavery," and most of these laws remained in place for nearly a hundred years, until repealed by the Civil Rights Act of 1964.[28]

The end of the Civil War also brought about a shift in the economic value of a black life. The system of slavery allowed masters absolute control over their slaves and they often engaged in brutal treatment in order to control and punish, but their financial investment tempered their violence, as maiming or murdering a slave would result in a substantial economic loss. White landowners, however, had no monetary outlay in sharecroppers and therefore possessed few reservations about using torture and murder to control newly freed African Americans.[29] The Ku Klux Klan, founded in 1865 by six Confederate veterans, evolved into the principal organization responsible for much of this violence. The Ku Klux Klan's crimes ranged from slaying African Americans and their supporters to stuffing ballots in order to elect Democratic candidates. The initiation oath clearly reflected this agenda. When asked, "What are the objects of the Ku Klux Klan?" the pledge's correct response was, "It is to suppress the negro and keep him in the position where he belongs, and to see that the Democratic party controls this country."[30]

Ida recalled overhearing the name of the Ku Klux Klan whispered between her parents. When her father went to Union League meetings, she remembered her mother pacing the floor with worry.[31] Lizzie had reasons to fear because despite threats of violence, African American groups such as the Union League continued to organize black voters. In Holly Springs, Nelson Gill, although white, became a target of the Ku Klux Klan due to his support of African Americans and his position as the head of the Freedmen's Bureau. Described by a local historian as a man who "preached and lived social equality," the former Union officer from Illinois remained undeterred by his hostile reception in Mississippi where local whites called him a "carpetbagger," a derogatory term for northern whites who came to the South after the Civil War.[32] Soon after his arrival, Gill joined the Lincoln's Legal Loyal League with Jim Wells, where he made political arguments and instructed African American men on how to vote, as well as helped establish Shaw University and co-found a Methodist church.[33]

At a political rally, a former Confederate Colonel took offense at Gill's message and charged the platform.[34] Gill recovered from his injuries only to have the Ku Klux Klan put a price on his head. Despite this, the Union League did not stop having their meetings, but Jim Wells and the other members did begin to require a password.[35] At one meeting of the Union League, held at Gill's residence, several Ku Klux Klan supporters hid under the house waiting for an opportunity to shoot him. When Klan member J. L. Holland aimed his gun at Gill, ready to fire, fellow Klansman Jim House knocked the barrel aside at the last minute, and the shot went wide, leaving Gill unharmed. House, it seemed, "couldn't bear to see him [Gill] shot," perhaps because he was a white man. The Klan felt the unexpected bullet, although it missed

Gill, "frightened the negroes very much."[36] In response to this attempted assassination, the Union League began posting armed guards outside Gill's house during meetings.[37]

Although debt and violence controlled African Americans to an extent, the Ku Klux Klan and the former elite planter class, unified by their desire to regain dominance, needed access to political power. In Marshall County, where Holly Springs was located, sixty percent of registered voters were black.[38] In order for the Democrats to win, African Americans needed to not vote, or barring that, not vote Republican. In the 1871 election, the Democratic Party sought to stuff the ballot box. During the voting period, a loyal Klansman named J. Alexander hid under a bed in the police department. When the authorities brought the ballot box to the station for safekeeping while everyone adjourned for dinner, Alexander crawled out of his hiding space and proceeded to open the ballot box, remove the Republican tickets, and replace them with a stack of Democratic ballots.[39]

The Holly Springs election of 1876, when Ida was thirteen, further demonstrated the deceptive tactics of the Democratic Party in regaining political power. Before the election, Nelson Gill sent J. L. Burton to a printer in Memphis to place an order for the Republican Party's ballots. Burton soon realized that a Democratic Party spy had followed him in hopes of discovering what color the Republican ticket would be. This vital information would allow the Democratic Party to make their ballots the same color and confuse voters. Burton delivered a decoy order in Memphis and then sailed up the Mississippi River to St. Louis to place the correct order for red ballot tickets. Despite his evasive maneuvering, the spy followed him, found out about the second order, and rushed back to Mississippi. After learning that the Democrats had also purchased red tickets, the Republicans took their ballots, stamped a tiger on them and began spreading this information to local African Americans. When a local Democrat found out about the change to the Republican ticket, he told the Chairmen of the Democratic Committee, Arthur B. Fant, who set his wife to creating a similar tiger on their ballots. Since voters folded the red tickets to fit in the ballot box, Republicans failed to realize until after the election that voters confronted two sets of red tickets with a tiger on them, the Republican one with the tiger going up the page and the Democratic ballot with the tiger running down it.[40] Many voters, seeing a red ticket with a tiger on it, thought that they were voting Republican but ended up casting a vote for the Democrats, who won the election.[41]

As a teenager, Ida recognized the increasing tensions around her, but at her parents' urging, remained focused on her education. She began attending Shaw University in 1877, and recalled her parents teaching their children that their role was "to go to school and learn all we could."[42] After the

Civil War, like many former slaves, Lizzie embraced education for herself and her children as a way to gain access to a better life. As historian Tera Hunter noted, for newly freed African Americans "the desire for literacy and education" represented a path for "achieving economic self-sufficiency, political autonomy, and personal enrichment."[43] Lizzie attended classes alongside her children in order to fulfill her lifelong dream of being able to read the *Bible*. As she did not have to work outside of the home, Lizzie's ability to devote time to her own education was a luxury available to only a few southern African American women after the Civil War.[44] Many black women, in order to support their families, returned to work in the fields and homes of whites, making them vulnerable to the same physical and sexual abuse they faced during slavery.[45]

Shaw University offered a curriculum focusing on faith, literacy, and practical skills. Lessons began at the elementary level, but as the principal's report of 1873 noted, "the pupils [are] proving their capacity for advanced study as well as more elementary work" and the school soon offered an education through to college level.[46] Students attended mandatory daily Chapel and were required to join two prayer meetings each week. While the religious aspects of her education certainly influenced Ida, she considered reading to be the most formative part of her youth. Prior to the Civil War in Mississippi, if a white caught a slave reading, the punishment was thirty-nine lashes.[47] Now free, African Americans embraced literacy, and Ida in particular devoured all the texts she could find. She read every book in her school and church library, including works by William Shakespeare, Charles Dickens, Louisa May Alcott, and Charlotte Brontë. These stories spurred her imagination and love of the written word.[48] In contrast, Ida dreaded her applied lessons, which included instructions on performing everyday household chores such as washing clothes and ironing.[49] In addition to these formal programs of study, Wells also learned etiquette from her white northern educated female teachers. They taught her the social expectations of polite society, including the proper ways to address people, how to present a calling card, how to avoid being unchaperoned with a man, and conversational conventions.[50] Unfortunately, her days of being "a happy light-hearted school girl" would soon end.[51]

Ida turned sixteen in the summer of 1878 and went to help with the cotton harvest on her Grandmother Peggy's farm. Jim's mother had married after the Civil War and lived with her husband a distance from Holly Springs.[52] Soon after Ida arrived, newspapers began reporting on a Yellow Fever outbreak in New Orleans, Louisiana that traveled up the Mississippi River to Memphis, Tennessee. No one knew that mosquitoes spread the disease until the turn of the century, but many people recognized a correlation between the illness and swampy land. Holly Springs had never suffered a single incident of the infection and the geography of the town—on high ground and away from stagnant water—made residents feel safe from the disease. In the middle of August, the *New Orleans Daily Picayune*'s headline read "Vicksburg Terrified—Holly Springs Not Afraid." In the article, the mayor of Holly Springs described the status of his town as clean, vigorous, and without any signs of the illness.[53] Indeed, the mayor allowed refugees fleeing from nearby areas with outbreaks to take sanctuary in Holly Springs. His positive interview contrasted with the descriptions coming out of New Orleans where one reporter noted, "Physicians are broken down... Many cases will die today... Gloom, despair, and death rule the hour, and the situation is simply appalling."[54]

On August 19, 1878, the first of the refugees in Holly Springs fell sick with the Yellow Fever. Soon another and another showed symptoms. Fearful, two thousand residents fled the town, while three hundred whites and twelve hundred blacks stayed to face the ensuing epidemic. Among the remaining residents were Ida's family and the mayor, who became the first casualty of the disease from Holly Springs. Soon other townspeople felt the symptoms, beginning with fever and chills, followed by headaches, back pains, bleeding gums, and broken blood vessels, making the victim look bruised. After a few days, massive kidney and liver failure began. The breakdown of these organs resulted in jaundice, the yellowing of the skin, which gave the fever its name. The final stage was massive hemorrhaging. Blood poured from every orifice and the patient coughed or vomited black blood, eventually falling into a coma and dying.[55] In some areas, including the nearby city of Memphis, more than half of the population died from the 1878 outbreak.[56]

Lizzie Wells, nursing nine-month-old Stanley, became the first in the family to exhibit symptoms. Fifteen-year-old Eugenia had developed a knot on her spine that left her bent double and unable to walk, and could do little to help care for twelve-year-old James, eight-year-old George, five-year-old Annie, and two-year-old Lily.[57] With Ida away, Jim hired a nurse to tend to his sick wife and the children while he worked during the day building coffins. Soon he also presented symptoms. Ida lost her father on September 26, 1878, and her mother on September 27.[58] She received word of their deaths several days later. Ida recalled, "I read the first page of this letter through, telling the progress of the fever, and these words leaped out at me, 'Jim and Lizzie Wells have both died of the fever. They died within twenty-four hours of each other.'"[59] Although Grandmother Peggy tried to convince her to wait for the epidemic to die down before returning to Holly Springs, a worried Ida rushed home.[60] The train conductor did not put her anxiety to rest, as he bluntly informed Ida that the fever remained in Holly Springs. Displaying both her commitment to her responsibilities and her rhetorical abilities, she asked why, if the chance of infection persisted, he was running the train into town. She remembered, "He replied that he did it because 'somebody had to do it.'" "That is," Ida retorted, "exactly why I am going home."[61]

Upon her arrival, she found the baby had also died. Stanley and her parents were among the four hundred fatalities in Holly Springs.[62] Eugenia recounted her parents' illnesses to Ida, including how after she saw the nurse going through Lizzie's pockets their father decided to entrust his life savings of three hundred dollars to the local physician, Dr. Gray.[63] With Ida back home, her father's Freemason lodge held a meeting to discuss the family's future. They advised Ida that two men would train James and George as apprentices. One family would take on Lily, and another would adopt Annie. At sixteen, Ida could support herself, while the crippled Eugenia would go to the poorhouse. Ida listened until they finished, but disagreed. Her parents, she informed them, would "turn over in their graves to know their children had been scattered like that." She offered an alternative plan— if they could help her find work, she would care for her family.[64] The Freemasons agreed.

Ida, suddenly the head of a household, first settled financial matters. Jim Wells owned his house and left no outstanding debts, so she proceeded to claim his savings. On market day, she went into town to find Dr. Gray, who told her he would bring the money to her house after his rounds. His evening visit and the resulting gossip became Ida's first lesson about the fragility of a black woman's moral reputation. Her neighbors, upon seeing a white man visit at night, immediately concluded that her desire to live on her own was for immoral reasons. Ida recalled, "[N]ever in all my life have I suffered such a shock as I did when I heard this misconstruction." The incident opened her eyes to the cultural beliefs about black women's sexuality and the need for her to preserve her reputation. She later recalled her naiveté in allowing a white man to visit her house alone: "I look back at it now I can perhaps understand… I was laying myself open to gossiping tongues."[65] She resolved to guard herself against any hint of impropriety and recognized that she would need an adult female chaperone with her in the house. Ida persuaded one of her mother's friends to move in with her and the children.[66] Another adult's presence soon became a necessity, as Ida passed the teacher's exam and received a job at a rural school six miles outside of Holly Springs. She prepared for her role as an educator by having the hem of her dresses lowered, outwardly demonstrating her shift from child to adult.[67]

For three years, Wells rode a mule six miles every week to teach reading, writing, and arithmetic in a one-room schoolhouse. On school nights she lodged with local families, traveling home on Friday evenings to spend the weekend catching up on the household chores of washing and ironing. During the summers, she attended classes at Shaw University in order to complete her college degree.[68] One term, Wells became upset when she observed the college president singling out another student for what she perceived as extra attention. President W. W. Hooper's exceptional interest in Annie Talbot, Wells concluded, resulted from her light complexion. Feeling the need to challenge this seeming inequality, Wells apparently confronted the college president. Although there is no record of what transpired, Hooper expelled Wells from Shaw University.[69] Several years later she reflected upon other possible reasons for the President's high regard of Talbot, conceding, "I've come to the conclusion that it was her obedient disposition, her extreme tractableness [sic] … and her evident ladylike refinement," which made her favorable.[70] In contrast to these feminine qualities, Wells confessed to her own "tempestuous, rebellious" nature, admitting she possessed a "hard headed willfulness," leading her to "question his [President Hooper's] authority."[71] This early incident foreshadowed many of Wells's tendencies. Always the first to confront a perceived inequality, she often acted without concern for the personal consequences she would face. Years later, the incident remained one of the most "painful memories" of her life.[72]

In 1881, Wells's household situation changed drastically. Her brothers, James and George, both began apprenticing to be carpenters, leaving her to care for only Eugenia, Annie, and Lily.[73] Fannie, her father's half-sister, wrote to Wells and invited her to come and live in Memphis, as the Yellow Fever epidemic had left her a widow with three young children. If Wells moved to the city, her aunt could help with her sisters and Wells's salary could contribute to the high costs of housing.[74] Eugenia preferred to live with her Aunt Belle, Lizzie's sister, therefore only Wells and her two youngest sisters relocated to Memphis in 1881. Not yet qualified to be a city schoolteacher, Wells obtained a rural teaching job in Woodstock, Tennessee, about twelve miles from Memphis, and too far away for daily travel. Wells took the train weekly and returned to Memphis on weekends, where she embraced the opportunities the city offered.[75]

About forty miles from Holly Springs, the city of Memphis, Tennessee rests on the banks of the Mississippi River. During the Civil War, Union troops occupied the city, making it a haven for runaway slaves and, after the conflict, many African Americans relocated to the town looking for work. In 1880, with forty percent of its population black, Memphis possessed a larger concentration of African Americans than many southern cities, and as one of the primary producers of cotton and lumber, became one of the few industrialized centers in the South. The city developed a modern infrastructure of roads, including streetcars for local public transportation. During the next twenty years, the population would steadily increase, tripling in size by 1900.[76] Due to the demographics and economy, Memphis developed a large and stable black middle class, and included among the town's

African American elite was millionaire Robert Church. African Americans became increasingly active within the city, participating on the City Council, developing strong churches, and fundraising to support local efforts.

Wells kept a diary while in Memphis, which served as a social calendar of people she met, the events she attended, and her extensive correspondence with dozens of friends and acquaintances. Although she recorded her anxieties with finances, her worry over her siblings, and the difficulties she experienced with several suitors, she wrote little about her day-to-day activities, barely mentioning her years teaching in the classroom. Wells never envisioned the diary published, yet as one scholar noted, while the pages allow readers to "learn much about Wells's social interactions" they "rarely yield the private Wells."[77] Miriam DeCosta-Willis, who edited her diary, noted the account's businesslike appearance, "There is a neat orderliness to her writing that bespeaks a clear and uncluttered mind."[78] Years later, a fire destroyed Wells's personal papers, making the diary the only surviving private writings from her time in Memphis.[79] The image of Wells that emerges is of a young black woman preoccupied with balancing her personal desires with the social requirements surrounding her.[80]

Wells's position as a teacher came with many expectations. Education offered one of the few avenues of consistent and respectable work available to African American women after the Civil War. Teachers, compared to other black women's employment opportunities as domestics, field workers, cooks, or in laundry work, received a measure of social status and a reasonable salary. Wells's role as an educator gave her the title of "Miss Wells," a change from the antebellum South, where address of "Mr., Mrs., or Miss," applied only to whites. In the 1840s, white southerner Anne Braden remembered her mother lecturing her when she mentioned meeting a "colored lady." "You never call colored people 'ladies,'" her mother scolded. "You say colored women and white lady—never colored lady."[81] Thus, in the post-Civil War South, to address a female as "Miss" or "Mrs." conferred the status of being a lady, one extended to select African American women during Reconstruction who demonstrated an indisputable virtuous reputation. The Memphis School Board, like many other educational bodies, expected all teachers to pass a written knowlege-based exam. Beyond that, the applicants needed to prove that they possessed "the purest and truest of natures."[82] Society believed that outward appearance reflected inward morality, and thus ladies needed to wear a modest dress accessorized with a coat, hat, gloves, and parasol.[83]

When Wells began teaching in Woodstock, much of her paycheck went to her family. In addition to helping Fannie with the household expenses and providing for Annie and Lily, she also sent money to her brothers and Eugenia. She needed the leftover money, and often more, to outfit herself in the wardrobe of a respectable middle-class lady. In one diary entry, she described a new outfit she liked "very much" but that "cost a good deal" at $7.60. Another ensemble she described cost more than double: "I have bought enough silk to finish my dress with, and buttons, thread, linings etc. amounting to $15.80 & yet have no parasol." In addition to appearing respectable, Wells often lamented on the "things I would like to have," and occasionally gave in to her desire to be fashionable, often at a high price and to her later regret, writing, "I am very sorry I did not resist the impulse to buy that cloak; I would have been $15 richer."[84] Even in 1884, after Wells passed the city teacher's exam and her pay increased, she still wished her money "was not so persistently sought after."[85] Complicating her financial situation, the School Board often failed to pay teachers on time. In one instance, she did not receive her January salary until April, and often had to borrow money in order to cover her expenses.[86]

The public schools in Memphis were segregated, with whites and "colored" students taught by teachers of their corresponding race. When Wells received a position in the city schools, her pay rose due to a resolution from the 1870s, when white reformer Elizabeth Meriwether fought the School Board for equal compensation for teachers regardless of gender. At the time, male teachers made more than double the salary of female educators. Meriwether brought a petition, signed by all of the female teachers of both races, before the School Board. The members did vote to implement a policy of equal pay, but not as the women hoped. Instead of raising the female teachers' salaries, the School Board decided to lower everyone's pay to their level, and because of the large reduction in salary, most men left the teaching profession. The single rate of pay for any teacher, however, translated into one of the highest paid opportunities for black women, who across the South made much less than their white counterparts.[87] In 1874, the average salary of an African American teacher in Tennessee was thirty-three dollars a month, whereas Wells received a starting salary in Memphis of fifty dollars a month, a raise of nearly twenty dollars from her previous job in Woodstock. With seniority, she could make as much as sixty dollars a month.[88]

Although they paid more, conditions in the Memphis public schools were far from ideal. In 1884, Wells, as one of twenty-two black teachers, taught first grade to forty-eight students.[89] This ratio stressed Wells, who wrote, "A day's worry with these children has brought my temper to the surface." In another entry, she commented on her own efforts to engage her pupils: "Friday was a trying day at school. I know not what method to use to get my children to become more interested in their lessons."[90] Outside of these fleeting mentions, Wells recorded little about her time in a classroom. She noted years later in her autobiography, "I never cared for teaching, but I had always been very conscientious in trying to do my work honestly."[91]

She recognized that any other career would not enable her to support herself or her family. "There seemed nothing else to do for a living but menial work, and I could not have made a living at that."[92] Despite its trials, teaching remained the logical choice of employment for a young, educated, and independent woman like Wells.[93]

Upon moving to Memphis, Wells became active in several black churches. She taught a Sunday School class at the African Methodist Episcopal Avery Chapel and often attended several church events on Sundays.[94] Although she often wrote of her need to pray for guidance and wisdom in her diary, Wells did not detail her personal religious beliefs.[95] Instead, she described the social world of the middle-class African Americans she met through church functions, such as the Memphis Lyceum, a club that met every Friday night at the Vance Street Christian Church. Members participated in a variety of literary-based entertainments and Wells described their meetings as consisting of "recitations, essays, and debates interspersed with music." At the end of each gathering, the participants read from the *Evening Star*, the "spicy" newsletter of the Lyceum that included literary reviews, poetry, and an advice column.[96]

For Wells, membership was "a breath of fresh air," and she became increasingly active in the group. In 1885, she performed a public reading as Mary, Queen of Scots with fellow member Virginia Broughton as Queen Elizabeth. The two women wore costumes and their recitations were a resounding success. Wells enjoyed her role so much that she began taking elocution lessons to develop her speaking ability. Even in times of financial stress, Wells often managed to pay fifty cents for her weekly lessons in pronunciation and speech.[97] In 1886, when the current editor of the Memphis Lyceum's newsletter left for a job in Washington, D.C., members elected Wells to replace him at the helm of the *Evening Star*. Although apprehensive about her ability to succeed at the position, Wells enjoyed the work of preparing, editing, and promoting the paper. In her autobiography, she proudly noted that under her leadership "lyceum attendance was increased by people who said they came to hear the *Evening Star* read."[98]

In addition to her involvement in the Memphis Lyceum, Wells went to lectures and saw her first baseball game, but she loved live theater above all other entertainments. Wells attended several plays, including "The Mikado," "The Burning of Moscow," "Humbug," and "The Count of Monte Cristo." She reviewed each performance in her diary finding "The Mikado," a humorous opera by Gilbert and Sullivan, to be a "Delightful fantasy!" but did not enjoy the production of "Humbug," noting "& humbug it was."[99] Several entries also reveal concerns about the propriety of a lady viewing these performances, as society viewed the theater as a place full of "professional liars and loose women."[100] Although Wells attended the theater with other women or in large groups, her presence at these performances became a point of contention. Fellow church member George Dardis, Jr. walked her home one Sunday in order to lecture her about the moral effects of the theater, claiming that going to plays could contaminate her virtue and suggested that her attendance set a bad example for her Sunday School students.[101]

For young black women, the issue of virtue was complicated. In the nineteenth century, an ideology called the Cult of True Womanhood regulated white middle-class women's behavior. This philosophy divided the world into two spheres, a public sphere outside the household, controlled by males, and a female-oriented private sphere inside the home. The domestic arena offered the only respectable space for women, where they remained protected from the corruption of the outside world. The True Woman's worth revolved around her household, husband, and children, with her virtue reflected in her gentle, passive, innocent, modest, and principled lifestyle. Her moral purity existed because she lacked knowledge of the public sphere of men, including politics or economics.[102] In contrast, any woman outside of the home became a target of speculation that her exposure to the public sphere had tarnished her morals. These beliefs, in claiming to protect women, effectively prevented them from gaining any authority or autonomy. Only a select group of white women with the economic ability to stay within the home could afford to practice this ideology, most working-class, immigrant, and former slave women could not meet these standards.

Black middle-class women attempted to embody the ideology of True Womanhood by adopting the beliefs, manners, and dress of the middle-class white woman, and teaching offered one of the few acceptable jobs for women in the public sphere, one that "a lady might openly engage without compromising her social status."[103] Wells aspired to conform to the values of True Womanhood during this time as well; she possessed impeccable manners and despite the financial struggle to do so, dressed every inch of the young, educated, and moral young woman. After the scolding she received for attending the theater, Wells swore she would never go again. Yet, she wrestled with her own nature. She liked to question authority and recognized that she was headstrong, willful, smart, and quick to anger. As her dismissal from Shaw University demonstrated, she often spoke without concern for consequence. Although these traits served her admirably in her lifetime, they caused Wells much grief as a young woman as she strove to control her "unfeminine" temper.[104]

As an orphan, Wells also lacked male relatives to lend her respectability and, after 1886, she lived alone when her Aunt Fannie decided to move to California. Wells never articulated the motive behind her aunt's decision to relocate, but as Lily and Annie had grown close to Fannie's daughters, she and Wells agreed that Lily and Annie would also go to California. After Fannie moved out West, Wells boarded with Josiah T. Settle and his wife. A lawyer serving in the state legislature, Settle became one of several mentors Wells cultivated to counsel her.[105] Another black man, Alfred Froman, a friend of her Aunt Fannie who lived in her neighborhood, was also an influential supporter in Memphis. In her diary, she often referred to him as "Pap," showing her affection for the man who became like a surrogate father to her. Froman, a former slave, settled in Memphis during Reconstruction, opening a saddle shop, and editing the *Memphis Planet* newspaper. In her diary, Wells mentioned discussing with Froman her financial issues, her career concerns, and her aspirations. In addition to advising her, as a member of the School Board, Froman supported her application to teach in the Memphis city schools. He also loaned her money on several occasions.[106]

Two other African Americans influenced her life during these years in Memphis. For a short time, Theodore W. Lott became an intellectual tutor to Wells after she became a teacher in the city school system. She borrowed books and magazines from him and the two often engaged in long academic discussions. Lott helped her with her diction and coached her public speaking. Yet when he attempted to transition from an intellectual mentor to offer advice on her personal life, their friendship ended. Lott criticized Wells for dating too many men and called her "a heartless flirt."[107] This reproach led her to cut off all contact with him. Although Wells often experienced difficulties making friends with women, she forged one fast female friendship in Memphis. She felt an instant connection with Mollie (Mary) Church, the daughter of wealthy African American Robert Church. The two women met when Mollie came to visit her father in Memphis after graduating from Oberlin, an integrated college in Ohio. Wells noted, "She is the first woman of my age I've met who is similarly inspired with the same desires hopes & ambitions." Despite their economic and educational differences, the two women talked for hours. Wells noted that "her ambitions seem so in consonance with mine."[108] Although of like minds, the two women would not maintain their friendship.[109]

Her mentors and friends aside, Wells, as an attractive, petite, "well proportioned," young woman with dark eyes, a sharp wit, and keen intellect, boasted more than her share of romantic suitors.[110] As a lady, and thus responsible for upholding the morals of True Womanhood required by society and the Memphis School Board, Wells attempted to adhere to the strict constraints of courtship. The few times she lapsed, she immediately scolded herself in her diary and resolved to follow social dictates. Despite her many suitors and her admission that she relished male attention, writing in her diary after an evening out, "I am enjoying existence very much just now," she was not anxious to marry.[111] Dating offered Wells a chance to be involved in Memphis's social life, yet, after spending most of her adult life caring for her siblings, she sought to preserve her independence. She noted, "I am an anomaly to myself as well as to others. I do not wish to be married but I do wish for the society of gentlemen."[112]

A pattern emerges in Wells's romantic life in Memphis. Although she tried not to find fault with those who courted her, once she found an imperfection, she drifted away from each suitor, one by one.[113] Her longest relationship involved fellow teacher Isaiah J. Graham, who engaged her in a convoluted courtship. Their romance became a power struggle, with Graham wanting Wells to pledge her love to him, and Wells, still dating other men, expecting Graham to be the first to make his feelings known. She wrote in her diary of his desire for her to express herself first: "I thought it was conceding too much considering he had never told me anything [about his feelings]."[114] Despite this tension, the two continued to spend time together. When Wells caught a cold, Graham brought medicine to her home, and they attended various parties and events together. Wells believed that he possessed strong feelings for her, but became impatient with his refusal to declare them. After a brief kissing session, Wells confessed to her diary that she blushed "to think I allowed him to caress me," without an accompanying declaration of love. One night Graham took her hat and ran off, an attempt to tease Wells that only angered her when he returned it "utterly ruined." After the hat incident, she became increasingly impatient with him. At his next visit, he "stood around like a mummy for a long while," and she resolved that he had lost his opportunity with her.[115] They remained on friendly terms until several months later when Graham finally confessed his love to her. Wells apparently felt his declaration too little and too late, and responded that she "was not conscious of an absorbing feeling for him." Her next diary entry described him only as "a friend to be kept," rather than a possible romantic partner.[116] Graham, by dragging of his feet in declaring his feelings for her, prompted Wells to lose interest.

Wells focused her attention on other suitors, and became intrigued by Louis M. Brown, a Memphian who now resided in Washington D.C., and edited the black newspaper *The Washington Bee*.[117] In a practice that continues today, many African American and female reporters of Wells's time employed pen names to protect themselves from reprisal if they offered an unpopular social viewpoint. Brown, in an allusion to his initials L. M. B., wrote articles under the pen name Elembee. Wells described him in her diary as "older" with "more varied experience."[118] During one of Brown's visits to Memphis, the two went on a midnight walk, but Wells scolded him when he pushed her for physical affection. Brown retreated and suggested they remain friends, referring to her as like a "little sister" to him, eradicating any romantic aspirations from their relationship. His rejection apparently did not dissuade her interest and the two continued to correspond.[119]

In the spring of 1886, he wrote to Wells and informed her that the newspaper had fired him and he would be returning to Memphis. She responded that she would be happy to see him again, and when he arrived, wrote, "I was real glad to see him" and mentioned that he had kissed her, twice.[120] Wells confessed to her diary that his kisses "blistered my lips," but this feeling of desire quickly turned to fear that she may violate the societal expectations of a moral woman. She began distancing herself from him and his brazen behavior. The next mention of him in her diary noted that she had "seen nothing of L. M. B. for nearly two weeks." Later, at a group outing, she "hardly noticed" his presence.[121]

Her third local relationship—with the Reverend A. A. Mosely—ended almost before their connection could develop, as a result of a sobering conversation with her landlord, Josiah T. Settle. Her mentor expressed concern at witnessing a stream of young men arriving at the house to court Wells. He explained that if she continued to date so many men, she would gain a reputation. To have socialized with several men, he noted, but not committed to any, made her seem heartless. Why, he asked her, could she not find happiness or marriage? Concerned about the consequences of her behavior, he warned her, "You are playing with edged tools." Wells, confronted with her failed relationships from a trusted advisor, took his advice to heart. Upon reflection, she chastised herself for not having the "courage" to send away or choose any of the men and felt she was "degrading" herself with her dating habits.[122]

A trip to California after the school year ended offered Wells a chance to visit her aunt and distance herself from her romantic affairs.[123] Wells departed on July 4, 1886, and stayed in Kansas City, Missouri for a few days to attend the National Teachers Association meeting. There she lodged with J. Dallas Bowser, the editor of the *Gate City Press,* and his wife.[124] After the conference, Wells traveled through Denver, Salt Lake City, and San Francisco, finally arriving in Visalia, California on August 1. Located about two hundred miles south and east of San Francisco, it offered Fannie a relatively inexpensive place to live.[125] As soon as she arrived, Fannie encouraged Wells not to return to Memphis, but remain in California. At first, Wells, thrilled to see the twelve-year-old Annie and nine-year-old Lily, agreed and sold her return ticket home. Hot, dusty, and remote, Visalia quickly disappointed and she noted, "Not a dozen colored families lived there," concluding that it must be "dull and lonely for my aunt and the five youngsters in the family."[126] Although she resolved to make the best of her situation, Wells remained miserable, complaining to her aunt about the lack of any recreation, which "was even worse for me, a young woman." Upset by Wells's change of heart, Aunt Fannie countered that if she wished to leave, then she must also take her sisters. As Wells could not afford two additional train tickets, and swayed by the eighty dollars a month the local school offered her as a teacher, she agreed to stay and teach in Visalia, a decision that made her cry "bitter tears of disappointment."[127]

Wells soon received two letters. The first one, from J. Dallas Bowser, encouraged her to apply for a teaching position in Kansas City and suggested she could also write for the *Gate City Press*. The second letter from Alfred Froman divulged the news that Mollie's father, the wealthy Robert Church, would loan her the train fare if she wanted to come home. Offered two options more appealing than teaching in the segregated, run-down, one-room school in Visalia, cemented Wells's decision to resign her position in California.[128] Fannie responded to this news by crying "half the night & all the morning."[129] Wells wrote to Froman, asking for a loan of one hundred and fifty dollars to cover train fare, noting "The schools in California opened on the first Monday in September; in Kansas City, on the second Monday; and in Memphis, Tennessee, on the third Monday." She informed him that if either the Kansas City or the Memphis School Board selected her, she would take the loan and return east. Soon she received a telegram offering her a teaching position in the Kansas City school district. When Fannie heard, she made such a scene that Wells felt compelled to turn the position down. "My aunt never left [my side] until I had written out and sent a reply...declining the position."

Nevertheless, after another day teaching in Visalia, Wells was resolute. She sent a second telegram, stating, "Leaving tonight. If too late to secure position there, will go on to Memphis. Ida B. Wells." When she informed her sisters of their departure, Annie refused to go. Wells wrote in her diary, "I did not blame her for doing so" since she did not want to leave Fannie's daughter, her close friend. "Besides," Wells concluded, it will be "much easier for me to manage with one instead of two half-grown girls on my hands."[130] Once on the train with Lily, Wells became "jubilant" at the thought of returning to a metropolitan area.[131] When she arrived in Kansas City, she began to feel apprehensive after learning that her fellow teachers regarded her as an outsider who had taken the job from a local teacher. After one day in her fourth-grade classroom of seventy students, she heard a rumor among the teachers that Lily was not her sister, but her daughter, a result of her "immoral conduct."[132] Angered, Wells resigned, unwilling to work where she was unwanted, and returned to Memphis, "the only home I know."[133] She recalled in her autobiography, "in the year 1886 I had taught in one month in the states of California, Missouri, and Tennessee. Four days in Visalia, one day in Kansas City, and the remainder of the school year in Memphis."[134]

After Wells resettled in Memphis, she referred to the following season as "[t]he winter of my discontent."[135] Historian Linda O. McMurry believed that Wells likely endured intense bouts of depression during her Memphis years. After returning from California, she struggled with her debt, work, and Lily.[136] In her diary, she recorded feeling poorly both physically and mentally. Wells observed that her "system was not in good order" and that she often felt "sluggish" and unmotivated.[137] Other entries such as, "My life seems awry, the machinery out of gear & I feel as if there's something wrong" speak to her mental stress. Her previous suitors only added to her melancholy. During her time in California, they had moved on; Louis Brown relocated to Kansas City and Isiah Graham abruptly married another woman a few weeks after Wells returned to Memphis.[138] Despite her feelings of isolation, she remained faithful to her earlier decision to no longer date, and Lily's presence likely helped temper her enthusiasm for romance. Soon Wells's legal proceedings would occupy her time. In 1883, two employees had forcefully removed her from the first-class ladies car of a train, despite an 1881 state law requiring equal first-class accommodations for members of both races. Angry and humiliated, Wells hired a lawyer to sue the Chesapeake, Ohio, Southwestern Railroad Company.

When Wells filed her case in 1883, she was not the first African American woman to challenge her treatment on transportation in a court of law, and she likely knew of an earlier, successful attempt to fight against eviction from the first-class car. In 1879, employees threw African American Jane Brown out of the ladies car on a Memphis and Charleston Railroad train.[139] In Brown's suit, a federal court heard her case, since the incident occurred on an interstate train. Brown testified to the "brutal violence" she experienced, which included being choked during her removal from the ladies car.[140] The defense attempted to discredit Brown, using a state statute that limited riders in the first-class carriage to "persons of good character, and genteel and modest deportment," which allowed an educated, well-dressed, and moral black woman to gain access to the first-class car. They argued that employees removed Brown from the train because she did not meet the criteria of having a "good character," claiming she was a "notorious courtesan," and "addicted to lascivious and profane conversation and immodest deportment in public places."[141] Regardless of this defamation, the court, applying the Federal Civil Rights Act of 1875, which prevented discrimination in public accommodations, awarded Brown $3,000 in damages.

Jane Brown's 1879 suit represented one of the first challenges by an African American to maintain the legal rights granted after the Civil War. With slavery abolished, whites sought ways to increase racial segregation. Once the Federal government's oversight of the southern state governments during Reconstruction ended in 1877, southern states began reducing African American liberties, with transportation as one of the first sites in which de jure, or legalized segregation began. In Tennessee during the 1870s and

1880s, passenger trains usually contained two cars; directly behind the engine was a smoker's car followed by the first-class car, reserved for ladies and those accompanying them. The division of where a passenger rode depended largely on class and gender. When African American women claimed the status of ladies by exhibiting the same gender behaviors and class traits in mannerisms and dress as white women, the only way that companies could justify removing black women from the first-class car was to demonstrate that they failed to meet the social requirements to be a lady.

In 1881, two years after Jane Brown's successful lawsuit and the same year that Wells moved to Memphis, the state of Tennessee enacted the first railroad segregation law in the nation.[142] This act required railroad companies to provide "separate cars, or portions of cars" for first-class black passengers.[143] This statute sought to undermine the Federal Civil Rights Act of 1875 the final act of Reconstruction, which stated that all persons "shall be entitled to the full and equal enjoyment of accommodations, advantages, facilities, and privileges of inns, public conveyances on land or water, theaters, and other places of public amusement" regardless of race.[144] The 1881 Tennessee state statue soon extended its influence to match the 1875 Act, and enforce segregation in all public spaces.

In Memphis, an incident involving Julia Hooks demonstrated the declining rights of educated and respected African American women to occupy public spaces. Hooks purchased a ticket for a performance in a Memphis theater near the front orchestra section. After sitting where her ticket indicated, an employee asked her to relocate to the balcony with the other African Americans. The theater, he explained, had recently determined that the front section existed for "whites only." Hooks, who had paid for a seat in that section and had sat there on many previous occasions, refused to move until two police officers arrived. As they dragged her to an exit, tearing her dress in the process, Hooks told the men, "Let go of me, I am a schoolteacher." In mentioning her profession, she attempted to inform the police that she was a respectable woman, but her declaration did not stop the officers, who removed her from the theater and arrested her for disorderly conduct. Undaunted, Hooks filed a complaint against the police officers, but her defiance contradicted her status as a lady, triggering several unflattering portrayals of her in the press. Newspaper accounts referred to her as "uppity" and noted how even "perfumed to the highest essence" and wearing "her best store clothes," she was little more than a "cheeky wench."[145] A judge dismissed her case against the police officers and the court ordered Hooks to pay a five-dollar fine for her disorderly conduct.[146]

Two years later, Wells encountered nearly the same treatment on a train and, like Hooks, fought for her right to occupy the seat she purchased. Although the law now required railroad companies to offer equal, if separate, accommodations to all customers, the only way that railroad companies could meet this mandate was by pulling three cars: one smoker, one white first-class car, and one black car. Yet most companies continued to pull only two passenger cars.[147] When the conductor ejected Wells from a train in 1883, there was only one first-class car, and this deficiency became the successful basis for Wells's lawsuit. In 1884, she won her case after her lawyer, Thomas Cassells, called several witnesses to testify to the inequity of the two cars; one noted the presence of an intoxicated white man in the smoker's car, while another confirmed that several men were smoking in the car. A third witness described the atmosphere of the smoker's car as "rough" and filled with vulgar talk, concluding that it was "no fit place for a Lady."[148] Since those behaviors were not occurring in the first-class car, the judge, James Pierce, a Union veteran from Minnesota, noted in his opinion that "she was thereby refused the first class accommodations to which she was entitled under the law. The policy of Tennessee upon this subject has been embodied in statutes." He continued to clarify his ruling, noting that the issue of segregation was not at the heart of Wells's suit, but rather equal accommodations. "The wrong complained of is the failure to furnish with the classification, accommodations for the colored passengers equal to those accorded to the white passengers."[149] Judge Pierce ruled in Wells's favor and awarded her five hundred dollars.[150] On December 25, 1884, the *Memphis Daily Appeal* detailed the outcome of her court case with the headline "A Darky Damsel Obtains a Verdict for Damages against the Chesapeake & Ohio Railroad—What It Cost to Put a Colored School Teacher in a Smoking Car—Verdict for $500" and concluded this was as "it should be."[151]

For the next three years, the Chesapeake, Ohio, Southwestern Railroad Company challenged the ruling and the case worked its way through the Tennessee legal system until it reached the State Supreme Court in 1887. After winning in the Circuit Court, Wells noticed that her lawyer appeared to have lost his enthusiasm for representing her and even discouraged her from fighting the appeal. The railroad, Cassells told Wells, assured him that they would not evict her again from the first-class car. Wells, concerned about his attitude, felt his change in heart resulted from a bribe that the railroad offered Cassells in return for poorly representing her case on appeal. After some investigation she claimed, "I found he had been bought off…and as he was the only colored lawyer in town I had to get a white one," and so she did, James M. Greer.[152] She never offered any direct proof of Cassells's corruption; he denied her charges and never forgave her for leveling such accusations against him.[153]

In between her original lawsuit and the appeal case, the practice of racial exclusion on public transportation increased, and African American women suing railroad companies demanding equal accommodations faced a rhetorical shift from justifying the separation of passengers by race rather than reputation.[154] During the 1887 appeal of her case, Wells and her lawyer presented the same evidence as in 1884; they established that the smoker car accommodations were in no way equal to the ladies first-class car and that the railroad had failed to provide a separate and equal space for first-class black passengers.[155] Greer noted, "If the cars were truly equal, white women would be indifferent as to which car they rode in."[156] Holmes Cummins, the Chesapeake, Ohio, Southwestern Railroad's lawyer, chose to focus on Wells's behavior, characterizing her as a disgraceful troublemaker seeking only to aggravate the company.[157] Her actions in physically fighting back did not contradict this depiction.

The Court agreed with the railroad, with the opinion finding Wells's lawsuit likely an effort to make a test case out of her treatment and that Wells intended to "harass" the railroad company. The judgment found her refusal to move to the smoker car to be not "in good faith" for her to "obtain a comfortable seat for the short ride." Her ensuing fight with the railroad's employees occurred, therefore, "without the slightest reason."[158] Indeed, the court ruled that the two cars were "alike in every respect as to comfort, convenience and safety" at least for a "mulatto passenger." As such, the court determined that Wells had no legal right to "arbitrarily determine" which coach she would ride in.[159] The Court also reversed the previous award of $500 in damages.[160] Furthermore, the court held her liable for $200 in court fees. To Wells, who had spent a considerable amount of her own money to fight her unjust treatment, the verdict was a personal blow as well as a setback for her entire race.[161] Reflecting on the appeal she wrote in her diary, "I felt so disappointed because I had hoped such great things from my suit for my people generally." She realized that her belief in the legal system was misplaced. "I have firmly believed all along that the law was on our side and would, when we appealed to it, give us justice."[162]

Wells's experience with the legal system foreshowed the evolution of segregation.[163] A few months after her appeal case, the State Supreme Court cited its ruling in Wells's case as setting the legal precedent for allowing "a railway company may make reasonable regulations concerning the car in which a passenger might be required to ride." Having already ruled that the smoking car offered a "reasonable" accommodation for an African American woman, Wells's case supported the right of railroad companies to prevent blacks from riding in the first-class car.[164] This subsequent ruling clarified any confusion as to the objective of the State Supreme Court decision on Wells's appeal case; it was clearly the court's intent to create a legal basis for the establishment of racial segregation in Tennessee.[165] In her autobiography, Wells contextualized her lawsuit by noting that if the State Supreme Court justices had upheld the original ruling, then her case would have opened the door to claims across the South. Her legal loss foreshadowed similar rulings that would constrain the social and political freedoms of southern African Americans. A few years later, in 1891, the Tennessee legislature passed a statute that defined segregation in public spaces and "empowered conductors to eject passengers seated in the other race's coach." It also prohibited "passengers from challenging the conductor's decision in any Tennessee court," therefore cutting off the legal system as an avenue to fight unequal treatment.[166]

Anna Cooper, a black southern author, educator, and activist described an incident in her book *A Voice from the South* (1892) that illustrates the social consequences of these legal decisions for African American women. Cooper writes of her own experience when she encountered a set of restroom doors at a train station. The label on one bathroom door identified it as "For Ladies" and the other "For Colored People." Cooper's initial reaction was puzzlement as to which door she should choose.[167] Realization soon dawned on her that her skin color now determined her social status, regardless of her gender, wealth, morals, or education. Cooper, in gazing at the two doors, recognized the decisive shift in racial life in the South that had occurred. Under segregation, she realized, she was only a black body.

Wells's early experiences shaped the rest of her life. Young Ida saw the importance of political power in making social progress as she watched her father and others fight against white oppression, often at great physical risk. After the Yellow Fever epidemic, Wells applied the education she received during Reconstruction to support her family. When she moved to Memphis, she struggled as a single, young, urban, black woman to conform to the requirements of True Womanhood. Although Wells sought to temper herself in order to preserve her reputation, she could contain herself no longer after the incident on the train in 1883. In that moment, her manners, dress, education, and morals failed to matter. Her race became her defining characteristic, an idea that challenged her view of herself. During her legal battle, she recognized the erosion of African American civil liberties all around her as regulations enforcing segregation sprang up in every southern state. Even though she ultimately lost her appeal before the Tennessee Supreme Court, the ruling inspired her to continue to fight against other instances of social discrimination. To begin, she published about her court struggles, sharing her experience with a wide-ranging audience and entering the next phase of her career as a journalist.

NOTES

1 Giddings, *Ida: A Sword among Lions*, 22; Davidson says fifty-nine times, 15.

2 McMurry, 6–7.

3 Giddings, *Ida: A Sword among Lions*, 17.

4 Numbers calculated from those provided in McMurry, 5.

5 Ruth Watkins, "Reconstruction in Marshall County," *Publications of the Mississippi Historical Society* 12 (1912): 156.

6 Although Jim did not experience much physical violence during slavery, the same is not true of his mother. The day after Morgan died, Polly ordered Jim's mother Peggy, "stripped and whipped" as retaliation for having a son with her husband. Wells, *Crusade for Justice*, 10.

7 Davidson, 18; Giddings, *Ida: A Sword among Lions,* 10, 19; McMurry, 4.

8 Mia Bay, *To Tell the Truth Freely: The Life of Ida B. Wells* (New York: Hill and Wang, 2009), 22; Giddings, *Ida: A Sword among Lions,* 15.

9 Reginald Washington, "Sealing the Sacred Bonds of Holy Matrimony Freedmen's Bureau Marriage Records," *Prologue Magazine,* spring 2005, http://www.archives.gov/publications/prologue/2005/spring/freedman-marriage-recs.html (accessed March 21, 2016).

10 Schechter, *Ida B. Wells-Barnett and American Reform*, 11.

11 "15th Amendment to the Constitution," *The Library of Congress*, 1870, loc.gov/rr/program/bib/ourdocs/15thamendment.html (accessed March 21, 2016).

12 Giddings, *Ida: A Sword among Lions*, 26.

13 Cory Campbell, "Revels, Hiram Rhoades," *The Online Reference Guide to African American History*, 2007–15, http://www.blackpast.org/aah/revels-hiram-rhoades-1827–1901 (accessed March 21, 2016).

14 Senate Historical Office, "Former Slave Presides over Senate," *United States Senate: Senate History*, https://www.senate.gov/artandhistory/history/minute/Former_Slave_Presides_Over_Senate.htm (accessed March 21, 2016). Bay, *To Tell the Truth Freely*, 26. Bruce also took on the same name as his former master. Watkins, "Reconstruction in Marshall County," 172.

15 Editorial, "The Freedmen's Bureau The Bills Before Congress To-Day," *The New York Times*, Feburary 9, 1865, http://www.nytimes.com/1865/02/09/news/the-freedmen-s-bureau-th (accessed March 21, 2016).

16 Fritz Hamer, "Wade Hampton: Conflicted Leader of the Conservative Democracy?," *Wade Hampton III—A Symposium* (Columbia: University of South Carolina, 2008), 94.

17 Watkins, "Reconstruction in Marshall County," 176.

18 Eric Foner, *Reconstruction: America's Unfinished Revolution, 1863–1877* (New York: Harper-Collins, 1988), 31, 75–78, 96.

19 Giddings, *Ida: A Sword among Lions,* 19.

20 Bay, *To Tell the Truth Freely*, 16.

21 Giddings, *Ida: A Sword among Lions*, 11; Davidson, 21; Duster, ed., *Crusade for Justice,* xv.

22 Davidson, 21.

23 Davidson, 23–24; Bay, *To Tell the Truth Freely,* 21.

24 "Sharecropper Contract, 1867," *The Gilder Lehrman Institute of American History*, n.d., http://www.gilderlehrman.org/history-by-era/reconstruction/resources/sharecropper-contract-1867 (accessed March 21, 2016).

25 Watkins, "Reconstruction in Marshall County," 204.

26 Ida B. Wells-Barnett and Jacqueline Jones Royster, *Southern Horrors and Other Writings: The Anti-Lynching Campaign of Ida B. Wells, 1892–1900* (Boston: Bedford Books, 1997), 6; Foner, 93.

27 Foner, 94.

28 Bay, *To Tell the Truth Freely,* 19–20.

29 Preston King, "Ida B. Wells and the Management of Violence," *Critical Review of International Social and Political Philosophy* 7, no. 4 (2004): 141.

30   Watkins, "Reconstruction in Marshall County," 178.
31   Davidson, 27.
32   Watkins, "Reconstruction in Marshall County," 168.
33   Giddings, *Ida: A Sword among Lions,* 24–25.
34   Watkins, "Reconstruction in Marshall County," 186–87.
35   Bay, 25.
36   Watkins, "Reconstruction in Marshall County," 178.
37   McMurry, 10.
38   Giddings, *Ida: A Sword among Lions,* 23; Davidson, 25.
39   Watkins, "Reconstruction in Marshall County," 189–90.
40   Watkins, "Reconstruction in Marshall County," 192–93.
41   Davidson, 30–31.
42   Wells, *Crusade for Justice,* 9; Giddings, *Ida: A Sword among Lions,* 31.
43   Tera W. Hunter, *To 'Joy My Freedom: Southern Black Women's Lives and Labors after the Civil War* (Cambridge, MA: Harvard University Press, 1997), 40.
44   Across the South, black women like Lizzie also embraced leadership roles in the newly forming black churches, using their talents to gain some control of their lives and help others. See Evelyn Brooks Higginbotham, *Righteous Discontent: The Women's Movement in the Black Baptist Church, 1880–1920* (Cambridge, MA: Harvard University Press, 1993).
45   See Jacqueline Jones, *Labor of Love, Labor of Sorrow: Black Women, Work, and the Family from Slavery to the Present* (New York: Basic Books, 1985), 4–5; Leslie A. Schwalm, *A Hard Fight for We: Women's Transition from Slavery to Freedom in South Carolina* (Urbana: University of Illinois Press, 1997), 262; Catherine Clinton, "Bloody Terrain: Freedwomen, Sexuality and Violence during Reconstruction," *The Georgia Historical Quarterly* 76, no. 2 (1992): 332.
46   Watkins, "Reconstruction in Marshall County," 201.
47   Davidson, 34.
48   Giddings, *Ida: A Sword among Lions,* 31; Bay, *To Tell the Truth Freely,* 28.
49   Bay, *To Tell the Truth Freely,* 24; Davidson, 37; Wells, *Crusade for Justice,* 21–2; Giddings, *Ida: A Sword Among Lions,* 31.
50   Davidson, 43.
51   Bay, *To Tell the Truth Freely,* 27.
52   Davidson, 44.
53   Quoted in Giddings, *Ida: A Sword among Lions,* 32–33; see also fn 62, p. 666.
54   McMurry, 14.
55   Davidson, 46, 44; Giddings, *Ida: A Sword among Lions,* 33.
56   McMurry, 15.
57   Her brother Eddie died either during childbirth or shortly afterward. Duster, ed., *Crusade for Justice,* xv; Giddings, *Ida: A Sword among Lions,* 27.
58   Davidson, 47; McMurry, 15.
59   Wells, *Crusade for Justice,* 11.
60   Giddings, *Ida: A Sword among Lions,* 35.
61   Wells, *Crusade for Justice,* 12–13.
62   Giddings, *Ida: A Sword among Lions,* 36, 42.
63   Wells, *Crusade for Justice,* 12–13.
64   McMurry, 16.
65   Wells, *Crusade for Justice,* 13, 17.
66   Giddings, *Ida: A Sword among Lions,* 38.
67   Davidson, 50.
68   McMurry, 16.
69   Davidson, 50.
70   McMurry, 14.

71 Ida B. Wells, *The Memphis Diary of Ida B. Wells: An Intimate Portrait of the Activist as a Young Woman*, ed. Miriam Decosta-Willis (Boston: Beacon Press, 1995), 78.

72 Bay, *To Tell the Truth Freely*, 37.

73 McMurry, 17.

74 Davidson, 56.

75 Wells, *Crusade for Justice*, 18; Davidson, 53, 64; Bay, *To Tell the Truth Freely*, 38, 40.

76 Davidson, 56; McMurry, 18, 21.

77 P. Gabrielle Foreman, "The Memphis Diary of Ida B. Wells by Miriam DeCosta-Willis (review)," *African American Review* 31, no. 2 (1997): 364.

78 Decosta-Willis, ed., *The Memphis Diary of Ida B. Wells*, xxii.

79 Bay, *To Tell the Truth Freely*, 105–6.

80 Joy James, "Shadowboxing: Liberation Limbos—Ida B. Wells," in *Black Women's Intellectual Traditions: Speaking Their Minds*, eds Kristin Waters and Carol B. Conaway (Lebanon: University of Vermont Press, 2007), 346–47; Duster, ed., *Crusade for Justice*, foreword.

81 Anne Braden, *The Wall Between* (New York: Monthly Review Press, 1958), 21.

82 Giddings, *Ida: A Sword among Lions*, 55–56.

83 Giddings, *Ida: A Sword among Lions*, 94.

84 Quoted in Bay, *To Tell the Truth Freely*, 40–41. In December 1885, she wrote in her diary of her splurges at the department store Menken, noting that she had received her bill "of $78 and I have no money to pay it" and in another entry lamenting, "My expenses are transcending my income; I must stop." Decosta-Willis, ed., *The Memphis Diary of Ida B. Wells*, 26, 59.

85 Quoted in Schechter, *Ida B. Wells-Barnett and American Reform*, 50.

86 Giddings, *Ida: A Sword among Lions*, 93.

87 Giddings, *Ida: A Sword among Lions*, 47; Schechter, *Ida B. Wells-Barnett and American Reform*, 45.

88 McMurry, 77–78; Giddings, *Ida: A Sword among Lions*, 74.

89 Giddings, *Ida: A Sword among Lions*, 74.

90 Decosta-Willis, ed., *The Memphis Diary of Ida B. Wells*, 20, 37.

91 Wells, *Crusade for Justice*, 31.

92 McMurry, 34.

93 McMurry, 78.

94 Davidson, 58–59. She also worshiped at the Beale Street Baptist Church, the Immanuel Episcopal Church, and the Colored Methodist Episcopal Church. Less often, she attended the Second Congregational Church or the LeMoyne Institute. Many of these churches had African American bishops and learning from an African American was a new experience for Wells. She recalled in her autobiography, "All my teachers had been the consecrated white men and women from the North who came into the South to teach immediately after the end of the war." Wells, *Crusade for Justice*, 22.

95 Schechter, *Ida B. Wells-Barnett and American Reform*, 50–51, 67.

96 Wells, *Crusade for Justice*, 22–53.

97 Giddings, *Ida: A Sword among Lions*, 74–75; McMurry, 35.

98 Wells, *Crusade for Justice*, 22–23.

99 McMurry, 36; Davidson, 61–62.

100 Schechter, *Ida B. Wells-Barnett and American Reform*, 43.

101 McMurry, 36.

102 McMurry, 53–54; see also Barbara Welter, "The Cult of True Womanhood: 1820–1860," *American Quarterly* 18, no. 2 (1966): 151–74; Linda M. Perkins, "The Impact of the 'Cult of True Womanhood' on the Education of Black Women," *Journal of Social Issues* 39, no. 3 (1983): 17–28; Amii Larkin Barnard, "The Application of Critical Race Feminism to the Anti-Lynching Movement: Black Women's Fight against Race and Gender Ideology, 1892–1920," *UCLA Women's Law Journal* 3, no. 27 (1993): 2.

103   Giddings, *Ida: A Sword among Lions,* 55–56; Brittney Cooper, "A'n't I a Lady ?: Race Women, Michelle Obama, and the Ever-Expanding Democratic Imagination," *MELUS (Multi-Ethnic Literatures of the U.S.)* 35, no. 4 (2010): 42; Bay, *To Tell the Truth Freely,* 74.

104   Giddings, *Ida: A Sword among Lions,* 85.

105   McMurry, 52–53.

106   McMurry, 51; Giddings, *Ida: A Sword among Lions,* 60; Decosta-Willis, *The Memphis Diary of Ida B. Wells,* 8.

107   McMurry, 53.

108   Decosta-Willis, ed., *The Memphis Diary of Ida B. Wells,* 150.

109   McMurry, 64.

110   Giddings, *Ida: A Sword among Lions,* 98; Bay, *To Tell the Truth Freely,* 59.

111   Decosta-Willis, ed., *The Memphis Diary of Ida B. Wells,* 80.

112   Bay, *To Tell the Truth Freely,* 59.

113   Among the characteristics Wells wrote that she would not tolerate were "sugaring men, weak, deceitful creatures, with flattery to retain them as escorts." Decosta-Willis, ed., *The Memphis Diary of Ida B. Wells,* xi.

114   As quoted in Giddings, *Ida: A Sword among Lions,* 101.

115   Decosta-Willis, ed., *The Memphis Diary of Ida B. Wells,* 44.

116   Decosta-Willis, ed., *The Memphis Diary of Ida B. Wells,* 74.

117   Giddings, *Ida: A Sword among Lions,* 105.

118   Decosta-Willis, ed., *The Memphis Diary of Ida B. Wells,* 41.

119   Giddings, *Ida: A Sword among Lions,* 106.

120   Decosta-Willis, ed., *The Memphis Diary of Ida B. Wells,* 59.

121   Decosta-Willis, ed., *The Memphis Diary of Ida B. Wells,* 66. Wells may have been distracted from Brown by her long-distance correspondence with two men, Charles S. Morris and Edwin Hackley. Morris, a journalist from Louisville, Kentucky, lost her interest after he sent a photo of himself, an image, she felt, of a "mere boy." This prompted her to ask his age, disappointing her when she discovered that he was her junior by two years. Decosta-Willis, ed., *The Memphis Diary of Ida B. Wells,* 31. Wells, nevertheless, continued to write to him, but stopped when his letters discussed his need for a traditional wife and disgust at her public performances as part of the Memphis Lyceum. Giddings, *Ida: A Sword among Lions,* 103–5. Her letters with Hackley similarly began with mutual interest but, over time, Wells felt he became slower and slower to respond back. She noted in her diary, "I would write again but it would have the appearance of eagerness." When he did not return her letter but instead enclosed a news clipping of his recent nomination for the Colorado legislature, she was unsure if this constituted a response. She concluded that his slacking communication demonstrated a lack of serious interest, and her last reference to him in her diary describes him as "my Denver one-time-friend." McMurry, 59.

122   Decosta-Willis, ed., *The Memphis Diary of Ida B. Wells,* 83.

123   Her travel preparations left little of her life in Memphis. She paid off her account at Menken's, the local clothing store, and withdrew all of her savings, about eighty-five dollars, from the bank. Giddings, *Ida: A Sword among Lions,* 111.

124   McMurry, 44; Giddings, *Ida: A Sword among Lions,* 111.

125   Decosta-Willis, ed., *The Memphis Diary of Ida B. Wells,* 93.

126   Wells, *Crusade for Justice,* 24–25.

127   Giddings, *Ida: A Sword among Lions,* 119; Decosta-Willis, ed., *The Memphis Diary of Ida B. Wells,* 103.

128   The town's history, founded by Kentucky slave-owners and Confederate sympathizers, may offer an answer for these inequalities. Davidson, 98.

129   McMurry, 49. She recalled how in Visalia the black families had asked for a segregated school and felt that offered a "tacit acknowledgment of the inferiority" that whites expected. McMurry, 109.

130 Wells, *Crusade for Justice*, 26–27.

131 Decosta-Willis, ed., *The Memphis Diary of Ida B. Wells*, 88.

132 Giddings, *Ida: A Sword among Lions,* 120, 125; McMurry, 49–51.

133 Decosta-Willis, *The Memphis Diary of Ida B. Wells*, 113.

134 Wells, *Crusade for Justice*, 31.

135 Decosta-Willis, ed., *The Memphis Diary of Ida B. Wells*, 27.

136 Decosta-Willis, ed., *The Memphis Diary of Ida B. Wells*, 59.

137 Bay, *To Tell the Truth Freely*, 68–69.

138 Davidson, 99.

139 Prior to 1865, the law required that railroad companies give "passengers a right to passage," but this did not include the "right to choose their seat." Bay, *To Tell the Truth Freely*, 50.

140 Kenneth W. Mack, "Law, Society, Identity, and the Making of the Jim Crow South: Travel and Segregation on Tennessee Railroads, 1875–1905," *Law and Social Inquiry* 24 (Spring 1999): 388.

141 Giddings, *Ida: A Sword among Lions*, 52, Mack, 388.

142 Mack, 383.

143 *Corporation Laws of Tennessee: Including Counties and Municipalities, Also Federal Corporation Income Tax Law, Revised and Annotated*, James L. Watts, ed. (Nashville: Marshall & Bruce Co. Publishers, 1910), chapter 155 (April 7, 1881), 400–1.

144 Civil Rights Act of 1875, 18 Stat. 335 (March 1, 1875). See also Bertram Wyatt-Brown, "The Civil Rights Act of 1875," *Western Political Quarterly* 18 (1965): 763–75 and John Hope Franklin, "The Enforcement of the Civil Rights Act of 1875," *Prologue Magazine* 6, no. 4 (1974): 225–35.

145 McMurry, 26; Schechter, *Ida B. Wells-Barnett and American Reform*, 43; Giddings, *Ida: A Sword among Lions*, 55–56.

146 McMurry, 26, 30.

147 Davidson, 66–67.

148 Giddings, *Ida: A Sword among Lions*, 64–65.

149 David S. Bogen, "Why the Supreme Court Lied in Plessy," *Villanova Law Review* 52, no. 3 (2007): 429–30.

150 Chesapeake, O. & S.W. R.R. v. Wells. 1885a. Trial Record. No. 312, Circuit Court of Shelby County; Davidson, 73; Giddings *Ida: A Sword among Lions*, 64.

151 McMurry, 28.

152 Wells, *Crusade for Justice,* 19.

153 McMurry, 27.

154 Mack, 384.

155 Chesapeake, O. & S.W. R.R. v. Wells. 1887. 4 S.W. 5 (Tenn.).

156 Bogen, 430.

157 McMurry refers to him as Holeman, McMurry, 28, but other accounts refer to him as Holmes, see Davidson, 71.

158 Giddings, *Ida: A Sword among Lions,* 136–37.

159 Bay, *To Tell the Truth Freely*, 54; Giddings, *Ida: A Sword among Lions,* 136–37.

160 McMurry, 29.

161 Decosta-Willis, ed., *The Memphis Diary of Ida B. Wells*, xiv.

162 Duster, ed., *Crusade for Justice*, xvii.

163 One black Louisiana man reflected on the consequences of this for African Americans observing that "the very men that held us as slaves" now controlled "[t]he whole South – every state in the South." Quoted in Foner, 244–45. Northerners, intent on the industrialization of their economy after the Civil War, barely noticed the end of Reconstruction, while abolitionists considered the plight of African Americans to be resolved with the end of slavery. See Heather Cox Richardson, *The Death of Reconstruction: Race, Labor, and Politics in the Post-Civil War North, 1865–1901* (Cambridge, MA: Harvard University Press, 2001), x, and

Michael Hatt, "Sculpting and Lynching: The Making and Unmaking of the Black Citizen in Late Nineteenth-Century America," *Oxford Art Journal* 24, no. 1 (2001), 5.

164   Bogen, 430.

165   Bay, *To Tell the Truth Freely*, 54. Her case was the first one with a black plaintiff to reach the State Supreme Court since 1875.

166   Mack, 400; *Acts of the State of Tennessee Passed at the General Assembly* (Nashville: Albert B. Tavel, Printer to the State, 1891), chapter 52 (March 27), 135–36.

167   Anna J. Cooper, *A Voice from the South* (Xenia: The Aldine Printing House, 1892), 96.

CHAPTER 2

MEMPHIS AGITATIONS, 1887–92

After Wells won her initial lawsuit in 1884, her fight against the Chesa-peake & Ohio Railroad garnered public attention. A new African American newspaper, *The Living Way,* one of the increasing number of black-owned newspapers emerging across the South, inquired as to whether Wells was interested in writing about her experience in court. When readers offered positive feedback on her unpaid article, she continued to write occasionally for the paper.[1] During Reconstruction, the rise of black presses reflected a desire by African Americans to define their own perspectives on race relations, education, politics, and society. As the practice of segregation entrenched during the 1880s, blacks recognized the necessity of creating presses separate from the white media. This desire to discuss the issues of the day, combined with technological developments lowering the cost to print newspaper, led to the increasing publication of newspapers and magazines by and for African Americans. Black-owned presses published nearly two hundred weekly newspapers in 1884, and as conditions in the South worsened, black newspapers became a principal site rallying for social change.[2]

Wells entered the arena of journalism through her court case and, in 1886, when the Memphis Lyceum elected her as the editor of the *Evening Star,* her delight in writing intensified. After the loss of her appeal in 1887, in which the court not only ruled against her but also saddled her with two hundred dollars in court costs, Wells began working as a correspondent for the national periodical, *The American Baptist Magazine.* This exposed her writings to a larger audience and, more importantly, the publication compensated her with what she described as the "lavish sum" of one dol-lar for each weekly article. Wells "never dreamed" of being remunerated for her journalism, and felt privileged that anyone would "pay me for the work

I had enjoyed doing."[3] Soon, Wells's prose and unique point of view led to other solicitations by newspapers and magazines for her articles.[4]

A growing number of women entered the field of journalism during the 1880s. Writing offered women, both black and white, the chance to articulate their ideas to a large audience with minimal risk. Many, like Wells, began by reporting for local or church publications and occasionally achieved regional or national recognition. Gertrude Mossell, a black Philadelphian, earned enough money from her writings to support herself, as did Mary, or as she preferred, "Meb" Hooks, the younger sister of Julia Hooks, the woman dragged from a Memphis theater for refusing to relinquish her purchased seat.[5] Most journalists, especially African Americans, chose to write under a pen name, allowing them to keep their anonymity for their own personal safety.[6] Wells wrote under the pen name "Iola," and although she never explained the origin of the name, it may have evolved from how her siblings pronounced her name when they were young.[7] In choosing "Iola," Wells identified herself as female to the public, and her work in primarily African American publications reflected her race. Indeed, she appears not to have guarded her identity closely, often signing letters to friends using her pen name, suggesting their familiarity with her dual identity.[8]

As "Iola," Wells drew upon her experiences teaching in rural areas to imagine those country people as her audience. Her *The Living Way* column, she felt, considered "problems in a simple, helpful way," using "plain, common-sense" writing. She recalled, "Knowing that their [her readers'] education was limited, I never used a word of two syllables where one would serve the purpose."[9] Despite claiming to prefer a straightforward writing style in her diary, the intellectual and logical arguments of "Iola's" eloquent prose soon became her trademark style.[10] Wells began her writing career by discussing her lawsuit, and so unlike many of her fellow women journalists, whose editors often limited them to writing about "women's" issues, she never faced content restrictions. Instead, she commented on political, economic, and gender issues, and her use of language presented "an outlet through which to express the real 'me.'" Her writing, she realized, satisfied her "to the utmost."[11] This fulfillment made her less content with her teaching position, but as a black single woman, she could not support herself as a writer. Few male journalists lived solely from their publications without a second full-time career, and her only paying job for *The Living Way* could hardly compare to her current teaching salary of sixty dollars a month.[12]

In one of her earliest articles, "Women's Mission" (1885), Wells applied the tenets of the Cult of True Womanhood to African American women, encouraging them to strive for a "pure" lifestyle free of "all vicissitudes and temptations."[13] She criticized "idleness" and instead encouraged an "earnest, thoughtful, pure noble womanhood."[14] She revisited this discussion of African American women bearing responsibility for appearing virtuous and industrious again in 1888 after she lost her appeal before the Tennessee State Supreme Court, likely provoked by the court's focus on her behavior to justify her removal from the train. This second article, entitled "The Model Woman: A Pen Picture of the Typical Southern Girl," continued to emphasize the need for black women to appear respectable and moral in order to put the black race's best image forward.[15] Writing "Women's Mission" and "The Model Woman" presented Wells an opportunity to encourage these attributes in others and perhaps reaffirm the desirability of these traits for herself. In her diary she also openly admired Mrs. Settle as a woman who embodied the ideas of True Womanhood, describing her as "the sweetest, quietest and most lady like little creature," a contrast to her own self-incriminations for losing her temper and behaving in an "unladylike way."[16]

Wells, still single, mentioned in her diary that she remained the only unmarried teacher at her school. While Wells enjoyed her independence, the choice not to marry often raised questions about her virtue and prevented her from reaching a higher social standing, as marriage offered women both a male protector and economic security. Married women also avoided having their bodies and actions watched as closely in the public sphere.[17] Yet, Wells held fast to her previous choice to remain single and apparently grew accustomed to it. When she served as a bridesmaid in her friend Stella's wedding, she expressed no envy, merely commenting, "Everybody said we looked 'sweet' & I guess we did." In another passage, she wrote dismissively of a recently married woman accompanied by her "inevitable baby."[18] As Wells formed her activist identity, she abandoned some of her earlier ideas about conforming to a white standard of True Womanhood and instead created her own moral code based on righting social wrongs.

In 1887, an article Wells wrote advocating for blacks to consider independence from their historical political allegiances attracted the attention of T. Thomas Fortune, the well-known African American editor of the *New York Age*, often considered the "best Negro paper of its day."[19] Fortune, who had been born into slavery, wrote essays attacking the system of white supremacy in the South, using strong language and sarcastic humor.[20] Two years before Wells's article, in 1885, Fortune had composed a piece on the subject of race and politics, suggesting that African Americans stop blindly voting for Republicans and instead consider both candidates' policies. Many blacks perceived Fortune's article as a betrayal of the Republican Party and he faced substantial criticism for daring to suggest that the party of the emancipator, President Lincoln, might not always represent the best interests of African Americans. In her *Living Way* article, Wells recognized him for his bravery in voicing an unpopular opinion. She noted, "Mr. Fortune has always claimed to be working in the interests of the race, which he holds to be superior to those of any party, and not for party favors or interests; and his position is the right, the true one." [21] Wells's defense earned her an ally in Fortune and the two began a regular correspondence.

In 1887, Fortune founded the Afro-American League, a non-partisan group open to both men and women. He envisioned the organization as unifying blacks across the nation in order to agitate for the return of their political rights, arguing, "[W]e have got to take hold of this problem ourselves." Fortune stated his belief that "agitations are inevitable" and "as necessary to [the] social organism as blood to [the] animal organism." [22] He identified several key grievances facing the black race, beginning with the loss of voting rights for African American men in the South. He also sought to end the lynchings of African Americans, unequal schools, disparate treatment of the blacks before the law and the subpar accommodations that blacks suffered under segregation. [23] Fortune's approach to activism influenced Wells, and she spent the remainder of her life fighting against each of the issues he recognized as the root sources of racial inequality.

Wells admired Fortune's outspokenness and agitation for social justice, and through her association with him identified the power of the press to shape ideas and stimulate change. She praised the organization for drawing attention to white southerners' treatment of African Americans, in particular Fortune's recognition that the violence employed by southerners reinforced white supremacy, remarking, "Innocent men and women are victims of mob and lynch law." She also appreciated his focus on unfair accommodations, noting from her own experiences, "cultured and refined ladies and gentlemen are insulted and proscribed on the railways every day...why?" [24] Another of Fortune's early advocates for the Afro-American League was Booker T. Washington. Born a slave in Virginia in 1856, Washington attended the Hampton Institute after the Civil War while working as a janitor. His intellect and work ethic gained the attention of the Institute's president, who nominated him to head a new vocational school in Alabama for blacks, the Tuskegee Institute. [25] Washington wrote to Fortune, "Let there be no hold-up until a League shall be found in every village." [26] Although Wells and other African Americans supported Fortune's vision, whites condemned the organization. The Charleston (SC) *News and Courier* warned, "The colored people...have nothing whatever to gain by organizing... [T]his merely strengthens racial divisions." In a similar tone, the *Constitution* in Atlanta, Georgia reported, "There is no conceivable direction in which an organization can do the Negro race any good, and it might do great harm." [27]

In the fall of 1887, Wells traveled to the National Colored Press Association meeting in Louisville, Kentucky, where she made her national debut as a journalist. The editor of *The American Baptist Magazine*, Reverend

William J. Simmons, offered to pay Wells's expenses in return for her proxy vote (on his behalf) at the convention. She agreed, and at the event finally had the opportunity to meet Fortune face to face. His physical description, she felt, failed to match his literary talent. "With his long hair, curling about his forehead and his spectacles he looks more like the dude of the period than the strong, sensible, brainy man I have pictured him."[28] Fortune, in response to seeing Wells for the first time, favorably described her as "rather girlish looking in physique, with sharp regular features, penetrating eyes, firm set lips and a sweet voice," and noted that from "a mere, insignificant country-bred lass she has developed into one of the foremost among the female thinkers of the race." She was, he felt, as "smart as a steel trap" and he appreciated how she had "no sympathy for humbug."[29] He described her increased exposure, with her writings appearing across the nation, making her "a great success in journalism and we can feel proud of a woman whose ability and energy serve to make her so."[30] He concluded, "She has become famous as one of the few of our women who handle a goose quill with diamond point as easily as any man in newspaper work. If Iola were a man, she would be a humming independent in politics" for "[s]he handles her subjects more as a man than as a woman."[31]

Along with Fortune, Wells saw Frederick Douglass at the meeting, as well as the former U.S. Senator Blanche K. Bruce from Mississippi. Her treatment among such distinguished black leaders pleasantly surprised her. She noted, "I suppose it was because I was their first woman representative," but nonetheless noted she was "tickled pink" over the attention she received.[32] News correspondents also took notice of Wells at the conference. The journalist Lucy Wilmot Smith commented, "None struck harder blows at the wrongs and weaknesses of the race" than Wells and concluded, "She is an inspiration to the young writers."[33] A New Orleans report on the convention found "Iola" to be "the most prominent correspondent" at the meeting and characterized her as "brilliant" and "earnest." The article continued on a cautionary note, remarking that the author hoped all the attention she received at the conference would not "suffer her head to become unduly inflated."[34]

The widespread practice in the African American press of reprinting editorials and commentaries from various papers exposed Wells to a broader audience, including the *Marion Headlight,* located in Marion, Arkansas, directly across the river from Memphis. The editor, African American J. L. Fleming, publically criticized the treatment of blacks by whites. Meanwhile in Memphis, the Reverend Taylor Nightingale, the pastor of the Beale Street Baptist Church, began a new newspaper in 1887, named *The Free Speech.* Wells chose not to write for this new local paper, as she greatly disliked Nightingale. In her diary, she discussed the root of this aversion, beginning when Nightingale decided to run against the black incumbent, Fred

Savage, Jr., for a position on the city's School Board. During the 1886 campaign, she felt he "boasted so and conducted himself generally in such an obnoxious manner that it completely disgusted me with him." Additionally, Wells believed Nightingale to be a "toady," that is, a flunky recruited by local whites in order to split the black vote, a successful tactic that resulted in the election of an all-white School Board.[35]

In 1888, armed men who claimed that they were the town's "best white citizens," escorted nearly one hundred African Americans from Marion, Alabama, including four elected town officials, a doctor, the schoolteacher, and two preachers. Claiming a desire to liberate themselves from "Negro rule," the vigilantes marched their captives to the town limits and gave them the choice of getting on a train or a boat.[36] J. L. Fleming, the editor of the *Marion Headlight,* was among those rounded up, and he chose to cross the river to Memphis. Shortly after his arrival, fellow newspaperman Nightingale offered Fleming a place at *The Free Speech.* The men combined the names of their respective papers, creating *The Free Speech and Headlight.*[37] The Memphis location offered "a prime playing field" for the newspaper with its sizable African American population, and the revamped paper quickly gained a reputation for advocating for the rights of African Americans.[38] Nightingale especially encouraged resistance, publishing rousing statements including one urging blacks to "contend for their rights" even "if they had to die in the ditch up to their necks in blood."[39]

In light of Wells's popularity and similar views on equal rights, Nightingale and Fleming approached her about writing for them. Wells's rising aspiration to edit her own paper made the offer appealing, but she no longer desired to be a minor partner. She agreed only if the men brought her on board as an equal and sold her a one-third interest in the paper. She later recalled, "Since the appetite grows for what it feeds on, the desire came to own a paper," and she seized her chance.[40] The three owners divided the duties among themselves. Nightingale, as the sales manager, sold advertising and the paper to his congregation at church on Sunday, often distributing around five hundred copies each week. Fleming managed the office and Wells provided most of the editorial content.[41] Reflecting the change in ownership, the paper returned to its original moniker, *The Free Speech.* Wells struggled to balance caring for her sister, her day job, her commitments to write for other publications, and her role as editor. Her schedule might have resulted in the erratic timetable of *The Free Speech,* which missed at least one publication date entirely.[42]

Once writing for her own newspaper, Wells turned her pen to issues that she felt were affecting her community. In 1888, she wrote a series of articles criticizing members of the black clergy in Memphis. Concerned about the virtue of certain ministers who, in some cases, she felt, failed to practice what they preached, Wells spared little sympathy for those who abused their power.[43] A clergyman, she argued, should be "noble of purpose and consecrated to his work."[44] Instead, she expressed dismay at "the most corrupt, immoral and incompetent ministry" inhabiting several African American churches in Memphis.[45] She urged her readers to take action, advising them to refuse to "support and uphold one who is not worthy" in order to protect the perception of their race.[46] The impetus for her article stemmed from the antics of a well-respected Reverend, who, after Sunday services, strolled home with one of his married female parishioners. One afternoon he was "surprised by her husband," who "ran him out of the house in his night clothes."[47]

After "Iola's" public criticism of the black ministry, several preachers formed an alliance and threatened to have their congregations boycott *The Free Speech*, and, if this occurred, the loss of revenue would likely damage the fledgling paper. When the ministers informed the office of *The Free Speech* of their intent, Wells responded in a manner representative of her emerging boldness: the next edition of the paper listed every minister she knew of engaging in immoral conduct. The concluding remarks of the article asked readers to consider "if they were willing to support preachers who would sneak into their homes when their backs were turned and debauch their wives."[48] The threatened boycott never materialized. In 1890, Booker T. Washington continued to draw attention to this issue in his article on the subject, claiming "two-thirds" of ministers as "unfit, either mentally or morally, or both, to preach the Gospel to any one or attempt to lead any one." Pleased to find another like-minded person, Wells wrote to Washington praising his "criticism of our corrupt and ignorant ministry." She encouraged him to continue the "clean up" of immoral ministers and enclosed copies of her own writings on the subject.[49]

In a similar theme, Wells in her article "Functions of Leadership," discussed how ambitious black leaders seemed to "get all they can for themselves, and the rest may shift for themselves."[50] Wells asked her audience, "What benefit is a 'leader' if he does not devote his time, talent, and wealth to the alleviation of the poverty and misery, and elevation of his people?"[51] This practice, she continued, existed not just in Memphis, but also across the South, resulting in a large number of duplicitous black leaders. Bluntly, she concluded, "in every community there are Negroes who persecute and betray their race of their own accord to curry favor with white people and win the title of 'good nigger.'"[52] The topics Wells took on in *The Free Speech* reflect the foundation of her identity as an activist and her emerging role as an unhesitating spokesperson for her race, gender, and region.[53] "We have to fight," she argued, as simply writing about these concerns represented only the first part of the struggle towards equality. Her articles led to a level of celebrity and earned her the nickname "The Princess of the Press," likely inspired by the popular play *Princess Ida*.[54] Now a renowned public figure within the African American population, Wells also faced a considerable amount of public condemnation. Although her supporters, including Fortune, quickly defended her, Wells's writing placed her in the public sphere and her calls for action not only often overstepped the social dictates of behavior for an African American, but especially those for an African American woman. As her reputation grew, critics targeted her in an effort to silence the rising activist in Memphis.

One of the most revealing efforts to disparage Wells occurred in 1890, when the Indianapolis African American newspaper the *Freeman* published a cartoon titled, "Fortune and His Echo."

Under the title, the copy begins, "There is a species of the canine tribe known as fice—and one well developed characteristic is their propensity to bark." In the foreground two smaller dogs bay at the larger dog, one labeled "The Age" and the other the "Free Speech," representing Fortune's *New York Age* and Wells's Memphis *The Free Speech*. As a yapping dog, the comic

Figure 2.1 Political cartoon.
Source: "Fortune and His Echo," *Freeman,* April 19, 1890, p. 4

portrayed Wells and Fortune as noisily pestering bigger African American papers.

The cartoon criticized Wells in several ways. First, the title, "Fortune and his Echo," as scholar Jean Marie Lutes noted, "[r]educes her to a man's echo," suggesting her points are not her own.[55] Although the image does not explicitly name Wells, that she was the editor targeted in this image is further clarified by the cutout box in the upper-left corner, where Wells, dressed in a man's suit complete with a tie and cane, stands next to the phrase "I Would I were a Man." The words recalled Fortune's praise of Wells from the National Press Association meeting of "If Iola were a man." Edward Cooper, the editor of the *Freeman*, defended his disparagement of another African American paper and "Iola" in particular by claiming in his editorial response that she had "been petted and spoiled by a very generous press, and forgets that in a journalistic sense she must sometimes take a man's fare."[56] Yet, if Wells needed to face the same criticism as a man, why was her appearance the focus of the *Freeman*'s campaign? The media did not routinely mock male journalists' physical features. Instead, Wells's gender offered her detractors a way to devalue her by mocking her appearance and femininity.

Another unattractive drawing of Wells soon appeared in the white newspaper the Louisville *Courier Journal*, and the *Freeman* commented on the unsightly likeness, remarking, "Iola will never get a husband so long as she lets those editors make her so hideous."[57] The African American-owned *Cleveland Gazette* defended Wells, remarking that the image "hardly does her justice," but the *Freeman* chose to disagree, claiming the depiction "flattered her" and readers should remember, "Beauty and genius are not always companions…Iola makes the mistake of trying to be pretty as well as smart."[58] Although her appearance offered an easy target for her critics who exploited it to undermine her work, worse yet were those who did not concede, as even the *Freeman* did, to her talents as a writer. William Calvin Chase, the editor of the *Washington Bee*, attacked "Iola's" prose, noting that her "trenchant pen is the most conspicuous for grammatical and typographical errors." He dismissed her work as "scribbles," unworthy of space within most newspapers.[59] This critique of her writing abilities wounded Wells; she wrote in her diary, "I would not write for him for any great pay & I will write something some day [sic] that will make him wince."[60] She, however, restrained herself from publically responding to these attacks.

Wells expanded her influence beyond her writing to public speaking. Through performances at the Memphis Lyceum and elocution lessons, she honed her verbal skills. In 1887, she delivered a well-received speech at the LeMoyne Normal Institute in Memphis titled "What Lack We Yet?"[61] In 1891, Fortune asked Wells to speak at the Afro-American League meeting in Knoxville, Tennessee, her first national address. Her speech, he reported, "kept the audience in a bubble of excitement" and was "eloquent, logical, and dead in earnest." Her words, he hoped, would "arouse the women of the race to a full sense of duty in the work of the Afro-American League."[62] Although Fortune, as her supporter, may be guilty of overstating her impact in his notes from the meeting, the *Knoxville Daily Journal*'s account of her speech supported his approving tone, mentioning how Wells "captured the house by her apt and clear illustrations of the points in her address."[63]

Wells remained, until 1891, relatively unscathed from direct action against her person, primarily due to her "Iola" persona. This ended after one of her articles in *The Free Speech* targeted the conditions within the Memphis public school system. The piercing narrative discussed overcrowded classrooms and dilapidated buildings, along with an accusation of favoritism by the all-white Memphis School Board. The piece charged that some of the black female teachers received their teaching jobs based on their "illicit friendship with members of the school board" and not for their knowledge and virtue.[64] As she readied the article for printing, Wells recognized the consequences of these allegations for herself, as "I was still teaching and I wanted to hold my position." Despite this, she resolved that "some protest should be made over conditions in the colored schools." She approached Nightingale and asked if he would sign his name to the article, protecting her from reprisal. Nightingale refused, and Wells published the article without any authorial attribution.[65]

Wells, in reporting on the relationships between some black teachers and white School Board members, desired to expose these underqualified teachers who, she felt, provided African American students with a subpar education. Despite drawing public attention to the issue, Wells noticed several of these relationships continuing unabated. One teacher, from her own school, not only maintained her involvement with a white lawyer on the Board of Education, but the two grew bolder. One Saturday night Wells observed that her fellow teacher stayed out all night in the company of this white man. Although Wells never named the teacher, the Memphis newspaper the *Appeal-Avalanche* reported on the outcome of this incident. According to the report, Hattie Britton, Julia Hooks's sister, was living with Julia and her husband, Charles. When Hattie returned home early Sunday morning, her brother-in-law confronted her. After an acrimonious argument about her behavior, the young teacher ran to her room where she "snatched a pistol out of her trunk, rammed it as far into her ear as it would go and blew her brains out," leaving, as the paper luridly described, "blood and brains oozing from the wound."[66] Although not directly responsible for the young teacher's death, Wells's editorial attempt to shame her and others in her situation deserved some blame and Wells likely knew this, but she continued to defend her publication of the article as necessary to expose the conditions of the black schools, which "deserved criticism."[67]

Even though *The Free Speech* published the editorial without an author, only one owner of the press possessed an extensive knowledge of the public schools. In the fall of 1891, the Memphis School Board evidently made the same connection, and after seven years of teaching, did not renew Wells's contract. Wells did not receive notice of her termination until the first day of school, preventing her from finding another teaching job. Desiring an explicit explanation, Wells sent her lawyer to the Board of Education to determine the grounds for her dismissal. In response to his queries, the School Board simply directed him to read the editorial in *The Free Speech*, "showing criticism of them," and remarked that "[t]hey didn't care to employ a teacher who had done this." The parents of her students also failed to support Wells, much to her surprise. Her goal, to better the conditions of African American schools, she felt, warranted their support. Instead, "They simply couldn't understand why one would risk a good job, even for their children." Wells bitterly recorded one parent's response, that she "might have known" her actions would result in her dismissal but remained resolute, writing in her diary, "I thought it was right to strike a blow against a glaring evil and I did not regret it."[68]

In light of losing her teaching job, Wells devoted herself to writing for *The Free Speech* full time and a month later another anonymous editorial ignited controversy. After discussing the recent lynching of James Dudley in Georgetown, Kentucky, the author described how members of the black community retaliated against the town. In an admiring tone, the story praised African Americans for setting fire to white property in order to end the violence against blacks, and supported the necessity of "burn[ing] up whole towns" in order to discourage future attempts at racial violence. The author carefully advocated only for attacks against property, not people.[69] Wells never took credit for writing the piece, even years later in her autobiography, but historian Linda O. McMurry analyzed the writing style in comparison to her other works, and concluded that Wells likely authored the editorial.[70] Locals, however, attributed the article to Nightingale, finding the sentiments similar to his previous remarks and labeling the contents "vile." Nightingale's heavy-handed approach to his ministry and his calls for reform made both white and black Memphians view him as increasingly militant. This disapproval mounted when he began using the pages of *The Free Speech* to "abuse" his enemies. When members of his congregation asked him to recant the editorial on the Georgetown lynching, Nightingale refused. Several members of his church, angry at his "incendiary and exciting speeches on the race question," hired lawyers Josiah Settle and Thomas Cassels to bring charges of assault against

Nightingale. In return, Nightingale hired Wells's former lawyer James Greer, but despite his defense, a jury convicted Nightingale and sentenced him to eighty days in prison. Rather than serve his sentence, Nightingale sold his interest in the newspaper to Wells and Fleming and fled for Oklahoma Territory, recently opened to settlement.[71]

Now half-owner of the paper, Wells committed herself to making the press a financial success. Taking over Nightingale's role as the sales manager, Wells sought to make money by increasing the paper's subscriptions. As a newspaper badge allowed journalists free passage on railroads, Wells began traveling to the states bordering Tennessee in order to solicit subscribers and found that "people received me cordially and gave me their warm support." During her trips, she recruited correspondents to write for her paper and published her own descriptions of her travels. Her direct approach to townspeople achieved immediate success. She recalled how in Greenville, Mississippi an appeal "at the state bar association" resulted in "the subscription of every man present." At a Masonic Lodge in Water Valley, Mississippi, she left so "weighted down with silver dollars," that she immediately had to proceed to a nearby bank. She recognized these accomplishments as stemming in part from her gender, for "[a] woman editor and correspondent was a novelty."[72]

Only one incident colored her experience as an independent newspaperwoman. When she visited Vicksburg, Mississippi, Wells stayed with a minister and his wife, whom she felt "made me very welcome as their guest." She experienced a "delightful" week during her stay, meeting new people, among them several young men in whose company she enjoyed "good times." To Wells's surprise, after her departure word soon reached her that the minister was castigating her virtue. In particular, he appeared upset by her fraternization with these young men, and commented on the "very suspicious" loss of her teaching job, implying that immorality led to her dismissal. Incensed by this attack on her honor, Wells returned to Vicksburg. No longer a timid young woman, she confronted the minister and he "acknowledged that he had made the derogatory remarks." She explained to him, "my good name was all that I had in the world, that I was bound to protect it from attack by those who felt that they could do so with impunity because I had no brother or father to protect it for me."[73] He apologized, but Wells, her name tarnished, demanded a public retraction of his slander. "I said I would accept his apology provided he made it from his pulpit the following Sunday in case anyone else in town had heard of his remarks." Not content to leave him to his own devices, she wrote the following statement for him to read aloud to his congregation, "I desire to say that any remarks I have made reflecting on the character of Miss Ida B. Wells are false. This I do out of deference to her as a lady and myself as a Christian gentleman."

As an independent newspaperwoman, Wells used her power to shame the minister into offering a public apology in order to protect her reputation and her business.

By March 1892, subscriptions had increased from about fifteen hundred to approximately four thousand, and Wells's income from *The Free Speech* approached her former teacher's salary.[74] The demand for her paper grew as porters sold it on railroad routes and whenever Wells boarded a train, workers asked her for a copy, with one man remarking how "he had never known so many colored people to ask for a newspaper before."[75] As her paper's reputation grew, she began printing the editions on dyed pink newsprint, so that even those who could not read could purchase a copy for others to read to them, and soon *The Free Speech* became known in the Mississippi Delta area as the "pink paper."[76] As a result of her successes, Wells "felt sure" of her calling as a full-time journalist.[77] The spring also marked a return visit to Holly Springs, where she sold her parents' house, likely to pay off her share of *The Free Press*.[78] Only days later in Natchez, Mississippi, Wells received the life-changing news of a lynching in Memphis that killed three black men, one of them her close friend, Thomas Moss.

In its earliest form, lynching referred to executions by vigilante committees in the West, but during the Civil War and Reconstruction, the act came to possess its modern meaning of a mass mob killing.[79] In the late nineteenth and early twentieth centuries, lynchings functioned to demonstrate to African Americans the deadly consequences for disruptive racial behavior.[80] In 1892, mobs lynched two hundred and forty-one people, with southern whites targeting African Americans eighty percent of the time.[81] Although racial violence occurred outside of the South, the motives behind lynchings differed regionally. Northern lynchings offered working-class whites a vehicle for "rough justice," often aimed at repressing crime, while the objective of similar brutality in the South focused on controlling the African American population.[82] Wells, aware of lynchings occurring across the South, had never experienced one in her own town, let alone that of a friend. She had known Moss, a postal worker, since 1885 and saw him every day as he dropped off *The Free Speech*'s mail. They both taught Sunday school at Avery Chapel and Wells was the godmother of Tom and Betty's daughter Maurine.[83]

Wells returned to Memphis and immediately devoted herself to reconstructing the events leading to the deaths of three prominent black men. She traced the origin of the violence to an interracial game of marbles. Two grocery stores occupied the same block near "The Curve," an area just outside of the city limits named for a bend in the streetcar rail line. W. H. Barrett's white-owned grocery store for years "had had a monopoly on the trade of this thickly populated colored suburb."[84] In 1889, Thomas Moss,

Calvin McDowell, and William Stewart formed a partnership and opened the People's Grocery.[85] The competition between the two stores grew, and Barrett lost revenue. Tensions increased as the black residents felt Barrett's business practices harmed the neighborhood; the city cited Barrett ten times for selling liquor illegally.[86] On Wednesday, March 2, 1892, a game of marbles near the stores between two white boys and two African American boys escalated into a fight. Several white adult men joined in the fray to assist the white boys, prompting Will Stewart, working at the People's Grocery store along with fellow owner Calvin McDowell, to wade into the brawl, ended by the arrival of the police.[87]

The next day, Barrett filed a formal complaint against Stewart, claiming he struck him during the altercation.[88] When Barrett and a police officer entered the People's Grocery store to follow up on the charges, Calvin McDowell answered the door and informed the men that no one matching Stewart's description remained in the building. According to McDowell, a frustrated Barrett grabbed his revolver and pistol-whipped him hard enough to drop him to the floor and send the gun flying. McDowell recovered, picked up the gun, aimed at Barrett and shot. He missed, and Barrett and the officer retreated from the store. Hours later, police officers arrested McDowell on the charge of assault and battery against Barrett.[89]

The sight of McDowell, released on bail the next day, angered Barrett, who went before the grand jury seeking an indictment against the owners of the People's Grocery store on the charge of supporting a public nuisance. In response to Barrett's allegations, the black community held a public meeting. Several African American men expressed their anger, with one participant referring to Barrett as "damned white trash," and two others suggesting violence as a means to permanently end the conflict. Men in the white community, angered that blacks dared to threaten a white man, began arming themselves.[90] Moss, McDowell, and Stewart, fearful of an attack upon their store by a gun-toting mob, consulted a lawyer, who informed the men of their legal right to defend themselves. The storeowners proceeded to organize a rotation of armed men to patrol inside the store in case of trouble.

For unknown reasons, at ten o'clock in the evening on Saturday night, while dressed in civilian clothes, the police approached the People's Grocery store in order to serve a warrant for Will Stewart. According to Wells's findings, "shots rang out in the back room of the store. The men stationed there saw several white men stealing through the rear door and fired on them without a moment's pause. Three of these men were wounded, and others fled and gave the alarm." Although completely unaware they were shooting at police officers, the white newspapers reported the incident as an organized ambush with the explicit intent of killing white policemen. The African American newspaper *St. Paul Appeal* claimed that once the guards realized that the white men were police officers, they dropped their weapons.[91] Regardless, the incident resulted in armed black men shooting three white deputies, and the extent of their injuries remained unknown.

The following night, white police officers patrolled The Curve neighborhood, arresting every black male they could find, including McDowell and Stewart. Moss had yet to have his name mentioned in the press in connection to these incidents. Of the dozen black men arrested, only four admitted to being in the store during the shooting. The next day, armed white men traversed the streets and white police officers began breaking into black homes, arresting thirty additional "conspirators," including Moss.[92] Held without bond, the arrested men faced brutal treatment in custody, as authorities beat them, injuring one detainee badly enough that he required crutches. The police denied the men visitors, kept their wrists bound in irons, and made them remain standing during their incarceration. McDowell's defiance in custody resulted in his confinement in a "sweat-box," a coffin-like enclosure.[93]

Fearful that a white mob would break into the jail, remove, and lynch the prisoners, representatives of the Tennessee Rifles, an African American state militia of which McDowell was a member, guarded the building for the next two nights. As the three deputies began to recover from their injuries, news spread that they would survive. The black community began to hope that the tensions would subside, but the sight of armed black men outside the jail alarmed white citizens, and a white city magistrate, Judge DuBose, ordered all black citizens, including the Tennessee Riflemen, relinquish their firearms. He also issued a court order forbidding the selling of any gun to any African American. Unarmed, the Tennessee Rifles could not protect the black prisoners, and in the early hours of the next morning, a band of white men entered the jail. They removed Thomas Moss, Calvin McDowell, and Will Stewart from custody and took the three storeowners by gunpoint a mile outside of town, where they shot and killed them. Moss, his Sunday school sermon still tucked into his pocket, begged for his life, pleading on behalf of his wife Betty, currently five months pregnant. When asked for his last words, he reportedly said, "Tell my people to go West—there is no justice for them here." McDowell did not submit quietly, he lunged for one of the guns, but his attempt failed. After his death, the men gouged his eyes out.[94]

The white men apparently notified reporters of their intentions and representatives from both white papers attended the lynching. The next day, the Memphis *Appeal-Avalanche* and *Commercial* recounted the event from an eyewitness perspective, praising the white men for being "orderly."[95] The lynchers, one report noted, administered "sharp, swift, and sure...vengeance" but without "whooping, not even loud talking, no cursing in fact, nothing boisterous," as if the solemnity of the participants lent the event credibility.[96] Despite the attorney general's asserted desire to prosecute the lynchers, the authorities continued to claim that they were unable to identify any of the white lynchers. Inquiries into the violent deaths of African Americans, even those where prominent men and officials within the community attended, usually resulted in the declaration that the death occurred at "the hands of persons unknown," despite obvious evidence to the contrary.[97]

The community buried the murdered men on March 11, 1892. Avery Chapel overflowed with thousands of African Americans, both from Memphis and nearby towns, wishing to pay their respects.[98] Wells missed the funerals but, upon her return, comforted Tom Moss's widow, Betty. The following year Moss moved to Indiana and Wells visited her, commemorating her stay with a photograph of herself with Betty, her godchild Maurine, and the baby, Tom Jr. Wells dealt with her grief for Tom by using her pen. She wrote editorials on the lynching, the disbanding of the Tennessee Rifles, and the selling of the People's Grocery store and its contents, which Barrett purchased for one-eighth of their value.[99] Wells's articles on the incident, backed by her research, became widely reprinted and earned her praise from Detroit to Kansas.[100] Her editorials on the lynching also received support from other black activists, including a Chicago lawyer Ferdinand Barnett, who wrote of the act as an "unspeakable disgrace," in his newspaper the *Conservator*.[101]

Meanwhile, tensions between the races remained high, and Wells purchased a gun to carry in her purse, recalling, "I had bought a pistol the first thing after Tom Moss was lynched," in preparation for any "retaliation from the lynchers" that may occur. So armed, she felt that if she could "take one lyncher with me, this would even up the score a bit." Wells considered such self-protection commendable, as "one had better die fighting against injustice than to die like a dog or a rat in a trap."[102] Despite arming herself, Wells remained steadfast in only advocating for self-defense and, from 1892 on, she consistently urged African Americans to rely only on themselves. The events in Memphis, where the police failed to protect African Americans and the legal system disarmed those who sought to protect black citizens, left Wells to conclude that white authorities would "neither protect our lives and property."[103]

Despite advocating for self-protection, Wells felt that black emigration from Memphis offered the best option for the protection of African Americans.[104] She used her newspaper to mobilize her readers, explaining how whites had murdered her friend with "no more consideration than if he had been a dog." Determined to spread Moss's final words, Wells adopted the mantra of "go West," within the pages of *The Free Speech*. She suggested her African American readers "save our money and leave a town" that "takes

Figure 2.2 Ida B. Wells standing with Tom Moss's widow and two children.
Source: Special Collections Research Center, University of Chicago Library

us out and murders us in cold blood when accused by white persons."[105] Another black newspaper in Memphis tempered Wells's message, realistically noting, "It is easy enough to cry go! go! but it takes a little longer to figure the cost." In response, Wells wrote that leaving "is one thing left that we can do," and urged black community members to "save their nickels and dimes."[106]

Black Memphis residents were not the only people seeking to leave the South. As whites constructed the racial system of segregation, African Americans across the South began leaving the region in large numbers. Throughout the 1880s and 1890s, in an attempt to escape exploitation and violence, African Americans headed west.[107] The "back to Africa" movement, seeking to transport blacks to Liberia, Africa, also gained some momentum, but the majority of African Americans did not wish to "return" to a country they had never lived in. They wanted the rights granted to them under the Constitution: life, liberty and the right to own property. In the West, many felt that these objectives might still be possible. The recent opening up of two million acres in Oklahoma Territory in 1889, coined the mantra for many southern blacks of "On to Oklahoma."[108]

In April 1892, Wells spent three weeks touring Oklahoma to experience for herself the conditions in the West. On her journey, she encountered several other journalists whom the railroad paid to write positive reviews of opportunities to encourage westward travel, but she vowed to report the truth of "exactly what I saw and of the chance they had of developing manhood and womanhood in this new territory."[109] Wells encountered a combination of positive and negative factors, finding prospects for skilled workers and middle-class blacks who were financially secure, but she admitted concern about the future in the West for those without training or savings. Despite her honest appraisal of African Americans prospects out West, many black Memphis residents, if they could afford to, chose to leave the city. Without accurate records, it is difficult to track the exact number, but historians estimate from two thousand to six thousand Memphis residents emigrated West in the months after the lynching.[110] This sizable drop in population in a relatively short period affected Memphis's economy.

In 1892, a streetcar fare cost a nickel or a dime, depending on the destination, and as African American families saved every cent they could to leave the city, most stopped paying to ride. The City Railway Company noticed a decline in sales and Wells received a visit from the superintendent at the offices of *The Free Speech*. He informed her of the recent drop in the company's biggest customer—African Americans. The reason for this reduction, he assumed, stemmed from a rumor that "Negroes were afraid of electricity." He requested that Wells print in the paper assurances that "there was no danger" in riding the streetcars. Wells "couldn't believe" his reasoning, as the company had converted the streetcars to electricity more than six months ago. She asked, "How long since you have observed the change?" The superintendent replied, "[S]ix weeks," and Wells pointed out, "[I]t was just six weeks ago that the lynching took place." The white administrator, unclear how the two were associated, reminded Wells that "the streetcar company had nothing to do with the lynching." Wells retorted, "We have learned that every white man of any standing in town knew of the plan and consented to the lynching of our boys." "Southern lynchers," she continued, ran the streetcars and African Americans were keeping their money in order to "get away from this town." Wells, realizing the success of her earlier campaign, instead of printing the reassuring article that the company wanted, transcribed the interview, published it, and exhorted her readers to "keep up the good work."[111]

Wells, in researching the Memphis lynching, examined other newspaper reports on the deaths of Moss, Stewart, and McDowell. Universally, the white media portrayed the three middle-class black businessmen as crooks and troublemakers.[112] The reports puzzled Wells, as she knew Moss as a good man, a father, a husband, and an honest citizen, with his only crime being his ownership of a successful business in competition with a white store.[113] Recognizing disparities, Wells turned a critical eye to the white press coverage of other lynchings and traveled to several towns where lynchings had recently occurred to research the events and interview local witnesses for herself. She soon realized that the white newspaper stories contained so much inaccurate information as to be effectively false. As a result, Wells launched an investigation into every lynching in the South from the past decade.[114]

Wells researched 728 lynchings and discovered that from 1882 to 1892 there had been an increase of more than two hundred percent in the number of African Americans lynched.[115] According to the newspapers accounts, the charge of raping white women dominated the justifications for the violence, yet Wells's investigation into the accusation of rape revealed it to be, if not downright false, tenuous at best. After reading "every case of rape reported," she recognized that the accusation of a black man attempting a sexual assault on a white woman, regardless of its veracity hid the primary motivation of the violence, which was "get[ing] rid of Negroes who were acquiring wealth and property."[116]

Wells organized her findings into a lengthy article titled, "Eight Negroes lynched since last issue of the *Free Speech*," detailing a recent lynching where whites murdered African American men, allegedly for the crime of raping white women, as the foundation for disseminating her findings. Wells established in the recent murders that no evidence existed to support any charge of sexual assault. She also detailed another case where the lynched man, portrayed in the white newspaper as a black "big, burly brute," had been murdered for the crime of raping a seven-year-old white girl. Upon visiting the town, Wells discovered the victim's age to be seventeen, not seven and that the teenage girl's "mortified" father had caught her in bed with a black man and organized the mob to kill her lover "in order to save his daughter's reputation."[117] If the rape accusations against black men were often false, then why did nearly every account include the charge? Wells argued that the idea of black men as rapists who violated pure white females offered whites a rhetorical excuse for targeting black males. The allegations of rape, Wells concluded, remained nothing more than an "old thread-bare lie" that "[n]obody in this section believes."[118]

Wells sent the article to press without any author attribution and boarded a train to attend the African Methodist Episcopal Church conference in Philadelphia and then visit Thomas Fortune in New York. Although she planned the trip months in advance, Wells likely timed the printing of her article to guarantee some distance between her and Memphis when the piece became public. After her stopover in Philadelphia, Fortune met her at the train in New York City, greeting her, "Now you are here I am afraid you will have to stay... From the rumpus you've kicked up I feel assured of it."[119] Wells's editorial in *The Free Speech* resulted in an immediate outcry from the white community. The Memphis *Commercial* threatened, "There are some things the Southern white man will not tolerate, and the obscene intimations of the foregoing have brought the writer to the outermost limit of public patience."[120] The Memphis *Scimitar* suggested tying up "the wretch who utters these calumnies to a stake" and branding them with a hot iron.[121] Luckily, someone warned her business partner J. L. Fleming and he fled Memphis before the white townspeople targeted him.[122] The sheriff then confiscated *The Free Speech*'s office and auctioned off the contents not stolen by angry community members. Wells noted in her autobiography how, for a long time, the city officials desired to destroy her paper, but "had not dared because they had no good reason until the appearance of that famous editorial." Authorities posted a notice on the building declaring that any attempt to revive the paper would be "punished by death." The destruction of the office was so complete that no copies of *The Free Speech* survive today; only excerpts reprinted in other papers offer evidence of its existence.[123]

Wells could not return to Memphis. She wrote to Lily, visiting her aunt and sister in California to stay in Visalia. Friends sent Wells telegrams notifying her of white men at the railway station waiting for her return.[124] A neighbor wrote to her warning of men watching her home with the intention of killing her on sight. Wells attempted to make peace with her fate and live in New York. She exchanged her *Free Speech* subscription list for a one-quarter interest in *New York Age*.[125] Just over a month later, on

June 25, 1892, the front-page headline of Fortune's paper read "The Truth about Lynching," and contained column after column of Wells's research.[126] The *New York Age* distributed ten thousand copies of her exposé across the nation under the author byline of "Exiled." Wells no longer wrote as "Iola," demonstrating a shift in her identity from a southern black woman immersed in fighting the inequalities of the South to a banished woman focused on drawing attention to issues from the outside.

For the next few months, Wells continued to publish in the *New York Age* regularly and always signed her work "Exiled."[127] Her initial writings provoked little response from her northern audience, prompting Wells to conclude that her readers must "not know the facts," or worse "had accepted the southern white man's reason for lynching and burning human beings in this nineteenth century of civilization." Determined to counter the white rhetoric of lynchings, Wells wrote about the realities of southern life for African Americans in an attempt to demonstrate to northern blacks and whites the brutal experiences of white supremacy in the South. She soon found allies in her cause. Two months after her first article appeared in the *New York Age*, Victoria Earle Matthews and Maritcha Lyons, both black activists in New York, approached her about creating an event "to show appreciation of my work and to protest the treatment which I had received."[128] The women wanted Wells's research to gain a wider audience and Wells agreed that speaking for her cause could gain publicity for her message.[129]

Forming the Ida B. Wells Testimonial Reception Committee, Matthews and Lyons reached out to black women in nearby Boston and Philadelphia to support their idea of a night of speeches about lynching and Wells's experience. Utilizing their church and community connections, the women organized the function at Lyric Hall in New York City on October 5, 1892. Among the more than two hundred guests were many renowned members of the northern black elite, including Dr. Susan M. McKinney, a black female physician, Sarah Garnett, the first black principal in the New York public school system, Gertrude Mossell, a writer and activist from Philadelphia, and Josephine St. Pierre Ruffin, a journalist and reformer from Boston. The committee attended to every detail. Floral arrangements decorated the room as ushers, wearing silk badges with "Iola" written across them, seated audience members before an enormous stage lit by gas jets also spelling out her former pen name. The programs even mimicked the formatting of *The Free Speech*.[130]

Wells offered the women an ideal spokesperson; African American, attractive, and thirty years old, she exhibited both poise and a strong passion for her subject.[131] Her keynote speech did not disappoint. Although no copy of the lecture she delivered at Lyric Hall exists, Wells presented the same talk several times in the ensuing months, and those copies offer a glimpse at the content of the Lyric Hall speech. Wells began her presentation by explaining the events leading up to the lynching of Moss, Stewart, and McDowell. Talking her audience through the violence of their deaths, she also revealed to her listeners how the brutality of the event lived on in the damage it did to the survivors. She spoke about her visit with Betty Moss, her friend Tom's widow, and how his toddler daughter hugged and kissed his postal uniform. She reminded her audience that Moss would never again be able to "clasp his daughter's form" or see his wife rock their infant son to sleep.[132] During her account, tears began to run down Wells's face. Undaunted, she "beckoned even as I kept reading" for a handkerchief. In her autobiography Wells recalled, "It was the only time in all those trying months that I had so yielded to personal feelings. That it should come at a time when I wanted to be at my best in order to show my appreciation of the splendid things those women had done!"[133] Despite claiming, even years later in her autobiography, of her show of "weakness" tarnishing her message, Wells's tears may have been a calculated move.

In publishing and speaking about lynchings, false accusations of rape, and white women's sexuality, Wells conceivably violated a criminal statute in addition to social expectations. The Comstock Law, passed in 1873, defined anything viewed as an "obscenity," including information deemed "lewd," "lascivious," or "indecent," to be illegal.[134] Although the law's initial intent was to outlaw the sending of contraceptive knowledge and birth control methods through the mail, it could also have applied to Wells's writings on black men and white woman's sexuality as a distribution of "licentious" information. By showing her emotions while discussing such socially charged issues, Wells humanized herself and, perhaps, tempered criticisms of her topic, shifting the discourse from vulgarity to tragedy. An adept speaker, Wells often adjusted her rhetorical style to the expectations of her audience. In order to demonstrate the impact of her arguments to northern blacks, who she was desperate to have understand the brutality their race experienced in the South, she employed every tool in her arsenal.[135] This is not to deny that Wells, alone in the North and explaining acts of violence on stage, did not experience genuine emotion and sorrow at her friend's passing, but as historian Mia Bay noted, anger was "antithetical" in the portrayal of virtuous womanhood.[136] In channeling grief rather than rage, Wells maintained the public appearance of constraint.

At the end of the program, the Reception Committee presented Wells with a donation of five hundred dollars and a brooch "in the shape of a pen, an emblem of my chosen profession." Inscribed on the pen-shaped pin, which she wore "for the next twenty years on all occasions," was the word "Mizphah," a Hebrew word meaning "lookout," reflecting Wells's identity as a guardian of justice, calling attention to the issues of inequality. Wells, in embodying this role, would soon transform herself from an exile into a national figure.[137]

NOTES

1 McMurry, 90.
2 Giddings, *Ida: A Sword among Lions*, 76; McMurry, 87.
3 Decosta-Willis, ed., *The Memphis Diary of Ida B. Wells*, 124.
4 Davidson, 88–100; Bay, *To Tell the Truth Freely*, 74.
5 Meb, like many women writers, restricted herself to domestic topics. Davidson, 102–3.
6 Melina A. Abdullah, "The Emergence of a Black Feminist Leadership Model: African-American Women and Political Activism in the Nineteenth Century," in *Black Women's Intellectual Traditions: Speaking Their Minds*, ed. Kristin Waters and Carol B. Conaway (Lebanon: University of Vermont Press, 2007), 333–34.
7 Giddings, *Ida: A Sword among Lions*, 78; Schechter, *Ida B. Wells-Barnett and American Reform*, 17.
8 Schechter, *Ida B. Wells-Barnett and American Reform*, 17.
9 Wells, *Crusade for Justice*, 31.
10 This assertive approach contrasted with the majority of female black journalists. Abdullah, 334.
11 Wells, *Crusade for Justice*, 31.
12 McMurry, 77.
13 McMurry, 10.
14 Bay, *To Tell the Truth Freely*, 72.
15 McMurry, 56.
16 McMurry, 63; Decosta-Willis, ed., *The Memphis Diary of Ida B. Wells*, 66.
17 Patricia A. Schechter, "'All the Intensity of My Nature': Ida B. Wells, Anger, and Politics," *Radical History Review* 70 (1998): 52, 54.
18 Decosta-Willis, ed., *The Memphis Diary of Ida B. Wells*, 120, 38.
19 McMurry, 90.
20 Emma Lou Thornbrough, "The National Afro-American League, 1887–1908," *The Journal of Southern History* 27, no. 4 (1961): 495.
21 McMurry, 90–91.
22 Quoted in Tommy J. Curry, "The Fortune of Wells: Ida B. Wells-Barnett's Use of T. Thomas Fortune's Philosophy of Social Agitation as a Prolegomenon to Militant Civil Rights Activism," *Transactions of the Charles S. Peirce Society* 48, no. 4 (2012): 468.
23 Thornbrough, 495–96.
24 Giddings, *Ida: A Sword among Lions*, 142.
25 Giddings, *Ida: A Sword among Lions*, 165.
26 Thornbrough, 497.
27 Quoted in Thornbrough, 497.
28 Decosta-Willis, ed., *The Memphis Diary of Ida B. Wells*, 52.
29 Curry, 459; McMurry, 92.
30 Wells, *Crusade for Justice*, 33.
31 McMurry, 111.
32 Wells, *Crusade for Justice*, 31–32.
33 Wells, *Crusade for Justice*, 32–34.
34 Davidson, 107.
35 Decosta-Willis, ed., *The Memphis Diary of Ida B. Wells*, 29.
36 Giddings, *Ida: A Sword among Lions*, 158; David M. Tucker, "Miss Ida B. Wells and Memphis Lynching," *Phylon* 32, no. 2 (1971): 113.
37 Davidson, 112–13; McMurry, 113; Giddings, *Ida: A Sword among Lions*, 158.
38 Robin Hardin and Marcie Hinton, "The Squelching of Free Speech in Memphis: The Life of a Black Post-Reconstuction Newspaper," *Race, Gender & Class* 8, no. 4 (2001): 78.
39 Giddings, *Ida: A Sword among Lions*, 158.
40 Wells, *Crusade for Justice*, 35.

41 McMurry, 113.
42 Giddings, *Ida: A Sword among Lions,* 163.
43 These men, Wells felt, possessed the opportunity to improve people's lives, but instead abused their power. Duster, ed., *Crusade for Justice,* xxvi.
44 Schechter, *Ida B. Wells-Barnett and American Reform,* 64.
45 Giddings, *Ida: A Sword among Lions,* 151.
46 Schechter, *Ida B. Wells-Barnett and American Reform,* 64.
47 Wells, *Crusade for Justice,* 39–41.
48 Wells, *Crusade for Justice,* 40.
49 Giddings, *Ida: A Sword among Lions,* 164–65; Schechter, *Ida B. Wells-Barnett and American Reform,* 65.
50 McMurry, 104.
51 Giddings, *Ida: A Sword among Lions,* 81.
52 McMurry, 127.
53 Preston King, "Ida B. Wells and the Management of Violence," 126; McMurry, 91; Giddings, *Ida: A Sword among Lions,* 151.
54 Giddings, *Ida: A Sword among Lions,*160–61, 169.
55 Jean Marie Lutes, *Front-Page Girls: Women Journalists in American Culture and Fiction, 1880–1930* (Ithaca: Cornell University Press, 2006), 55.
56 McMurry, 116.
57 Giddings, *Ida: A Sword among Lions,* 160–61.
58 Tucker, 113.
59 Giddings, *Ida: A Sword among Lions,* 89.
60 Decosta-Willis, ed., *The Memphis Diary of Ida B. Wells,* 36.
61 Schechter, *Ida B. Wells-Barnett and American Reform,* 48.
62 McMurry, 110.
63 During this time, Wells also served as the National Colored Press Association secretary, the first female officer in the organization. McMurry, 110.
64 Davidson, 114–15.
65 Wells, *Crusade for Justice,* 36–37.
66 Giddings, *Ida: A Sword among Lions,* 167; Wells, *Crusade for Justice,* 36–37.
67 Wells, *Crusade for Justice,* 36–37.
68 Wells, *Crusade for Justice,* 36–37.
69 Adam Fairclough, *Better Day Coming: Blacks and Equality, 1890–2000* (New York: Penguin Books, 2002), 31.
70 McMurry, 129.
71 Schechter, *Ida B. Wells-Barnett and American Reform,* 70; Giddings, *Ida: A Sword among Lions,* 173–74; Tucker, 115.
72 Wells, *Crusade for Justice,* 39.
73 Wells, *Crusade for Justice,* 42–44.
74 Davidson, 122.
75 Wells, *Crusade for Justice,* 41.
76 Davidson, 119–21.
77 Wells, *Crusade for Justice,* 39.
78 Giddings, *Ida: A Sword among Lions,* 177.
79 Thomas F. Gossett, *Race: The History of an Idea in America* (New York: Oxford University Press, 1997), 269. Although it is difficult to define lynchings during the Jim Crow period, as various classifications result in discrepant statistics, the designation of a lynching as three or more people intending to inflict bodily harm on their victim based on their race or heritage, encapsulates the format of race-based lynchings that occurred throughout the New South. I am using William Fitzhugh Brundage's definition, as described in *Lynching in the New South: Georgia and Virginia, 1880–1930* (Urbana: University of Illinois Press, 1993), 292.

80 Mary Jane Brown, *Eradicating This Evil: Women in the American Anti-lynching Movement, 1892-1940* (New York: Garland Publishing, 2000), 28.

81 From 1882 to 1930, eight out of every ten victims of white mobs were African American. Brundage, *Lynching in the New South*, 8. E. M. Beck and Stewart E. Tolnay, "When Race Didn't Matter: Black and White Mob Violence against Their Own Color," in *Under Sentence of Death, Lynching in the South*, ed. William Fitzhugh Brundage (Chapel Hill: University of North Carolina Press, 1997), 149.

82 Michael J. Pfeifer, *Rough Justice: Lynching and American Society, 1874-1947* (Urbana: University of Illinois Press, 2004), 4–12.

83 Davidson, 137.

84 Wells, *Crusade for Justice,* 47–48.

85 Wells refers to the owner as Henry Stewart, but he is predominantly referred to as Will or William. See Wells, *Crusade for Justice*, 47; Bay, *To Tell the Truth Freely*, 82; Giddings, *Ida: A Sword among Lions*, 177.

86 Giddings, *Ida: A Sword among Lions*, 178.

87 McMurry, 131.

88 Giddings, *Ida: A Sword among Lions*, 176.

89 Bay, *To Tell the Truth Freely*, 82.

90 Tucker, 115.

91 Giddings, *Ida: A Sword among Lions*, 179–80.

92 McMurry, 132.

93 Giddings, *Ida: A Sword among Lions*, 182; McMurry, 132.

94 Wells, *Crusade for Justice*, 51.

95 Bay, *To Tell the Truth Freely*, 84.

96 Giddings, *Ida: A Sword among Lions,* 183.

97 See Phillip Dray, *At the Hands of Persons Unknown: The Lynching of Black America* (New York: Random House, 2002).

98 Giddings, *Ida: A Sword among Lions*, 186.

99 Wells, *Crusade for Justice,* 55.

100 McMurry, 138.

101 Giddings, *Ida: A Sword among Lions*, 194.

102 Wells, *Crusade for Justice*, 54, 62.

103 Bay, *To Tell the Truth Freely*, 94. See also Rychetta N. Watkins, "The Southern Roots of Ida B. Wells-Barnett's Revolutionary Activism," *Southern Quarterly* 45, no. 3 (2008): 114.

104 After the Civil War, a wave of people had emigrated from the South to benefit from President Lincoln's 1862 Homestead Act. In order to encourage western migration, settlers could receive 160 acres of public land once they had lived on it for five years and paid a nominal filing fee. Bay, *To Tell the Truth Freely*, 90.

105 Davidson, 150.

106 Davidson, 151.

107 Giddings, *Ida: A Sword among Lions,* 190.

108 Tucker, 116.

109 Wells, *Crusade for Justice,* 57.

110 Tucker suggests two thousand (p. 116) while Schechter in *Ida B. Wells-Barnett and American Reform,* estimates four thousand (p. 78) and Davidson suggests four to six thousand (p. 153).

111 Wells, *Crusade for Justice*, 54–55.

112 The white newspapers created a narrative in which armed black men had shot white officers when they had attempted to clean out a den of black criminals at "a low dive in which drinking and gambling" occurred. Wells, *Crusade for Justice,* 48–49.

113 Paula J. Giddings, *When and Where I Enter…: The Impact of Black Women on Race and Sex in America* (New York: William Morrow, 1984), 22.

114 Davidson, 153.

115 The number of lynchings researched is taken from Paula J. Giddings, *When and Where I Enter,* 24. The increase is discussed in Ida B. Wells and Jacqueline Jones Royster, *Southern Horrors and Other Writings: The Anti-Lynching Campaign of Ida B. Wells, 1892–1900* (Boston: Bedford Books, 1997), 10.

116 Wells, *Crusade for Justice,* 64.

117 Bay, *To Tell the Truth Freely,* 101.

118 Wells, *Crusade for Justice,* 66.

119 Davidson, 158.

120 Tucker, 117.

121 Davidson, 157.

122 Fleming moved to Chicago, where he attempted to start another paper, but he lacked the capital and it soon folded, leaving him "very bitter." Bay, *To Tell the Truth Freely,* 105.

123 Wells, *Crusade for Justice,* 63.

124 Davidson, 160.

125 Bay, *To Tell the Truth Freely,* 105.

126 Although Giddings in *When and Where I Enter,* on page 25 notes it is published on June 5, the actual date was June 25. See also Christopher Waldrep, *African Americans Confront Lynching: Strategies of Resistance from the Civil War to the Civil Rights Era* (New York: Rowman & Littlefield Publishers, 2009), 47.

127 She lived in Brooklyn where she was a racial minority, outnumbered by the Irish and Italian immigrants. Giddings, *Ida: A Sword among Lions,* 231. She published regularly in the reporting on southern events and asked her former *Free Speech* subscribers to support the *New York Age.* McMurry, 148.

128 Wells, *Crusade for Justice,* 77–78.

129 Bay, *To Tell the Truth Freely,* 113.

130 Davidson, 159; Giddings, *Ida: A Sword among Lions,* 236–37; Bay, *To Tell the Truth Freely,* 114; McMurry, 171; Wells, *Crusade for Justice,* 78–79.

131 Wells recalled in her autobiography marveling that a "homesick" young "exile" could command all this attention. Wells, *Crusade for Justice,* 79.

132 Bay, *To Tell the Truth Freely,* 115–16.

133 Wells, *Crusade for Justice,* 78–79.

134 John D'Emilio and Estelle B. Freedman, *Intimate Matters: A History of Sexuality in America,* second edition (Chicago: University of Chicago Press, 1998), 60, 159.

135 See Gary Totten's discussion of her performances in "Ida B. Wells and the Segregation: Embodying Cultural Work of Travel," *African American Review* 42, no. 1 (2008): 47–60, and Nicole King, "'A Colored Woman in Another Country Pleading for Justice in Her Own': Ida B Wells in Great Britain," in *Black Victorians/Black Victoriana,* ed. Gretchen Holbrook Gerzina (New Jersey: Rutgers University Press, 2003), 88–109.

136 Bay, *To Tell the Truth Freely,* 117.

137 Schechter, *Ida B. Wells-Barnett and American Reform,* 30, 19; Wells, *Crusade for Justice,* 80.

CHAPTER 3

NEW HORIZONS, 1892–1900

The five hundred dollars that the Ida B. Wells Testimonial Reception Committee raised and presented to Wells at her October 1892 speech funded the publication of the pamphlet version of her investigation, titled *Southern Horrors: Lynch Law in All Its Phases.* In this tract, Wells became the first person, black or white, to distribute a systematically researched explanation for the rise in lynchings in the South during the previous decade.[1] This knowledge revealed to her, with startling clarity, the objectives of racial violence.

With the system of slavery, white southerners felt secure in their dominance, but in order to continue the system of segregation, whites needed to maintain a racial binary. Interracial liaisons became the weak point where the system could fail, and black men emerged as the primary threat to the continuation of white supremacy. Black males' potential relationships with white females could destabilize the race-based social order, and this made white female sexuality, or rather the protection of white female sexuality, the fundamental justification that whites utilized, regardless of its accuracy, for engaging in racial violence against black men.[2] This belief allowed whites to attack any African American man, as each one offered the potential to disrupt segregation.[3] Such practices, which also allowed whites to dominate members of the black community through terrorism, produced a rape-lynch complex or rhetoric that portrayed African American men reverting to brutality without the chains of slavery to control them.[4]

The differences in the media's portrayal of the black men lynched in Memphis and Wells's firsthand knowledge of Moss, Stewart, and McDowell, drove her initial research. In her widely circulated *Southern Horrors,* she sought to contradict society's prevailing images of the black race. She prefaced her research by noting that "[t]he Afro-American is not a bestial race" and if her writing "can contribute in any way toward proving this…I shall feel I have done my race a service."[5] To Wells, the media perpetuated the belief that black male sexuality offered the primary danger to the future of white southern society by claiming that African American males possessed an uncontrolled sexual desire for white women.[6] Mississippi Governor Theodore Gilmore Bilbo, in his speech "Mississippi Will Attend to All Brutes," warned his white constituents that African Americans sought to gain equality by acquiring sexual access to white females and encouraged white southerners to use racial violence to remove potential problems from the black community.[7] The northern media also accepted the beliefs articulated by Bilbo and southern newspapers. *Harper's Weekly* magazine published an article on "The New Negro Crime," implying that northern blacks, like their southern brethren, were losing their respect for "woman of the superior race" and warned readers that they sought "social equality."[8]

Augmenting these media accounts were prominent scholars publishing research supporting white racial superiority and the inferiority of African Americans. The early white political scientist John W. Burgess taught his students at Columbia University that "black skin" was the "antithesis of both white men and civilization."[9] Scholar Philip A. Bruce's 1889 study, *The Plantation Negro as a Freeman: Observations on his Character, Condition, and Prospects in Virginia,* shaped the scholarship on race for several generations. Bruce began his work by discussing the effects of freedom on African Americans, arguing, "slavery stepped in to restrain these instincts when uncontrollable otherwise." He explained "these instincts" to be the black race's inherent capacity to be "morally obtuse and indifferent" and "openly and unreservedly licentious."[10] These racial susceptibilities, Bruce explained, resulted in black men's desire to rape, as "[t]here is something strangely alluring and seductive to them in the appearance of a white woman…it moves them to gratify their lust at any cost and in spite of every obstacle." Bruce believed these findings to be common knowledge to all southerners, especially white women "of every class, from the highest to the lowest" who "are afraid to venture to any distance alone, or even to wander unprotected in the immediate vicinity of their homes."[11] The act of rape by black men against white women, he concluded, "will be committed more often in the future than it has been in the past."[12] For the females of the black race, Bruce argued, these racial traits manifested themselves as a "sexual laxness," making it impossible for an African American woman to be raped.[13]

Academics widely accepted Bruce's findings and he influenced many scholars and notable people, including white author Thomas Nelson Page, whose work appeared in the popular pages of *Scribner's* magazine and in a variety of fiction, children's, and non-fiction writings.[14] In part, Page's popular appeal resulted from him embracing southern white claims about African American innate racial inferiority and using these traits for entertainment. His work, *Two Little Confederates* (1888), began as a monthly children's publication about two young boys and their adventures during the Civil War. In one vignette, Old Balla, the oldest slave on the plantation, locks a drunken Union soldier in the hen house, only later to find that he escaped through the roof, supplying the story with comic relief when the two boys ridicule Old Balla for his failed attempt at outsmarting a white man; even a drunk, northern, one.[15]

Page also wrote an article, "A Southerner on the Negro Question," in 1892, the same year as Wells's *Southern Horrors*.[16] In this essay, Page noted how African Americans "[f]resh from slavery" were "enfranchised" to vote and ended up being "drafted" into the Union League by northern "carpet-bag officers." Page urged his readers to correct the "great mistake" of Recon-struction in allowing African Americans access to political power, and provided several examples "to establish the fact that the negro [sic] does not possess the elements of character, the essential qualifications to conduct a government even for himself." These inabilities, he argued, are not "because he was a slave, but because he does not possess the faculties to raise himself above slavery. He has not yet exhibited the qualities of any race which has advanced civilization or shown capacity to be greatly advanced."[17]

Joseph Alexander Tillinghast, a scholar of history and political science, also found that racial inferiority explained the failure of African Ameri-cans to maintain any rights after Reconstruction.[18] His paper "The Negro in Africa and America" extensively quoted Bruce's research on the "primi-tive, savage passions" of African Americans. Tillinghast examined property records during the 1880s and declared that many blacks had been unable to gain or retain control of land. This, he concluded, supported his arguments about African Americans inherent lack of work ethic and inability to handle money.[19] His findings became part of a body of scholarship, along with sim-ilar examinations, to overlook the rise of the Redeemers, Democratic ballot stuffing, sharecropping, or racial violence as causes for African American's inability to prolong their social progress.[20]

In a culture where academics and the media perpetuated the idea that blacks were inherently inferior to whites, Wells's findings offer a true counter-narrative. Wells argued that whites utilized the belief of black men's sex-ual desire for white women not on account of its accuracy, but because it offered a socially acceptable excuse for killing black men. Wells demon-strated the weaknesses in these widely accepted arguments by revealing the economic and political motives behind the majority of lynchings. She never denied that black men could or did commit the crime of rape, but the large number of false accusations suggested to her that the allegation of sexual assault hid the real motive of murdering any black failing to remain submissive to the dictates of white supremacy. Instead of focusing on the alleged offenses of the lynch victim, she examined the crimes whites committed by taking the law into their own hands. If an African American man did rape a white woman, Wells asked, how did one accusation of a wrongdoing justify extralegal death at the hands of white men? If blacks broke the law, Wells argued, authorities needed to legally hold the accused accountable for their actions in a court of law, rather than allow white community members to execute them.[21]

Although Wells became the most successful person to point out the incongruity between the justification of lynchings for perceived sexual assault and the reality that lynchings targeted prosperous blacks, Wells was not the first to publish on this issue. Four years before the Memphis lynching or *Southern Horrors,* in 1888, African American journalist Jesse Duke published an article in the Montgomery, Alabama African American paper *Pine Bluff Weekly Echo* about a mistaken accusation of rape in a recent lynching.[22] Duke discussed how a local white mob lynched a black man for the crime of raping a white woman, only to later discover that the allegation was false, as the white woman and black man were engaged in a consensual affair.[23] Duke wrote of "the growing appreciation of white Juliets for colored Romeos" and noted an increase in white women willing to engage in sexual liaisons with black men. The "bloodthirsty mob," Duke suggested, used the excuse of rape to justify attacking an educated African American attempting to make social progress. White townspeople responded to his editorial with threats of violence, forcing Duke to flee town.[24] This reaction to Duke's commentary foreshadowed the same response that Wells's *Free Speech* article received, demonstrating how commenting on white women's willingness to engage in a sexual relationship with a black man was intolerable to white southerners whether the charge came from an African American man or woman.

Wells considered acts of extralegal murder as a microcosm of the larger issues in the South. The violent and brutal killings of black men at the hands of white mobs resulted from southerners' attempts to reinforce white supremacy. When white mobs attacked a black man, this act was not simply against one person, but rather an assault on the humanity of every African American.[25] In using violence as a form of terrorism, lynching prevented not just individual blacks from gaining access to political power, it also served to undermine all African Americans' efforts at social progress. Her debunking of the rape-lynch rhetoric exposed lynchings as acts of racial violence necessary for the maintenance of white patriarchy and the economic, social, and political power that it bestowed.

The disparate responses that community members offered to the news of a white woman's accusation of rape versus a black woman's report of sexual assault clearly demonstrate the racial nature of lynching. Wells bitterly noted how the threat against white women's virtue resulted in violent death, but if the "victim is a colored woman it is different."[26] Indeed, she remarked, every African American knew of the numerous "assaults by white men on black women," for which "nobody is lynched, and no notice is taken."[27] Black women, according to the accepted narrative constructed to justify white supremacy, were lustful and thus incapable of experiencing unwanted sexual advances. As a result, Wells wrote, the white man "is free to seduce all the colored girls he can," as he possessed the power to have sex, willingly or not, with both white and black women. The same white men, Wells noted ironically, could not abide any threat to their sexual authority, and retaliated when a black man infringed on their prerogative by "succumb[ing] to the smiles of white women."[28] Yet whites, unlike African Americans, faced no legal repercussions for their crimes.

After laying out her arguments about the realities behind lynching, Wells rallied African Americans. In the section of *Southern Horrors* subtitled "Self-Help," she urged every African American to "do for himself what no one else can do for him." She set forth goals for her race, suggesting that they continue to work towards gaining an education and securing "financial strength." She also believed that boycotting white businesses and emigrating out of the South remained the most effective methods to gain whites' attention. Wells recounted the success of these approaches for black Memphians, who after waiting for the "authorities to act in the matter and bring the lynchers to justice" only to find "[n]o attempt was made to do so," left town or stopped patronizing white business. Finally, she urged, a "Winchester rifle should have a place of honor in every black home, and it should be used for that protection which the law refuses to give." The measure, she insisted, was necessary, as "there is no protection for the life and property of any Afro-American citizen." The black community, she felt, could no longer afford to be passive victims; they needed to defend themselves. For Wells, this fortification did not encourage offensive retribution, but rather presented a deterrent towards further violence. If armed African Americans no longer offered the mob easy victims, it might produce a "greater respect for Afro-American life," and break the cycle of victimization.[29]

The publication of *Southern Horrors* garnered a reaction from the most influential African American leader of the time, Frederick Douglass, widely known for his abolitionist work and autobiography, *Narrative of the Life of Frederick Douglass* (1845). In July of 1892, a few months before Wells's pamphlet, Douglass published an essay attempting to understand the rapid rise of lynchings in the South. As he lived in the North, Douglass relied on newspaper accounts of lynchings to understand what was happening.[30] In "Lynch Law in the South," he noted, "It is evident," that the blame for lynchings, "is not entirely with the ignorant mob." He continued, "The men who break open jails and with bloody hands destroy human life are not alone responsible."[31] Unlike Wells, Douglass did not fault whites but instead believed the increase in lynchings resulted from African Americans' lawless behavior and insufficient leadership.[32] After Douglass read *Southern Horrors*, he wrote to Wells, praising her work and expressing relief that the rise in lynching was not due to "an increasing lasciviousness on the part of Negroes." Recognizing the effect that his support could have in garnering attention to her efforts and protecting her from backlash, Wells responded that his letter "highly honored" her and asked if he would allow his opinion of her work to serve as an introduction to future versions of the pamphlet.[33] Douglass agreed and Wells published his letter at the beginning of the 1893 edition of the pamphlet and in every version thereafter.[34]

In *Southern Horrors,* Wells not only exposed the false rhetoric behind southern racial violence, but also humanized African Americans. As in her Lyric Hall speech, those she discussed emerge as fully realized people, with families, dreams, and hopes for the future. Wells's research allowed her to focus on the humanity of the mob's victims, usually upstanding male citizens in the black community. Her exposure of the treatment that black women received by white men, their presence a mere excuse for sexual assault, existed alongside portrayals of these women as intelligent, educated, and caring, if largely powerless.[35] She not only contradicted the mainstream representations of African Americans but, in *Southern Horrors*, Wells reversed the roles of whites and blacks, as her depictions of the white mob committing illegal and unjustified violence left her readers without a doubt as to which race was acting as "savages."

Wells recognized the need to introduce her reader to the arguments in *Southern Horrors* carefully in order to establish her credibility. She began by drawing upon her feminine moral authority, noting in her preface of her reluctance to enter into the discussion. She directly addressed the reader, explaining, "It is with no pleasure I have dipped my hands in the corruption here exposed" but "[s]omebody must show that the Afro-American race is more sinned against than sinning."[36] In opening the pamphlet with these remarks, Wells recognized the unfeminine topic she was about to discuss and situated herself as a reluctant participant compelled by her ethics into action. By explicitly employing the moral authority of True Womanhood to justify her position, Wells attempted to prevent criticism for overstepping her role as a black woman in the public sphere and endeavored to undermine any challenge against her virtue.[37] *Southern Horrors* was the last public treatise in which Wells validated her writing by explicitly referring to the tenets of True Womanhood. After *Southern Horrors* established her as an expert, she no longer justified her work as consistent with her feminine virtue. Instead, her attempts to highlight social injustice offered enough reason to substantiate her efforts.

After years of honing her skills in newspapers and magazines, Wells infused *Southern Horrors* with her distinctive writing style. In the work, she engaged in a call-and-response technique, an approach often used in churches, to captivate her reader. Wells wrote a question, prompting her audience to consider an issue and then offered a response, occasionally mocking, sometimes educational, but always thought provoking. In *Southern Horrors,* one such exchange began with Wells adopting a white point of view regarding African Americans, stating the oft-repeated complaint in the white press, "The Negroes are getting too independent," and the need for people to "teach them a lesson." Wells transitioned from these points into her question, "What lesson?" before supplying an answer that would ring true to African Americans: "The lesson of subordination."[38] This style of approach allowed her reader to engage with her topics informally, as a conversation rather than a lecture.

Wells, as both a speaker and a writer, supported her points with quotations appropriated from white newspapers. She enjoyed letting the words of others make her argument for her, and in doing so gained authority as a logical and composed narrator.[39] Drawn into her research after turning a critical eye to white newspaper accounts of lynchings, Wells, in order to help her readers do the same, interrogated the validity of various details using punctuation. She often inserted question marks into quoted text to serve as interjections, drawing the reader's attention to the word choice in the passage. In *Southern Horrors,* Wells wrote of how "[o]ne by one the Southern states have legally (?) disfranchised the Afro American," and "last Saturday morning where the citizens broke (?) into the penitentiary."[40] These question marks prompt the reader to pause and question the narrative. Is disenfranchisement legal? Did the white men break into the jail, or did they simply stroll in with the implied consent of local authorities?

Wells's use of punctuation became a powerful tool to draw attention to the language of the white narrative and encourage her readers to be aware of the linguistic implications of the white presses' accounts.[41] Similar to her question-mark technique, Wells offset certain phrases from the white papers in quotes, attracting the reader's notice to the wording, such as when she discussed "the 'leading citizens' who want to protect the 'honor' of *all* white women."[42] By quoting the phrase "leading citizens," Wells drew the reader's attention to the detail that these important community members were the same ones directing the mobs. In highlighting "honor" as the justification, Wells questioned its validity simply by extracting the word from its context. With a few quotation marks from white newspaper excerpts, Wells highlighted the animalistic behaviors of white lynch mobs who castrated, tortured, cut, burned, and shot black bodies.

Wells recognized that the publication of her viewpoints resulted from the support of other black women, who championed her and her cause. The dedication page of *Southern Horrors* acknowledged the aid of the "Afro-American women of New York and Brooklyn, whose race love, earnest zeal and unselfish effort…made possible its publication."[43] Their assistance helped Wells, but also allowed them to recognize the impact that an organized group of African American women could have on social issues. Inspired, Josephine St. Pierre Ruffin, an Ida B. Wells Reception Committee member, founded the Women's Loyal Union, the first African American women's club. The success of Ruffin's organization soon prompted other associations to form in nearby cities.[44]

Meanwhile, Wells's success with *Southern Horrors* and at Lyric Hall led to multiple requests to speak about lynchings across the North. She recalled that "invitations came from Philadelphia, Wilmington, Delaware, Chester, Pennsylvania, and Washington, D.C.," and at each she read her speech, "the same one that I had read at the first meeting in New York."[45] One of these talks occurred in Washington, D.C., where Frederick Douglass requested Wells's participation in a special address at his African Methodist Episcopal Church, along with several other prominent leaders for African American rights, including himself, T. Thomas Fortune, and Mary (Mollie) Church Terrell. Wells's friend from Memphis had married a Washington, D.C. lawyer, Robert Terrell, who would later become a judge. During the early 1890s, Mary Church Terrell emerged as a leader among black women in the North.[46] Despite the high profiles of the speakers and an advertisement in the *Washington Bee*, only a handful of people showed to the event. Disappointed, Douglass promised Wells that he would have her back soon to speak to a full house.[47]

By the end of 1892, Wells and Douglass had established a mentor and mentee relationship. Wells's straightforward writings about racial injustice and her treatment of Douglass's wife earned the older man's respect. In 1884, Frederick Douglass married for the second time. His wife, Helen Pitts, was a white woman, and their interracial relationship resulted in criticism from many in the black community who felt his private marriage affected his public attempts to enact social change. One newspaper noted after his wedding, "We have no further use for him."[48] When Wells visited the couple at their home, she mentioned meeting "his lovely wife." When, at the end of her visit, Frederick Douglass took her to the train, he told her, "[Y]ou are the only colored woman save Mrs. Grimke who has come into my home as a guest and has treated Helen as a hostess has a right to be treated by her guest." Wells, at first confused by this admission, understood when Douglass continued by describing how "many of her white friends had resented her marrying me" and how "my colored friends showed their resentment even in our home." Wells visited Frederick Douglass many times, and each stay "deepened and strengthened" her "admiration and love" for him. She recalled in her autobiography, "I felt then and now that he is the biggest and broadest American our country has produced."[49]

Southern Horrors, while generating supporters like Douglass, also led to increased public attacks upon Wells. This response is unsurprising, as the tract reproached white men for failing to act in an honorable manner and suggested that white women willingly engaged in sexual relationships with black men. These remarks, seen as disparaging to whites, resulted in a maelstrom of white media reports questioning her motives in order to undermine her findings. One paper called Wells "a poser for attention" and when the *Boston Courant* suggested that Wells was a "fake," they found support from New York City's *The American Citizen*, which agreed, "she seeks fame and gets notoriety."[50] On November 15, 1892, the Memphis *Commercial* newspaper published a story declaring that Wells was not the author of *The Free Speech's* spring editorial, but simply Fleming's mistress who claimed authorship in order to gain money and celebrity. The newspaper described "this Wells wench" as a "black harlot" and her move to the North merely an attempt to "marry a white husband."[51]

In response, several defenders came forward on Wells's behalf, among them the Kansas newspaper the *Topeka Weekly Call*, which rebuked the Memphis paper for "slandering the good name of Miss Ida B. Wells" and suggested they had proved her point about white masculinity, concluding, "Southern chivalry was a thing of the past."[52] Josephine St. Pierre Ruffin also openly supported Wells, condemning the Memphis paper and defending the "purity of purpose and character" of Wells.[53] Although she often publically ignored her detractors, these denunciations, dismissive of both her journalism and morality, spurred Wells to demand retribution. As a single black woman, she did not have the protection of her virtue that marriage offered, and as a rising national figure making her living speaking about lynchings, perhaps she recognized that if she failed to respond and these claims gained traction, she would no longer be able to continue her burgeoning efforts as a social reformer.[54] She decided to file a libel suit against the Memphis *Commercial* newspaper.

Wells asked Douglass for advice on how to proceed with her case, and he referred to her to Albion Tourgée, a well-known white lawyer. Tourgée had founded the National Citizen's Rights Association, the organization that recruited Homer Plessy, a light-skinned African American to ride in a "whites' only" car on June 7, 1892 in order to challenge segregation in the courts.[55] The esteemed lawyer, who had congratulated Wells after she published her lynching editorial, responded to her inquiry by noting that she may win a libel suit against the newspaper if she could "deny and sustain a denial of impropriety with any man."[56] Tourgée also felt that Wells's case required a black lawyer and recommended a Chicago barrister to her, Ferdinand L. Barnett. The owner of the *Conservator*, the first black Chicago paper, Barnett held a reputation for being a staunch defender of African American rights. As Wells and Barnett corresponded about her possible legal options, they ultimately decided not to pursue the case in court, fearing a repeat of Wells's 1887 appeal against the Chesapeake, Ohio and Southwestern Railroad. The libel case would require Wells to convince a white courtroom that a black woman possessed morality. A loss would serve as a public verdict on her virtue, irreparably damaging her reputation and hindering her ability to continue her work.

The year after the publication of *Southern Horrors*, the nature of lynchings began to shift, evidenced by the 1893 mass mob killing of Henry Smith in Paris, Texas. Across the South, the lynchings of black men evolved into public performances, functioning as a visible demonstration of segregation and no longer limited to the former method of a gang of white men at night, outside of the city limits. Instead, many lynchings of African Americans became community events witnessed by white women, boys, girls, and even young children. Historian Grace Hale categorized these events as "spectacle lynchings," emphasizing the crowd gazing at the ritual for entertainment. Such community participation functioned to create a sense of "collective, all-powerful whiteness" for the audience.[57]

On February 1, 1893, a train returned Henry Smith, an African American accused of murdering white four-year-old Myrtle Vance, to Paris, Texas, after a manhunt ranging from Arkansas to Michigan. The mayor, in celebration of Smith's lynching, granted the town's children a holiday from school, and these youths joined their families to watch as the posse paraded Smith through town on a float drawn by four white horses. The crowd followed the procession to a field, where several men placed Smith upon a scaffold and tortured him. For almost an hour, Myrtle Vance's father, brother, and two uncles scorched Smith's feet, legs, stomach, back, and arms with a hot poker. They then burned out his eyes and thrust the hot metal down his throat. During this torture, the crowd, including the white schoolchildren, reportedly shouted with approval. The men then doused both the scaffold and Smith with oil and set him on fire. After the flames had burned down, the crowd scavenged the body and site for souvenirs.[58]

Smith's murder created a ritualized pattern thereafter expected at most spectacle lynchings.[59] First, a manhunt began or a crowd amassed in order to remove the accused party from the local jail. Once procured, the mob brought their victim to the chosen lynching site, where representatives from the crowd leveled charges against them. Often, the mob shouted for the accused to affirm their guilt. Failure to admit wrongdoing often led to torture in an effort to gain a confession, but acknowledgment frequently did so as well, with the mob calling for such suffering as a form of punishment.[60] In cases where the accusation involved the rape or murder of a white female, male relatives of the victim often carried out this retribution.[61] The climax of the ritual arrived with the killing of the victim, with this culminating act allegedly imposing justice. The victim's death reinforced, for both whites and African Americans, the belief that violating the customs of segregation required a deadly punishment.[62] Afterwards, crowds took pictures and seized pieces of the scene as mementos of their experience.[63]

Upon learning of the lynching in Paris, Wells decided to "get the facts" for herself.[64] She hired a detective from the Pinkerton Detective Agency, but when the investigator concluded his inquiry by simply handing her clippings about the lynching cut from the local paper, Wells decided to travel to Texas and research the incident herself. Once there, she discovered through her interviews with local African Americans that Smith likely had committed the crime. Several residents who knew Smith suggested he suffered from a mental illness, and one local minister informed Wells that he tried to have the man committed into an institution.[65] Wells continued to tread cautiously on the subject of guilt or innocence, instead focusing on why Smith had not received his day in court. Unsurprisingly, Wells found the white press accounts exaggerated certain aspects of the alleged murder in order to excite their readers, including discussing fictional damage done to Vance's body in order to stress the brutality of her attacker. Wells returned from Texas and continued speaking across the North, adding the events of Paris, Texas to the content of her lectures.

During her previous tour in 1892, Wells met Catherine Impey after a talk in Philadelphia. Impey, a reformer from England, expressed shock over Wells's findings and informed her of her own efforts to fight on behalf of those oppressed in England's colonies. After Smith's lynching, Impey contacted Wells, aghast at the details reported in the English newspapers about Smith's torture and murder.[66] She wrote to Wells that while visiting her friend and fellow activist Isabelle Fyvie Mayo, a Scottish novelist, the two women decided to include lynchings in the United States in their efforts to fight against all forms of social inequality. After more discussion, the women wrote to Wells, noting, "The chief difficulty over here" is "people don't know & therefore don't care about the matter," and asked if she would help bring attention to their efforts by coming to England to speak about American lynchings.[67]

Wells accepted the invitation and on April 5, 1893, she set sail, arriving at Mayo's Scottish home on April 21.[68] Wells gave her first foreign address to various supporters in Mayo's living room, immediately inspiring them to establish an organization dedicated to opposing racial separation and injustice that they named The Society for the Recognition of the Brotherhood of Man (SRBM). In order to draw attention to their cause, the members planned to announce their formation in *Anti-Caste*, a publication edited by Mayo and Impey.[69] Wells stayed at Mayo's house for two weeks while the SRBM organized her speaking tour, and she met a variety of people, for, as part of her commitment to social change, Mayo opened her home to representatives of other countries pursuing higher education. Wells met Dr. George Ferdinands, a member of British Ceylon (present-day Sri Lanka), who was finishing dental school, as well as his cousin, also a student, and a German music teacher. All three, Wells recalled, "threw themselves wholeheartedly into the work of helping to make preparations for our campaign."[70]

After arriving in England, Wells's rhetorical approach shifted for her British audience. In England, nearly everyone she encountered treated her as an equal and so her message was independent of her racial identity or moral reputation. In response, Wells adopted a matter-of-fact lecture style that drew connections between slavery and segregation in order to encourage the British, whose anti-slavery movement affected American views, to fight against this racial injustice. She told her audiences of the "conditions in the South since the Civil War," the new laws preventing African Americans from exercising their rights, "of the cruel physical atrocities vented upon my race, and of the failure of the whites to allow a fair trial to any accused."[71] One audience member said of her demeanor, "She spoke with a cultivated manner with great simplicity & directness & with a burning intensity of feeling well-controlled. It was the most convincing kind of speaking—it sounded intensely genuine & real."[72]

After positive responses to her early talks, Impey continued to arrange meetings and the women traveled to Aberdeen, Huntly, Glasgow, and Edinburgh. Once in Edinburgh, a letter from Mayo arrived that would alter the remainder of Wells's English tour. Impey had recently sent Dr. Ferdinands a letter and he had shared its contents with Mayo. In the message, Wells reported, Impey "declared that she returned the affection she felt sure he had for her" but as "he was of a darker race," she felt the need to make the first move and "had written to her family...telling them to prepare to receive him as her husband." Impey's declaration startled Dr. Ferdinands, who claimed that he did not know of her feelings and did not return them. While seemingly a simple misunderstanding, to Mayo the letter represented an unforgivable moral breach. Outraged, she called Impey a nymphomaniac (a term unfamiliar to Wells), demanded that she withdraw from The Society for the Recognition of the Brotherhood of Man, and ordered all copies of *Anti-Caste* in which both of their names appeared, destroyed. Impey, Mayo noted, was the "type of maiden lady who used such work as an opportunity to meet and make advances to men."[73]

Whereas Mayo saw Impey's behavior as sexually forward and felt that her impropriety made her unable to work for social reform, Wells interpreted the situation differently. Perhaps having heard months earlier from Frederick Douglass about the responses to his interracial marriage, she felt sympathetic towards Impey. She wrote in her autobiography that just because Impey had fallen in love and "been indiscreet enough to tell him so," did not indicate moral corruption or make her unable to continue working for equality. Wells also likely felt compassion for the woman, as she too had suffered from assaults on her honor and been deemed an unsuitable messenger. Wells wrote to the Scottish reformer defending Impey, arguing that only four people knew about the letter and the event could be easily contained. Mayo retorted to Wells that Impey "was likely to write such letters to others who might strike her fancy and throw suspicion and ridicule on our cause." Wells noted, "I had never heard…the scorn and withering sarcasm with which she [Mayo] characterized her [Impey]."[74] After this exchange, Mayo claimed that Wells's defense of Impey also damaged their cause, and "she cast me into outer darkness with Miss Impey and I never saw her again."[75]

Mayo, the financial sponsor of Wells's trip, withdrew her support, which hindered the remainder of the tour. Wells accepted the invitation to speak in England based on the understanding that Mayo would not pay her but would cover her expenses. Despite the lack of funds, Wells and Impey decided to press forward to London, the last leg of her trip. Impey, now separated from her reformer contacts, could only organize a few small meetings and Wells decided to return home. Despite a disappointing conclusion to her tour, Wells enjoyed her return trip. Fifteen Englishmen traveling to Chicago for the World's Columbian Exposition were onboard and Wells recalled, "They were as courteous and attentive to me as if my skin had been of the fairest" and admitted, "I enjoyed it hugely."[76] The Englishmen's attitude towards her reflected her reception in Europe, which Wells described in an interview published in the London newspaper *The Sun*, as being "received in perfect equality" everywhere she went.[77]

The American newspaper coverage of Wells's international tour restored lynchings to a topic of discussion in the mainstream press. Wells noticed some hopeful changes in white rhetoric when one Memphis writer in the *Appeal-Avalanche* mentioned that "[m]istakes had been made" in lynching some African Americans. To Wells, this brief sentence signaled a small victory as anti-lynching sentiment grew. The majority of white presses, however, insisted on the same arguments as previously, suggesting that if African Americans stopped "committing rape and midnight murder" then lynchings would end. The personal attacks on Wells also continued with several white southern papers belittling her. The Memphis *Appeal-Avalanche* reprinted several press excerpts from England praising Wells in order to demonstrate that she remained a "negro adventuress" who "deftly gulled a number of credulous persons in England." In response to this round of denigrations, Wells remarked, "I know that the work has done great good, if by no other sign than the abuse it has brought me from the Memphis Appeal Avalanche, Atlanta (Ga.) Constitution and Macon Telegraph and Washington City Post."[78]

Upon her return to the United States, Wells settled in Chicago where she had accepted an offer to write for Ferdinand Barnett's African American newspaper, the *Conservator*. When news of her joining the Chicago newspaper spread, a fellow African American editor, C. H. J. Taylor, attacked Wells in the pages of the *Kansas City American Citizen*. Taylor editorialized that "we are sorry for the *Conservator*. It was once a clean paper" and suggested, "put[ting] a muzzle on that animal from Memphis. We are onto her dirty, sneaking tricks."[79] Despite this reaction greeting her, Chicago offered Wells an ideal location to devote herself to protesting the upcoming Chicago World's Fair treatment of blacks.

In 1893, the Columbian Exposition celebrated the four hundredth anniversary of Christopher Columbus's discovery of the New World. The tradition of World's Fairs began in 1851, as a way to display the achievements of a region or nation, and approximately twenty-eight million visitors from across the globe would visit the World's Columbian Exposition in Chicago.[80] Planned for almost a decade, the organizers intended to highlight the accomplishments of America. The only previous World's Fair in the United States, the 1876 Centennial Exposition in Philadelphia, excluded African Americans not only from attending, but also from being present on fairgrounds, even as employees. It appeared that little had changed in the ensuing decades, as the organizing board for the 1893 Exposition did not plan any exhibits featuring African Americans and did not allow any blacks to serve on the committee. Although several blacks attended the event, they were all foreign delegates. The only African American allowed access to the Chicago World's Fair was Frederick Douglass, who served as the representative from Haiti due to his position as the former ambassador to the country. In response to this prohibition against African Americans, Douglass proposed to Wells that they draw attention to the treatment of African Americans to visitors attending the World's Fair, and the two reformers decided to produce a pamphlet similar to Wells's *Southern Horrors*, cataloguing the outrages committed against blacks in America.[81]

Wells and Douglass envisioned the pamphlet printed in English, French, German, and Spanish, making it available to all who visited the Exposition. Upon her return from England, the project became Wells's top priority, but the financial support lagged. It would cost an estimated five thousand dollars to print four separate versions of a publication, and Douglass informed Wells that his fundraising efforts had largely failed. In light of this, he suggested forgoing the pamphlet entirely, but Wells, never one to step away from a project, began soliciting donations through her *Conservator* column and approached black churches for support. By July, with the Exposition well underway, Wells's efforts resulted in $275 worth of donations. Part of the difficulty in raising the funds stemmed from fellow African Americans criticisms of Douglass's and Wells's efforts. The Indianapolis *Freeman* opposed the venture as they felt little need to disclose the treatment that blacks received in America to foreign visitors, and other papers suggested that the funds requested were better spent by African Americans themselves, noting that the solicitation of donations contradicted Wells's earlier encouragements of gaining financial independence.[82] Hindered by their limited resources, Wells and Douglass modified their original plan and published the pamphlet only in English, but included a preface in English, German, and French. As they finished their collaboration, the issue of "Colored Jubilee Day" at the World's Fair divided Wells and Douglass.

Amidst growing protests on the exclusion of African Americans from the Exposition, the organizers compromised, declaring that since "[e]very other nationality had had its 'day,'" so would African Americans and scheduled "Colored Jubilee Day" for August 25, 1893.[83] Allowing African Americans to attend the Fair on just one day upset Wells for several reasons. First, she opposed any racial segregation, believing that accepting their own day would "certify to the world that the colored people of the United States are content with the treatment accorded to them as citizens of the great Republic in several states of the American Union."[84] She also felt that the committee's concession reflected an attempt to make money on African Americans without including them. By charging admission, the organizers profited from black attendance, but African American visitors would only be able to experience the achievements of the white race in "classically designed buildings finished with gleaming white paint," on the main thoroughfare, making the Exposition "literally and figuratively a White City."[85] The only exhibit with dark-skinned peoples, located at the far end of the grounds, displayed "the savage races," including the black race and the North American "Indian."[86]

Wells became further incensed when she encountered promotional materials for "Colored Jubilee Day" promising free watermelons. She wrote an editorial decrying this loss of "self-respect of the race" and worried that the image of "our people…roaming around the grounds munching watermelons, will do more to lower the race in the estimation of the world than anything else."[87] Douglass, however, "thought it better to accept half a loaf than to have no bread at all," and supported the day as an opportunity to speak out on social issues while highlighting African American accomplishments.[88] When the day came, Wells found her fears unsubstantiated, recalling, "I was so swelled with pride over his [Douglass's] masterly presentation of our case that I went straight out to the fair and begged his pardon for presuming in my youth and inexperience to criticize him."[89]

In August, with only two months left of the World's Fair, the pamphlets returned from the printers, and Wells frantically distributed them, succeeding in handing out ten thousand tracts before the Exposition closed in October.[90] The booklet, titled, *The Reason Why the Colored American Is Not in the World's Columbian Exposition*, brought several prominent black authors together to discuss the current position of African Americans in society. The work began with Frederick Douglass's chapter on the legal disenfranchisement of blacks and the "too shocking for belief" daily barbarities that African Americans experienced.[91] Wells authored three chapters on disenfranchisement, segregation, and lynching, reiterating many points from her *Southern Horrors* tract. Contributor I. Garland Penn, a black historian, followed her research with a discussion on the progress of African Americans in literacy, education, and the medical and legal professions. Ferdinand Barnett wrote the concluding chapter on employment discrimination and the societal view of the black race as menial laborers. Although no quantifiable action directly resulted from the dissemination of the pamphlet, the protests surrounding the World's Fair offered African American reformers a target against which to organize.[92]

The World's Fair in Chicago also illustrated the need for more leadership opportunities for African Americans, especially women. During the event, the Tourgée Club, a black men's club in Chicago named after lawyer, novelist, and long-time supporter of African Americans Civil Rights Albion Tourgée, created a "Ladies Day," allowing black women to entertain visitors at their clubhouse.[93] On the first day of this initiative, no women came. Members approached Wells and invited her to speak at the following "Ladies Day," hoping to spark interest, and she "gladly gave" her consent. At the next meeting, Wells encouraged her female audience to embrace "what an opportunity was theirs in having a clubhouse...and urged them to accept it regularly." She continued,

> I told them of the club movement in the East and how our women had started it in an effort to be of help to me. I also spoke of the opportunities I had in England to be present at women's gatherings and what it meant to the womanhood of that nation and urged them to consider establishing an organization of their own here in Chicago.[94]

From this talk onward, Wells found herself at the forefront of the black women's club movement. In response to her advocacy, in September 1893, the black women of Chicago started the Ida B. Wells Club, naming their organization after the driving force behind their formation, and soon boasted more than three hundred members, including prominent church-women, schoolteachers, and housewives.[95]

The white clubwomen movement that Wells alluded to in her initial "Ladies Day" speech consisted of the voluntary associations of white middle-class women whose economic positions allowed them leisure time in which to devote themselves to social issues such as sobriety, education, domestic violence, safe working conditions, sanitation, and suffrage. For black women, the clubwomen movement added an additional key compo-nent to these issues, one of "racial uplift," the belief in combating racism by working to better the conditions of African Americans. Historian Glenda Gilmore argues that with black men essentially disenfranchised by Jim Crow laws, black women stepped in as the advocates for the race and applied the same moral rhetoric utilized by white women as part of True Womanhood in order to claim a legitimate role in public spaces.[96] In carv-ing out a space for public female activism, black women began to gener-ate social change, and during the next decade, the clubwomen that Wells encouraged became increasingly influential within the black community.

In the spring of 1894, the executive council for one of the models for this movement, The Society for the Recognition of the Brotherhood of Man, contacted Wells with an invitation for her to return to England and con-tinue her anti-lynching campaign. Wells, hesitant to become involved again with Isabelle Mayo, negotiated not just for her expenses, but also a salary of two pounds per week. When the organizational board agreed to her terms, Wells accepted the invitation. Unfortunately, the money for her passage did not arrive before her departure date, and at the last minute, Wells asked Frederick Douglass to loan her twenty-five dollars for the fare. During her voyage, the council appraised Mayo of Wells's return, and Mayo demanded that the Council require she publically repudiate Impey. Apparently, the SRBM Council members refused to agree to the terms and Mayo withdrew her financial support. When Wells arrived, she encountered similar circum-stances to those of her first trip.[97]

Fortunately, Wells found a different supporter, the Reverend Charles F. Aked and his wife, who she met previously at the World's Fair. The couple invited her to their Liverpool home where "[t]he queen of England herself could not have been treated with more consideration than I was during the course of my stay with them."[98] Wells would later name her first son after Aked, reflecting her esteem for him. Without support from The Soci-ety for the Recognition of the Brotherhood of Man, Wells sought out her

own contacts and sponsors. Aked, a pacifist, Baptist, and Christian Social-
ist, suggested that she approach Frederick Douglass for an introductory
letter to open more doors for her, and Well did so, writing to her mentor of her arrival and circumstances, noting, "I am compelled to depend
upon myself somewhat," and enclosing a clipping praising her recent talk.
Douglass viewed her request poorly, apparently feeling that Wells assumed
his support of her too freely, remarking, "I see that you are already adver-
tised as accredited to England by me," and asked for more details about
her objectives in England.[99] Wells, recognizing his chastising tone, quickly
responded, stating, "I have never felt so like giving up as since I received
your very cool and cautious letter this morning, with its tone of distrust
and its inference that I have not dealt truthfully with you" and offered a
detailed explanation of events.[100] In Douglass's second, more positive
response, he reminded her that he had stood with her before and would
"for all time to come." He enclosed the requested letter of introduction,
and with her credentials in place, Wells proceeded to spend the next few
months delivering more than one hundred lectures and numerous interviews across England. Wells wrote of her experiences for her American
readers in the column "Ida B. Wells Abroad," published in the *Chicago
Inter-Ocean* newspaper.[101]

During her second trip, Wells spoke to large audiences and received
extensive press coverage.[102] In an effort to both financially support herself
and spread her message, Wells reprinted the *Southern Horrors* pamphlet,
selling it in England under the title *American Atrocities*. She convincingly
spoke about the motives behind lynching as being about race, not rape, and
her interpretation embroiled Wells in a conflict with another American
reformer in England, Frances Willard. President of the Woman's Christian
Temperance Union (WCTU), Willard headed the largest and arguably most
influential white clubwoman organization in America. The WCTU focused
on sobriety as a way to cure several social ills, especially those affecting
women, including spousal abuse and poverty. Created after the Second
Great Awakening to encourage moderation in drinking, by the end of the
nineteenth century the movement focused on implementing legislation
against all consumption of alcohol in order to better society. One of its
members, Frances E. W. Harper, believed the movement to be "one of the
grandest opportunities that God ever placed in the hands of the womanhood of any country."[103] By 1894, concerns over the social issues stemming
from alcohol abuse had extended to England, where Willard sought to
gain a victory for temperance from the Liberal Party. For Wells, drinking
alcohol was not necessary a central social ill, but a reflection of inequalities.[104] African Americans, Wells felt, should refrain from buying alcohol for
political and economic reasons, not moral ones. Drinking only gave "judges

and juries" justification for "filling the convict camps of Georgia alone with fifteen hundred Negroes," and purchasing of alcohol, Wells concluded, only served to fill the pockets of whites.[105]

The English press viewed Willard, whose parents were abolitionists, as a liberal social reformer, yet comments she made in an 1890 interview revealed her hostility to blacks and her racial prejudice. In the New York newspaper *The Voice*, Willard discussed how "the colored race multiplies like the locusts of Egypt," and believed lynching to be a result of black men reverting to brutality. She claimed, "The safety of women, of children, of the home is menaced in a thousand localities at this moment" by African American men.[106] The impact of these words from a national reform leader, Wells felt, damaged her cause, as Willard "practically condoned lynchings."[107] On her first trip to England, audiences asked Wells about Willard's view of lynchings, leaving Wells to reply that "the only public expression about which I knew [she made] had seemed to condone lynching." Her response she found "was promptly challenged by temperance workers in my audience." When Wells arrived for her second tour she had prepared for this question by not only bringing a copy of the interview with her that "I not only quoted," but also reprinting it in the English press. Willard, already in England a year, had enjoyed favorable press coverage, including a "lengthy article touching her wonderful crusade in the interest of temperance" that went so far as to name her "The Uncrowned Queen of American Democracy."[108]

In response to Wells publicizing her derogatory comments, Willard issued another interview, this one conducted by her hostess in England, Lady Henry Somerset. Appearing in the *Westminster Gazette*, the piece claimed Wells's criticism to be an "exaggeration of mind," and clarified her position as opposition to the enfranchisement of "illiterate, ignorant blacks." Willard claimed that she knew multiple tales of black men's "threatening behavior" reported to her "by upstanding citizens in the South" and believed them to be true.[109] In her autobiography, Wells believed that Willard's *Westminster Gazette* interview was an attempt by two elite white women to "crush an insignificant colored woman."[110] In addition to its dismissive tone regarding Wells, Willard reiterated her views of African Americans as largely uncivilized and upheld her previous comment that racial characteristics made African Americans undeserving of a role in politics. These remarks, however, also offered Wells an opening, the following day, she told the media that Willard's comments demonstrated that she did not seek to help African Americans. "With me," Wells declared, "it is not myself nor my reputation" but rather "the life of my people which is at stake."[111] Wells's response continued the conflict with Willard, and the two women feuded for several years.

Wells returned home from England in June, but before her departure, witnessed the culminating event of her second trip, the founding of the British Anti-Lynching Committee. During her 1894 tour, her message had reached more people, received more publicity, and increased her popularity in both England and America. Upon her return stateside, white southern newspaper attacks on her increased. The Memphis *Commercial* claimed that as a "saddle-colored Sapphira" (a reference to a biblical story of deception) Wells influenced the British press through "foul and slanderous" arguments. The paper published gossip from her Holly Springs teenage years, noting that "rumors had been rife about her unchastity," and reiterated its earlier claim that she was Fleming's "paramour."[112] In response to these allegations, Wells received encouragement from T. Thomas Fortune's Afro-American League and pledges of support from Josephine St. Pierre Ruffin and the Woman's Loyal Union. Additionally, northern news outlets began accepting Wells's viewpoint about lynchings, with *The New York Times* publishing a demand for "[e]very single report" of a lynching to "be investigated by detectives," including "the negro witness[es]," and to have their statements "published side by side with that of the lynchers."[113] As a result of the increased pressure to end lynchings brought on by Wells's international work, four southern states passed anti-lynching laws holding law enforcement accountable for protecting prisoners in their care in an effort to prevent the common practice of officers simply handing detainees over to mobs. While the enforcement of these new laws remained uneven, the creation of these regulations resulted from the public outcry begun by Wells and the publicity surrounding her second British tour.[114]

Upon her return, Wells embarked on another year-long lecture tour and, for the first time, addressed white audiences as well as black. She also made two major decisions. First, she resolved to publish an updated tract on her findings and, second, she accepted Ferdinand L. Barnett's offer of marriage. Wells and Barnett, despite fighting similar battles, had not met face-to-face until they began writing the pamphlet for the World's Fair in Chicago and had corresponded regularly by letter until her return.[115] After Wells agreed to marry Barnett, her busy schedule made setting a date difficult, and she pushed back her wedding until 1895 in order to concentrate on finishing her speaking tour and her next work, *The Red Record: Tabulated Statistics and Alleged Causes of Lynching in the United States*, which was published in early 1895. This one-hundred-page tract on lynching as a "nation's" crime expanded on her previous arguments about civilization and morality.[116]

Wells traveled from coast to coast, speaking in Illinois, Missouri, Nebraska, New York, Washington, D.C., Connecticut, Pennsylvania, Colorado, California, and Missouri.[117] In Kansas City, Missouri, Wells learned of Frederick Douglass's death from a heart attack on February 20, 1895.

She did not discuss his passing in her autobiography, only mentioning him again once, when she described a conversation with women's rights activist Susan B. Anthony. When Wells stayed with Anthony in April 1895 during her tour, the women's discussions over their methodologies highlighted Wells's differences from previous generations of female reformers. Anthony and Douglass, both abolitionists, shared the same desire for extending the right to vote to women. Anthony explained to Wells how she requested that Douglass step aside and not attend suffrage functions for fear that his presence would alienate southern white women. Wells, who respected the older woman, explained her dissenting opinion, responding that while Anthony's choice to push Douglass away may have made "some gains for suffrage," it also "confirmed white women in their attitude of segregation."[118] The two women appeared to have agreed to disagree on their divergent approaches.

During her visit, Anthony fired her stenographer for her racial attitude towards Wells. Anthony, observing her hand-written letters, asked Wells, "You didn't care to use my secretary, I suppose. I told her to come to your room when you came upstairs. Didn't she come?" Wells informed Anthony that the woman had never appeared. Anthony left the room and later returned, telling Wells, "Well, she's gone." Her employee had informed her, "It is all right for you, Miss Anthony, to treat Negroes as equals, but I refuse to take dictation from a colored woman."[119] Wells appreciated Anthony's support, and respected her willingness to "hear all sides of any question." Despite their discussions, the two women continued to clash on how to advance the issue of women's suffrage. Anthony felt that giving women the right to vote would solve most of the social problems facing America, but Wells believed that the ballot would do little for black women. Society, she argued, would effectively disenfranchise black women just as they had black men. To this point, Wells noted, "Miss Anthony seemed a little bit startled, but she did not make any contention."[120]

In June, with her speaking tour completed and *The Red Record* published, Wells married Ferdinand L. Barnett. In her surviving writings there is little about their courtship. A widower ten years her senior, Barnett's first wife, Molly Graham Barnett, was one of the first African American women to graduate from the University of Michigan and the couple had two sons before she died.[121] Chicago's black society considered Barnett a desirable catch, but he appeared reluctant to re-marry. The reason for this disinclination was hinted at several years after his wife's passing, when a rumor romantically linked him to another young woman. In response to this gossip he declared his intention to find not just a wife, but also a partner, claiming, "[W]hen I do think of marriage it will be to a woman—one who can help me in my career."[122] In Wells, Barnett found an uncompromising morality and commitment to social reform similar to his own. After postponing their wedding three times, on June 27, 1895, Wells and Barnett married. She planned a simple affair; as Wells recalled, "I had no relative, either to give me away or to tender me a reception." However, the Ida B. Wells Club asked to manage the function and Wells agreed.[123] Wells wore a white dress with a satin train trimmed in chiffon and orange blossoms. Her sisters Lily and Annie served as her attendants. She walked herself down the aisle.

Exhausted from the past two years, at the age of thirty-three Wells finally had a home and a supportive husband. Many female social reformers of her time, both black and white, were either unmarried or widowed, due to the amount of time that activism required. Black clubwoman Fannie Barrier Williams remarked on Wells's "determination to marry a man while still married to a cause."[124] With a household to run, many of her supporters questioned whether Wells could continue her work and, if so, if she would maintain her previous level of intensity. Susan B. Anthony worried about her now "divided duty" between home and reform. Anthony, now in her seventies and the newly elected president of the National American Woman Suffrage Association (NAWSA), had never married. Instead, Anthony devoted herself entirely to her cause, once telling an interviewer, "No woman is ever wholly independent who has yielded to her love nature either in marriage or out of it."[125]

Wells soon assuaged any concerns. The first indicator of her commitment to her autonomy occurred when she kept her last name as she "didn't want to lose the identity of Ida B. Wells," and all of the good work that she had accomplished with that name.[126] In an unusual move for a woman in the nineteenth century, she simply added Barnett's name to hers with a hyphen. Within a week of marrying, she also took on an editorial role at the *Conservator*. In order to support Wells-Barnett in her efforts, Barnett hired domestic help to assist with the household chores and moved his parents, who cared for his children from his first marriage, into another house when it quickly became apparent that a single residence could not accommodate both his mother and his wife.[127] During their marriage, the couple collaborated not just on their advocacy efforts, but shared domestic duties. Together, they formed a relationship in which Ida represented the public, vocal, and visible reformer with Ferdinand as the silent collaborator assisting her behind the scenes.

Shortly after her marriage, in the fall of 1895, Booker T. Washington spoke at the Atlanta Cotton States Exposition. His talk, often referred to as the "Atlanta Compromise Speech," urged black southerners to seek education and employment. While this call echoed the goals of other African American reformers, including the late Douglass and Wells-Barnett herself, who felt education offered African Americans a way to secure economic independence, Washington differed in his application of the ideology. He encouraged black southerners to embrace industrial instruction in order to provide the South with a viable workforce. Washington's support of a trade-based education was unsurprising considering his role as the head of the Tuskegee Institute, the first black industrial college in Alabama. "Friction between the races," Washington claimed, would "pass away as the black man gets a hold of the things the white man wants and respects, like the trades and mechanic arts."[128] Essentially, he argued for African Americans to focus on working for whites and not on gaining a higher education or political rights. Once the workforce in the South stabilized, he believed, lynchings would end. As his critics, including Wells-Barnett, noted, Washington essentially asked African Americans to accept segregation and the ensuing inequalities rooted in white supremacy.[129] In contrast, Wells-Barnett believed that only with the return of voting rights to African American men would the intimidation and violence inherent in the system of segregation end. Washington's conciliatory approach to reform offered stark contrast to Wells-Barnett, who demanded action, not appeasement, in order to gain social change. Predictably, Washington's plan appealed to whites, who liked his deferential approach to racial uplift, and in the vacuum in leadership left by Frederick Douglass's death, Washington had no one to oppose his methods.

Shortly after her marriage, Wells-Barnett returned to the lecture circuit, but soon realized that she was pregnant. The following March, she gave birth to a son, named Charles Aked after her British friend. Unwilling to stop her activism for motherhood, the couple hired a nurse to accompany Wells-Barnett to lectures. Soon, she made providing a nurse a part of her speaking contract. Although she continued her public efforts to end lynching, becoming a mother complicated Wells-Barnett's sense of self-identity. Even during her courtships in Memphis, she never imagined herself as a mother, and Wells-Barnett's desire to continue lecturing with her infant son by her side possibly reflected her fears of parenthood as much as her commitment to racial justice. In her autobiography, she attempted to pinpoint the reasons behind her ambivalence to motherhood, suggesting, "It may be that my early entrance into public life and the turning of my efforts, physical and mental, in that direction had something to do with smothering the mother instinct."[130] Ultimately, she wrote in her autobiography, she learned to embrace her role as a mother, and regardless of the extent to which she enjoyed parenting, having a child added an urgency to her efforts, as she worried that the social inequalities of her current world would be passed on to the next generation. This perspective reassured her as to the importance of her efforts, as she "traveled throughout the country with a nursing baby to make political speeches."[131]

In her new capacity as a mother, Wells-Barnett returned to her initial supporters—black women—to mobilize for reform. Elected the president of the Ida B. Wells Club, she began expanding her efforts beyond lynching to creating opportunities for African Americans. Her first project became opening a kindergarten for black children, as, in 1896 Chicago, the existing kindergartens allowed only white children. Like many black and white social reformers, Wells-Barnett viewed a kindergarten education as a necessity for children. When she first spoke of establishing a kindergarten, accessible to children of both races, the negative response from the African American community surprised Wells-Barnett, who characterized the discussion as "a battle royal." She could not understand how the black community would rather "our children be neglected and do without kindergarten service," than to attend an integrated nursery school. Wells-Barnett dismissed the dissenting view that establishing a kindergarten in a "colored" school district would result in African Americans "drawing the color line." In order to advance the race, Wells-Barnett felt, black children needed the same opportunities as their white counterparts and argued that the benefits of a program serving both whites and blacks outweighed any drawbacks.[132] Her arguments echoed that of many reformers who believed that childhood offer the ideal age for lessons in moral development.[133] Resolved in her commitment, Wells-Barnett dismissed the opposition as belonging to "a few narrow-minded men," and set about raising the necessary funds. She succeeded in opening the first kindergarten in Chicago accepting both black and white students, but her vision of an integrated classroom never materialized; only African American students ever attended.[134]

In 1896, the Supreme Court ruled on the case of *Plessy v. Ferguson*, and the decision, citing her 1887 appeal to the Tennessee Supreme Court in its holding, claimed separate accommodations, as long as they were equal, constitutional. As several historians note, the judgment received little notice at the time, as the system existed in practice already throughout the South.[135] Shortly after the verdict, in the summer of 1896, the two largest groups of clubwomen, the National Federation of Afro-American Women and the National League of Colored Women, merged into a new national organization, the National Association of Colored Women (NACW). With five-month-old Charles, Wells-Barnett attended the meeting and heard Josephine St. Pierre Ruffians advocate for an inclusive mission. The clubwoman declared, "we are not drawing the color line; we are women, American women, we are not alienating or withdrawing, we are only coming to the front, willing to joining any others in the same work and cordially inviting and welcoming others to join us."[136] NACW offered black women a safe space where they could work towards change. After the merger, the women elected Wells-Barnett's old friend from Memphis, Mary Church

Terrell, as president. With the motto "Lifting As We Climb," NACW focused on combating several social issues—housing, education, and unregulated working conditions—and by focusing on improving society for everyone, or "lifting" it as a whole, black women reformers sought to, through their actions, "climb" toward political and economic success.[137]

An election year, the fall of 1896 resulted in a vote that profoundly affected Wells-Barnett and her husband. The Republican Party established a national office in Chicago to organize black voters, and they selected local activist Ferdinand Barnett to direct the efforts. Barnett mobilized black men across the Midwest to vote, and his Chicago constituents successfully elected Edward H. Wright, a black man, to the position of Cook County Commissioner. In acknowledgment of Barnett's efforts, Wright asked the state's attorney, Charles S. Deneen, to appoint Barnett to the position of assistant state's attorney. Ferdinand became the first African American man in Illinois to hold the position, remaining in the office for the next fifteen years. Along with increased responsibilities and influence, the post also offered a salary of one hundred and fifty dollars a month.[138] The couple welcomed this well-paying opportunity, as Wells-Barnett was pregnant again. In November 1897, she gave birth to a second son named Herman, named for Herman Kohlsaat, one of the couple's supporters in Chicago.[139]

The lynching of a federal employee soon had Wells-Barnett back in the field. In Lake City, South Carolina, President McKinley appointed an African American man, Frazier Baker, as postmaster, incensing local whites with the selection of a black man to a coveted federal job. After months of harassment, violence erupted on February 22, 1898, when a mob of more than one hundred whites surrounded the building that served as both Baker's residence and the post office. With the family inside, the crowd set the house on fire. When the Bakers' fled the burning building, the mob opened fire upon them, shooting and killing Frazier and his three-year-old daughter. Mob members also shot Baker's wife and two of his other children, but all three managed to survive their injuries. The city's legal system found no one accountable for the lynching, claiming that the participants were "unknown." Outraged, Wells-Barnett traveled to Washington, D.C. for an audience with President McKinley and demanded he launch an investigation into the murder of his federal employee. Although President McKinley agreed to do so, before the inquiry could begin, the U.S. battleship the USS *Maine* blew up in the Havana Harbor, setting the Spanish-American war into motion and pushing the issue of the lynching aside.[140]

Although by 1898 T. Thomas Fortune's Afro-American League had largely ceased to function on a national level, the Spanish American War reinvigorated the group. The conflict presented African Americans with evidence as to the problematic nature of race and power in society, as the United States defended its occupation of Cuba as justifiable due to the atrocities committed by the Spanish.[141] During this conflict, Wells-Barnett noted that President McKinley's administration recruited both blacks and whites to fight in support of Cuba's independence against the Spanish.[142] She wrote a letter to the President, saying:

> Strange that this sentiment so exercised over barbarism in Cuba should rest so complaisant [sic] over barbarism at home. During the past fifteen years more than 2500 men, women, and children have been put to death through lynchings, hangings, shooting, drowning and burning alive. All this in our own land under our own flag and yet our government has not taken the first step to stop the slaughter.[143]

Fortune, feeling a national black political organization offered an ideal platform from which to point out these incongruities in American policies, issued a call in the *New York Age* to reconvene the group. Wells-Barnett eagerly attended to support her old champion. The Fortune she encountered at the meeting, however, disappointed her. He seemed bitter and had "no confidence." Not the only member to observe this shift in Fortune's outlook, pressure from the attendees resulted in Fortune's resignation as president and a new election of officers.[144] When the voting ended, Wells-Barnett became the group's secretary, gaining her first position as an officer in a non-clubwoman organization.

With Americans focused on their fight against the Spanish in Cuba, continued lynchings in the South highlighted race relations both domestically and internationally. The mob murder of Sam Hose in April 1899 began a series of events that would affect the future of African American social reform. The white press claimed that Sam Hose, a black sharecropper in Georgia, killed a white farmer, Alfred Cranford, and raped his wife.[145] As a manhunt ensued, the newspapers recounted with increasingly lurid details their version of events and offered a reward for Hose's capture. These newspaper reports did not even pretend that Hose would stand trial—instead they advertising his lynching before a posse even located him. Once captured, Hose's death contained all of the elements of a spectacle event, echoing Henry Smith's earlier death in Paris, Texas. A train transported Hose into town where a mob of more than two thousand men, women, and children, including "lawyers" and "doctors" proceeded to strip him and tie him to a tree. Representatives of the mob asked Hose to confess to the crime, and when he did not, tortured him by castrating him and cutting off his fingers. The men then poured oil over him before setting him on fire and burning him alive.[146] Immediately after his death, members of the mob cut his heart and liver out of his body and removed bones, crushing them into small bits for mementos. Those not present at the lynching could purchase these remains: bits of bone for twenty-five cents and slivers of the liver for ten cents.[147]

A professor with a Harvard Ph.D. and the author of several sociological books, W. E. B. Du Bois was teaching at Atlanta University and had written a "a careful and reasoned statement" about the recent lynching for the Atlanta *Constitution* when he passed by a grocery store and saw Hose's knuckles displayed in the front window. He turned around and walked away, committed to entering the arena of social advocacy. Du Bois never published his statement, whose tempered tone in hindsight must have seemed incompatible with such brutality.[148] Wells-Barnett published her findings on Hose's death in the pamphlet, *Lynch Law in Georgia,* revealing Hose to be a self-made man who taught himself to read and write. According to Wells-Barnett, when Crandford and Hose began arguing about his wages, Cranford drew a gun on Hose as he chopped wood. Threatened by the firearm, Hose threw an axe at his landlord. As Wells-Barnett discovered, Cranford's wife never leveled the accusation of rape and her assault was impossible, as she was not even home when the incident occurred.[149] While Wells-Barnett had offered a quick and decisive public response to the lynching, Booker T. Washington, at the time the most well-known African American leader in America, remained silent for two months, even when reporters directly questioned him about Hose's lynching. When he finally published his response, he failed to issue the hoped for repudiation of the mob's torture and murder. Instead, Washington believed that the mob's victims were sexual predators and that the African American men brutalized in these public killings were guilty "as a rule" because they had "no opportunity to secure an education and moral restraint."[150]

Wells-Barnett had admired Washington in 1890 for his campaign against corrupt members of the African American clergy, but after his 1895 speech, she grew disenchanted with him. As a result of his response to the Hose lynching, in which he essentially blamed the mob's victim and ignored the political and economic factors in lynchings, Wells-Barnett no longer supported him as a race leader. In her next editorial for the *New York Age,* she included a disparaging remark about Washington. Fortune, who often lectured at Tuskegee, was now a supporter of Washington, and as the *New York Age*'s editor, he took it upon himself to remove her negative remark. He then promptly wrote to Washington, warning him about Wells-Barnett's comment, noting that she was "a sort of bull in a China Shop."[151]

Wells-Barnett's criticism of Washington led to quick repercussions. In 1899, both the national meetings of the Afro-American League and NACW were held in Chicago. NACW president Mary Church Terrell did not ask Wells-Barnett for help in organizing the meeting in her hometown. When

Terrell arrived in Chicago, she informed Wells-Barnett that her estrange-
ment resulted from letters she received "from women in Chicago declaring
they would not aid in entertaining the National Association" if she involved
Wells-Barnett. Wounded by this "staggering blow" from the "women whom
I had started in club work," Wells-Barnett soon began to wonder about the
truth of her reply.[152] When Terrell invited Washington as one of the honored guests at the meeting, Wells-Barnett believed the pressure to shun
her originated from him. At the national meeting of the Afro-American
League, members blocked Wells-Barnett's officer nomination, claiming that
"the financial secretary of the Afro-American Council should be a man."[153]
Although he did not appear at the meeting, Washington met with key leaders behind closed doors and Wells-Barnett recalled in her autobiography,
"Mr. Washington had been sent to Chicago to hold the Afro-American
Council in check" and prevent members, including her, from speaking out
again against the president of the United States.[154]

Washington's attempt to alienate her exposed a growing division in the
ranks of African American reformers, resulting in a leadership split in the
fall of 1899. Wells-Barnett, her husband, Du Bois, William Monroe Trotter,
a Boston editor, and Calvin Chase, a Washington editor, constituted one
block, existing in opposition to Fortune, Washington, and Terrell. Shortly
after this divide, Du Bois spoke publically for the need to create a federation
of black businesses, and once he heard the idea Washington acted upon it,
creating the National Negro Business League. Wells-Barnett defended her
new ally Du Bois in the pages of *Conservator*, noting how Washington stole
Du Bois's idea so he could form and control the group as "the president,
moderator and dictator."[155] Such public dissent would become increasingly
difficult in the future, as Washington quietly gained control of several newspapers. With influence over the leadership of the Afro-American Council,
the National Negro Business League, and several major black presses, the
Tuskegee president quickly gained a reputation of having an "iron hand"
with his enemies.[156]

In the spring of 1900, Wells-Barnett formally published her complaints
against the leader in the essay "Booker T. Washington and His Critics." In
order to illustrate her charges that he pandered to whites at the detriment
of the black race, in her treatise she repeated a "joke" that Washington told
to a white Chicago Women's Club. The exchange begins with Washington
telling how he complimented a black farmer on his hogs. Slipping into a
deep southern dialect, Washington then narrated the alleged response,
"Yes, Mr. Washington, ebber sence you done tole us bout raising our own
hogs, we niggers round her hab resolved to quit stealing hogs and gwinter
raise our own." The audience apparently roared with laughter. Such stories,
Wells-Barnett noted, were an insult not only to the race, but overlooked

the "hundreds of Negroes" who bought land and raised stock "long before Booker Washington was out of school."[157] Wells-Barnett felt industrial education had not, as Washington promised, decreased lynchings and by claiming it as the only type of education African Americans should undertake, Washington's approach limited access to higher education for southern blacks, harming the race as a whole. Once she published her attacks on Washington, Wells-Barnett, from 1900 on, would be working against other prominent members of her own race in her efforts at social change and, as a result, during the next decade Wells-Barnett would shift both her methods and her focus, but not her objectives.

NOTES

1 Bay, *To Tell the Truth Freely*, 103.
2 The rhetoric of the bestial black rapist who violated pure white females and deserved torture and death, Wells concluded, served only as a convenient excuse for whites to justify their actions. Wells-Barnett and Royster, 3. See also, Pamela Newkirk, " 'Ida B. Wells-Barnett: Journalism as a Weapon against Racial Bigotry,' " *Media Studies Journal* 14, no. 2 (2000), http://www.hartford-hwp.com/archives/45a/317.html; Schechter, *Ida B. Wells-Barnett and American Reform*, 87; Davidson, 90, 155.
3 Most of the African American males lynched were young, usually in their twenties or thirties. Although the rhetoric of Jim Crow primarily focused on controlling African American men, black women occasionally became the targets of a lynch mob if they injured a white girl. In Shreveport, Louisiana, a white mob lynched Jennie Steers, a black woman, in 1903, for giving sixteen-year-old Elizabeth Dolan "a glass of poisoned lemonade, causing her death." A mob gathered, "took her to a tree, placed a rope around her neck, and demanded a confession. The woman refused and was hanged." *Chicago Record–Herald*, July 27, 1903 as quoted in Ralph Ginzburg, *100 Years of Lynchings* (Baltimore: Black Classic Press, 1988), 53–57; Brundage, *Lynching in the New South*, 82.
4 While the rape-lynch rhetoric portrayed African American men as savages desiring to rape white women, the ideology also implied that white women would not betray their race's future by having consensual sexual relationships with black men. Therefore, any contact between a black man and white woman must be unwilling on the part of the female. Lynching offered white men not only a way to exhibit their social, political, economic, and sexual prerogative over both black men but also white women, as they needed to be policed by white men in order to prevent them from willingly seeking out black sexual partners. See Hazel V. Carby, " 'On the Threshold of Woman's Era': Lynching, Empire, and Sexuality in Black Feminist Theory," *Critical Inquiry* 12, no. 1 (1985), 270; and J. William Harris, "Etiquette, Lynching, and Racial Boundaries in Southern History: A Mississippi Example," *The American Historical Review* 100, no. 2 (April 1995): 392.
5 Ida B. Wells, *Southern Horrors: Lynch Law in All Its Phases*, 2013 edition (CreateSpace Independent Publishing Platform, 1892), February 8, 2005, http://www.gutenberg.org/files/14975/14975-h/14975-h.htm (accessed March 21, 2016), preface.
6 As Hazel Carby summarized Wells, the "press acted as accomplices" doing the "the ideological work" that cloaked the political and economic motives of lynchings. Carby, 269.
7 *NAACP Collection*, Group I, Section C, Box 360, Subject File: Lynching, Ellisville Miss. 1919, News clippings.
8 Giddings, *When and Where I Enter*, 23.
9 Bay, *To Tell the Truth Freely*, 91.

10 Philip Alexander Bruce, *The Plantation Negro as a Freeman; Observations on His Character, Condition, and Prospects in Virginia* (New York: G. P. Putnam's Sons, 1889), 3, 5. Bruce's publication is but one example of scholars that drew similar conclusions about the biological nature of white supremacy.

11 Bruce, 83.

12 Bruce, 249.

13 Bruce, 85. This argument was widely circulated by pro-slavery theorists, including Judge Thomas R. R. Cobb of Georgia, who believed that inserting the race of a rapist in court documents was "superfluous" as being a black male equated with being a rapist. As quoted in Diane Miller Sommerville, *Rape and Race in the Nineteenth-Century South* (Chapel Hill: The University of North Carolina Press, 2004), 89. See also Paul Finkelman, "Thomas R.R. Cobb and the Law of Negro Slavery," *Roger Williams University Law Review* 5, no. 1 (1999): 75–115.

14 The University of Alabama, "Genesis & Apocalypse of the 'Old South' Myth: Two Virginia Writers at the Turn of the Century," *Publisher's Bindings Online, 1815–1930: The Art of Books*, 2005, http://bindings.lib.ua.edu/gallery/nelson_page.html (accessed March 21, 2016).

15 Thomas Nelson Page, *Two Little Confederates* (New York: Charles Scribner's Sons, 1888), 39–49, 189.

16 Thomas Nelson Page also wrote *Among the Camps, or Young People's Stories of the War* (New York: Charles Scribner's Sons, 1891). This novel described slave children as filthy and as all speaking in heavy dialect. The plantation owner's son Jack receives a slave (Jake) from his grandfather. Jack is envious of Jake who lounges around all day. The two engage in shenanigans when they go to a Yankee camp where Jack repeatedly shows his intellectual and moral superiority, his bravery, and his own manly self-worth. Gail Murray, *American Children's Literature and the Construction of Childhood* (London: Twayne Publishers, 1998), 115.

17 Thomas Nelson Page, "A Southerner on the Negro Question," *The North American Review* 154 (April 1892): 406, 402–3.

18 Joseph Alexander Tillinghast, "The Negro in Africa and America," *Publications of the American Economic Association* 3 (1902): 407–636. He supported the prevailing academic understandings of race, discussing African American's "primitive, savage passions," 606.

19 Tillinghast, 606.

20 Tillinghast, 598, 595.

21 Giddings, *Ida: A Sword among Lions*, 223, 225.

22 Duke's publication did not have any of the research or statistical backing that served as the backbone of Wells's writing.

23 Wells also began her pamphlet by acknowledging Jesse Duke, who, upon leaving town, "signed a card disclaiming any intention of slandering Southern white women." This, Wells went on to note, would not be happening with her. Wells, *Southern Horrors*, 4.

24 Davidson, 155; Bay, *To Tell the Truth Freely*, 103; Giddings, *Ida: A Sword among Lions*, 153; McMurry, 120.

25 This is discussed in detail in Gail Bederman, " 'Civilization,' the Decline of Middle-Class Manliness, and Ida B. Wells's Antilynching Campaign (1892–94)," *Radical History Review* 52 (1992): 5–30, and in Bay, *To Tell the Truth Freely*, 91.

26 Wells, *Southern Horrors*, 11.

27 Schechter, *Ida B. Wells-Barnett and American Reform*, 87.

28 Ida B. Wells, *Southern Horrors*, 6.

29 Ida B. Wells, *Southern Horrors*, 42.

30 Frederick Douglass, "Lynch Law in the South," *The North American Review* 155, July (1892): 17.

31 Douglass, "Lynch Law in the South," 23.

32 Schechter, *Ida B. Wells-Barnett and American Reform*, 81.

33 McMurry, 183.

34 Schechter, *Ida B. Wells-Barnett and American Reform*, 21.

35 Bay, *To Tell the Truth Freely*, 125; Schechter, *Ida B. Wells-Barnett and American Reform*, 85.

36   Wells, *Southern Horrors*, 2.
37   Caroline C. Nichols, "The 'Adventuress' Becomes a 'Lady': Ida B. Wells' British Tours," *Modern Language Studies* 38, no. 2 (2009): 56.
38   Wells, *Southern Horrors*, 19.
39   Simone W. Davis, "The 'Weak Race' and the Winchester: Political Voices in the Pamphlets of Ida B. Wells-Barnett," *Legacy* 12, no. 2 (1995): 83.
40   Wells, *Southern Horrors*, 13, 4.
41   Davis, 79.
42   Wells, *Southern Horrors*, 8; emphasis in original.
43   Wells, *Southern Horrors*, 3.
44   Wells, *Crusade for Justice*, 81.
45   Wells, *Crusade for Justice*, 82.
46   McMurry, 175.
47   Giddings, *Ida: A Sword among Lions*, 243.
48   McMurry, 185.
49   Wells, *Crusade for Justice*, 72–73.
50   Quoted in McMurry, 153.
51   Giddings, *Ida: A Sword among Lions*, 245.
52   Bay, *To Tell the Truth Freely*, 136–37.
53   Quoted in McMurry, 177–78.
54   Giddings, *Ida: A Sword among Lions*, 245–46; Schechter, *Ida B. Wells-Barnett and American Reform*, 91.
55   Mark Elliott, *Color Blind Justice: Albion Tourgée and the Quest for Racial Equality from the Civil War to Plessy v. Ferguson* (New York: Oxford University Press, 2008), 12.
56   McMurry, 182.
57   Grace Hale, *Making Whiteness: The Culture of Segregation in the South 1890–1940* (New York: Pantheon Books, 1998), 237, 202–3. Amy Louise Wood, *Lynching and Spectacle: Witnessing Racial Violence in America, 1890–1940* (Chapel Hill: University of North Carolina Press, 2009), 74. This enabled a previously impossible collectivity to form. Local and regional newspapers were also responsible for the publicity and promotion of a lynching, as well as playing a key role in the creation of a genre of lynching narratives. Stanley J. Tambiah, "A Performance Approach to Ritual" in *Readings in Ritual Studies*, ed. Ronald Grimes (New Jersey: Prentice Hall, 1996), 497. The mob's actions were, as Fitzhugh Brundage notes, "a highly ritualized choreography." Brundage, *Lynching in the New South*, 39. Later in the twentieth century, the new technology of radios, advertising the time and place of a lynching in advance, turned a previously local incident into a regional event. These mass mob spectacle lynchings followed a predetermined pattern that unified disparate lynchings across the South into consistent ritualized violence. Hale, 203–10.
58   Wells-Barnett and Royster, 92; Hale, 207. Hale describes Myrtle Vance as three years old.
59   A mass mob formed for only the most heinous of crimes, usually defined as the sexual violation of a white woman or an act of violence against a white. The public mass mob lynching offers insight, from the rendering of the accusation to the collection of souvenirs, of the racial and gender representations of white southerners during Jim Crow. Spectacle lynchings exhibited and demanded the acknowledgment of gender roles for white men and women as well as boys and girls, and allowed the white community to model, produce, and reinforce the distinct racial and gendered behavior needed by whites to enforce segregation. See Kristina DuRocher, *Raising Racists: The Socialization of White Children in the Jim Crow South* (Lexington: The University Press of Kentucky, 2011). These spectacles are part of what Saidiya Hartman terms "Negro Enjoyment," and a terrorizing example of everyday domination. Saidiya Hartman, *Scenes of Subjection: Terror, Slavery, and Self-Making in Nineteenth Century America* (New York: Oxford University Press, 1997), 7, see also chapter one.
60   In churches across the South, whites heard sermons and repeated in prayers and in hymns that sin deserved punishment. This possibility for redemption within the ritual maintains the

religious ideology that retribution and suffering are part of salvation. A mob's attempt to gain a confession from the accused not only endeavored to determine guilt or innocence, but also to extract a degree of salvation through pain. See Donald G. Mathews, "The Southern Rite of Human Sacrifice," *Journal of Southern Religion* v, no. III (August 2000), http://jsr.fsu.edu/mathews.htm (accessed March 21, 2016).

61 Torture as punishment is part of the lynching ritual; it controlled the level of pain, branded and marked the body to purge the crime, and its culmination marked the triumph of the mob over their victim. Michel Foucault, *Discipline and Punish: The Birth of the Prison* (New York: Second Vintage Books Edition, 1995), 33–34.

62 This public ritual served to unify whites against a common enemy, the black aggressor, which bonded whites along racial lines, minimizing class distinctions and preventing poor whites from recognizing that perhaps they had more in common with poor blacks than elite whites. Other early studies of lynching argued that this violence was the work of lower-class whites. See James Cutler, *Lynch-Law: An Investigation into the History of Lynching in the United States* (New York: Negro Universities Press, 1969) and Arthur Franklin Raper, *The Tragedy of Lynching* (Baltimore: Black Classic Press, 1933). Recent scholarship has complicated these views, noting that lynching united whites and oppressed blacks psychologically, economically, socially, and politically.

63 The collection of souvenirs allowed whites to consume the sacrificed body and remember the ritual and the (temporary) restoration of order that resulted after a lynching. James Allen, *Without Sanctuary: Lynching Photography in America* (Santa Fe: Twin Palms, 2000), 8–9.

64 Wells, *Crusade for Justice*, 84.

65 Giddings, *Ida: A Sword among Lions*, 250.

66 Bay, *To Tell the Truth Freely*, 135.

67 McMurry, 186.

68 McMurry, 189.

69 Giddings, *Ida: A Sword among Lions*, 262.

70 Wells, *Crusade for Justice*, 89.

71 Wells, *Crusade for Justice*, 90–91.

72 Quoted in Schechter, *Ida B. Wells-Barnett and American Reform*, 25.

73 Quoted in McMurry, 191–92.

74 Wells, *Crusade for Justice*, 103–4.

75 Wells, *Crusade for Justice*, 105.

76 Wells, *Crusade for Justice*, 113.

77 Bay, *To Tell the Truth Freely*, 139.

78 McMurry, 196.

79 McMurry, 206–7.

80 Norm Bolotin and Christine Laing, *The World's Columbian Exposition: The Chicago World's Fair of 1893* (Urbana: University of Illinois Press, 2002), vii.

81 Bay, *To Tell the Truth Freely*, 129–31; McMurry, 185.

82 Elliott M. Rudwick and August Meier, "Black Man in the 'White City': Negroes and the Columbian Exposition, 1893," *Phylon* 26, no. 4 (1965): 356.

83 Wells, *Crusade for Justice*, 118.

84 Bay, *To Tell the Truth Freely*, 156.

85 Schechter, *Ida B. Wells-Barnett and American Reform*, 94; McMurry, 200.

86 Bay, *To Tell the Truth Freely*, 159.

87 Quoted in McMurry, 203–4.

88 Wells, *Crusade for Justice*, 118.

89 Wells, *Crusade for Justice*, 119.

90 McMurry, 203.

91 Ida B. Wells, Frederick Douglass, Irvine Garland Penn and Ferdinand Lee Barnett, *The Reason Why the Colored American Is Not in the World's Columbian Exposition*, 1999 edition (Urbana: University of Illinois Press, 1893), 10.

92 Anna R. Paddon and Sally Turner, "African Americans and the World's Columbian Exposition," *Illinois Historical Journal* 88, no. 1 (1995): 36.

93 Tourgée rose to fame for his novels set in the South, including his 1879 work, *A Fool's Errand*, which described race relations during Reconstruction. Elliott, 1–2.

94 Wells, *Crusade for Justice*, 121–22.

95 Wells, *Crusade for Justice*, 123–24.

96 See Glenda Gilmore, *Gender and Jim Crow: Women and the Politics of White Supremacy in North Carolina, 1896–1920* (Chapel Hill: University of North Carolina Press, 1996).

97 Bay, *To Tell the Truth Freely*, 175; McMurry, 207–8.

98 Wells, *Crusade for Justice*, 127; Bay, *To Tell the Truth Freely*, 176; Giddings, *Ida: A Sword among Lions*, 286.

99 Giddings, *Ida: A Sword among Lions*, 294.

100 McMurry, 207–8; Giddings, *Ida: A Sword among Lions*, 293–95.

101 Giddings, *Ida: A Sword among Lions*, 296; McMurry, 209.

102 Wells praised these churches while criticizing American congregations for not speaking out against racial violence. C. L. Karcher, "Ida B. Wells and Her Allies against Lynching: A Transnational Perspective," *Comparative American Studies* 3, no. 2 (2005): 145; Giddings, *Ida: A Sword among Lions*, 291.

103 Quoted in Schechter, *Ida B. Wells-Barnett and American Reform*, 66.

104 Giddings, *Ida: A Sword among Lions*, 266; Schechter, *Ida B. Wells-Barnett and American Reform*, 66.

105 McMurry, 210.

106 "The Race Problem: Miss Willard on the Political Puzzle of the South," *The Voice* (New York), October 23, 1890. Also quoted in McMurry, 210; Schechter, *Ida B. Wells-Barnett and American Reform*, 102.

107 Wells, *Crusade for Justice*, 112–13.

108 Wells, *Crusade for Justice*, 202.

109 Giddings, *Ida: A Sword among Lions*, 302–3.

110 Wells, *Crusade for Justice*, 210.

111 McMurry, 212.

112 Giddings, *Ida: A Sword among Lions*, 305.

113 Giddings, *Ida: A Sword among Lions*, 318.

114 Bay, *To Tell the Truth Freely*, 196.

115 Barnett founded the Illinois Anti-Lynching League and also published articles criticizing lynchings. McMurry, 238.

116 Nichols, 55.

117 McMurry, 225; Giddings, *Ida: A Sword among Lions,* 321.

118 McMurry, 231.

119 Wells, *Crusade for Justice*, 228–29.

120 Wells, *Crusade for Justice*, 230.

121 Giddings, *Ida: A Sword among Lions*, 345–46; Bay, *To Tell the Truth Freely*, 168–69.

122 McMurry, 238, also quoted in Bay, *To Tell the Truth Freely*, 169.

123 Wells, *Crusade for Justice*, 240–41.

124 Schechter, *Ida B. Wells-Barnett and American Reform*, 28.

125 Ida Husted Harper, *The Life and Work of Susan B. Anthony: Including Public Addresses, Her Own Letters and Many from Her Contemporaries During Fifty Years, Volume III* (Indianapolis: Bowen-Merrill Company, 1908), 1,483.

126 Quoted in Bay, *To Tell the Truth Freely*, 214–15.

127 McMurry, 240.

128 Bay, *To Tell the Truth Freely*, 167.

129 See Michael Hatt, "Sculpting and Lynching: The Making and Unmaking of the Black Citizen in Late Nineteenth-Century America," *Oxford Art Journal* 24, no. 1 (2001): 7–8; McMurry, 254; Giddings, *Ida: A Sword among Lions*, 365; Schechter, *Ida B. Wells-Barnett and American Reform,* 109.

130 Wells, *Crusade for Justice*, 251.
131 Wells, *Crusade for Justice*, 244.
132 Wells, *Crusade for Justice*, 249–50.
133 Cheryl Nelson Butler, "Blackness as Delinquency," *Washington University Law Review* 90 (2013): 1,393.
134 McMurry, 268.
135 Giddings, *Ida: A Sword among Lions*, 371.
136 Quoted in Abdullah, 337–38.
137 See Dulcie Straughan, "'Lifting as We Climb': The Role of The National Association Notes in Furthering the Issues Agenda of the National Association of Colored Women, 1897–1920," *Media History Monographs* 8, no. 2 (2006): 1–19.
138 McMurry, 270.
139 McMurry, 242–43.
140 Bay, *To Tell the Truth Freely*, 234; McMurry, 258; Giddings, *Ida: A Sword among Lions*, 388–89.
141 Kristin L. Hoganson, *Fighting for American Manhood: How Gender Politics Provoked the Spanish-American and Philippine-American Wars* (New Haven: Yale University Press, 1998), 134, 171, 183.
142 Bay, *To Tell the Truth Freely*, 235.
143 Quoted in Trichita M. Chestnut, "Lynching: Ida B. Wells-Barnett and the Outrage over the Frazier Baker Murder," *Prologue* (Fall 2008), 23.
144 Giddings, *Ida: A Sword among Lions*, 391.
145 In several accounts Hose also is referred to as Samuel Wilkes.
146 Giddings, *Ida: A Sword among Lions*, 405–6.
147 Ginzburg, 12.
148 Edward Ayers, "An American Nightmare: A Heartbreaking History of Segregation and Its Target Population," *The New York Times on the Web*, May 3, 1998, https://www.nytimes.com/books/98/05/03/reviews/980503.03ayrest.html (accessed March 21, 2016).
149 Giddings, *Ida: A Sword among Lions*, 409.
150 Bay, *To Tell the Truth Freely*, 241.
151 Quoted in McMurry, 256.
152 Wells, *Crusade for Justice*, 258–59.
153 Schechter, *Ida B. Wells-Barnett and American Reform*, 116.
154 Wells, *Crusade for Justice*, 261–62.
155 Quoted in McMurry, 260.
156 Bay, *To Tell the Truth Freely*, 253.
157 McMurry, 263.

CHAPTER 4

PIONEERING EFFORTS, 1900–18

"Our country's national crime is lynching," Wells-Barnett wrote in her January 1900 article "Lynch Law in America," while discussing the celebratory and ritualistic nature of mass mob spectacle lynchings, concluding that "butchery is made a pastime and national savagery condoned."[1] A few months later, her research into the death of African American Robert Charles, published in *Mob Rule in New Orleans: Robert Charles and his Fight to Death, the Story of his Life, Burning Human Beings Alive, Other Lynching Statistics*, proved the veracity of these remarks. On July 23, 1900, Robert Charles and another black man, Leonard Pierce, strolled through town intending to visit a friend. Finding their associate not at home yet, the two men sat down to wait on the doorstep. The sight of two black men lingering in a predominantly white neighborhood prompted inquiry, and soon three white police officers approached the men, questioning what they were doing. Charles replied that he was "waiting for a friend," and "in less than three minutes" from the time the police approached the men, they "attempted to put both colored men under arrest."[2] While one officer grabbed Charles, the other struck him on his head, and Charles, a believer in self-defense, drew his gun. In the following scuffle, both the officers and Charles fired shots, and all were wounded. After an injured Charles fled the scene, a citywide manhunt ensued. The mayor issued the following public statement:

> Under the authority vested in me by law, I hereby offer, in the name of the city of New Orleans, $250 reward for the capture and delivery, dead or alive, to the authorities of the city, the body of the Negro murderer, ROBERT CHARLES...
> PAUL CAPDEVIELLE, Mayor.[3]

For the next few days, police searched the city for Charles, assisted by gangs of armed white men roaming the street. Lashing out in anger, these groups attacked and beat more than a dozen African American men they came across and, as tension escalated, so did the violence. White men began shooting at any black man fitting Charles's description, killing the innocent Louis Taylor on his way to work and a black woman when a stray bullet entered her home.[4] Other African Americans barely escaped with their lives after encountering angry white citizens. Esther Fields went outside her home to investigate a noise, "ran into the arms of the mob, and was beaten into insensibility in less time than it takes to tell it." Another African American, T. P. Sanders, was "sitting in front of his home when he saw the crowd marching out the street," and having "stayed to see what the excitement was all about," the mob "shot [him] in the knee and thorax and [he was] horribly beaten about the head."[5]

After four days of racial violence, authorities discovered the wounded Charles's location. The news spread and the police and a mob surrounded the residence. Charles, still armed, proceeded to shoot out a window at his pursuers. "He worked the weapon with incredible rapidity, discharging from three to five cartridges each time before leaping back to a place of safety." Doing this, he killed seven men and wounded twenty. Enraged, the mob set the house on fire and shot repeatedly inside, eventually killing Charles. Not yet satisfied, the crowd dragged his "bleeding body" out of the burning building where "[i]t was shot, kicked and beaten almost out of semblance to humanity."[6] Wells-Barnett remarked upon the actions of the mob, "In no other civilized country in the world, nay, more, in no land of barbarians would it be possible to duplicate the scenes of brutality that are reported from New Orleans."[7]

Wells-Barnett examined the accounts in the two white New Orleans newspapers branding Charles as a " 'monster,' 'an unreasoning brute,' 'bad nigger,' 'cocaine fiend,' 'woman beater,' 'dangerous agitator,' 'worthless, crap-shooting negro,' 'ruthless black butcher,' and 'blood thirsty champion of African supremacy.' " While the white press created an image of Charles consistent with a savage black man, Wells-Barnett's research told a different story of the mob's victim, evidenced by the representation of Charles wearing a suit, ascot, and derby hat on the cover of her pamphlet.[8] She found, "Even the most conservative of journals" lacked "evidence to prove that the dead man was a criminal, and that his life had been given over to lawbreaking." A search of his room revealed Charles supported "the *Voice of Missions*, a 'religious' paper," and these documents became, in the white newspaper accounts, "race propaganda" castigating Charles as a militant in order to maintain their narrative of him as "a lawbreaker and desperado."[9] In contrast to white accounts, Wells-Barnett concluded that Charles died for failing to submit meekly to white authority. This resistance, she argued, "made him an outlaw" to whites but for many African Americans his decision to fight back was heroic.[10] It is unsurprising that Wells-Barnett praised Charles for his act of self-defense, as she had advocated that African Americans arm themselves for the past decade in an effort to dissuade mob violence. Three days of unrestrained attacks on the black community at large in New Orleans extended beyond any previous spectacle, as whites attacked the entire black community and ultimately murdered three African Americans, foreshadowing the race riots that would soon spread across the county.[11]

The publicity surrounding the deaths of Sam Hose and Robert Charles led other social reformers to join Wells-Barnett's anti-lynching cause, including Chicagoan Jane Addams. While Wells-Barnett appreciated the attention that other prominent reformers could bring to her efforts, she struggled with those who condemned lynchings but failed to comprehend the motives behind white southerners' engagement in racial violence. With white reformers such as Addams, Wells-Barnett encountered resistance to her arguments that segregation was a system based on racial domination. In order to understand lynchings, Wells-Barnett believed, one first had to accept that this brutality served to control African Americans in order to protect whites' access to political and economic power. For white activists, this meant rejecting the oft-repeated ideology that African Americans were less evolved and accepting that the rhetoric about racial inferiority was a consequence of white supremacy, not the cause. This transition in racial thinking proved a difficult bias for many whites to overcome.

Jane Addams, an early sociologist, co-founded the Hull-House settlement in 1899. Settlement houses in urban areas encouraged educated, middle-class whites to live in poor metropolitan neighborhoods and serve the needs of the community by offering tutoring, daycare, employment services and other activities. Hull-House's Chicago location served a large number of Eastern European immigrants.[12] In 1901, Addams, who knew Wells-Barnett from NACW meetings and other local events, wrote an article for New York's *The Independent,* on "Respect for the Law," attempting to denounce lynchings. Wells-Barnett greatly admired Addams and appreciated her commitment to uplifting all members of society. In her autobiography, she referred to Addams as "the greatest woman in the United States."[13] As female reformers devoted to class, race, and gender issues, Addams and Wells-Barnett shared a similar perspective on social change, but Addams, well-known for her calm temperament, offered a stark contrast to the outspoken Wells-Barnett.[14] In "Respect for the Law," Addams offered a gendered analysis of white lynchers, noting, "We must remember that many of the most atrocious public acts recorded in history have been committed by men." She continued, "The woman who is protected by violence allows herself to…still be regarded as the possession of man."[15] She concluded, "that the bestial in man, that which leads him to pillage and rape, can never be controlled by public cruelty and dramatic punishment."[16]

Wells-Barnett felt compelled to address Addams's assumption of black men as "bestial" and uncontrolled. Her response to Addams, titled, "Lynching and the Excuse for It," sought not to "lessen the force" of Addams's appeal, but instead correct her "unfortunate presumption."[17] In failing to debunk the rape myth behind lynchings, she believed that Addams reinforced the ideology of racial inferiority.[18] Wells-Barnett maintained that only by confronting the racial reasons for lynching—upholding white supremacy, could society make progress. Addams, in making an argument based on gender, overlooked the primary issue of race. As one of the first white female reformers to oppose lynchings publically, this exchange with Addams offered Wells-Barnett a new audience, and although she found Addams's interpretation troubling, she agreed with the white activist's conclusion that "[b]rutality only begets brutality."[19]

In 1901, Wells-Barnett did not attend the NACW or Afro-American Council national meetings as she had recently given birth to her third child, a daughter she named Ida. During her absence, Booker T. Washington gained additional support for his leadership and Wells-Barnett lost influence in the organizations, as members did not elect her to any officer positions. One supporter commented to the Tuskegee president, "I am glad Mrs. Barnett was not there to complicate the situation."[20] Her husband delivered her report as the head of the anti-lynching committee to the Afro-American Council, which contained Wells-Barnett's proposal that the group pressure the President and Congress for a federal anti-lynching bill. Such an undertaking, Wells-Barnett believed, could become a reality if Washington took up the anti-lynching cause. After William McKinley's assassination in 1901, recently inaugurated president Theodore Roosevelt had invited Washington to the White House for dinner and considered him a valuable consultant on race issues. With this new influence, Wells-Barnett hoped that Washington was confident enough to push for reform. Instead, the opposite occurred: Washington desired to maintain his status and refused to publically make waves. His elevation in significance only increased his determination to silence his detractors and, to that end, he continued buying stock in African American presses responsible for publishing negative items about him.[21]

Although Wells-Barnett remained committed to drawing attention to and working for anti-lynching reform, she also recognized that discriminatory practices limited African Americans' access to education and high-paying jobs, which prevented them from making social progress. She continued her attempts at rectifying these disparities at the city level, believing that local successes would create forward progress. After the turn of the century, Wells-Barnett recognized the limitations of working with black clubwomen. Although they had made a difference in the region, perhaps as a result of the success of Jane Addams, she began to feel that creating interracial organizations with white women could further her causes. In a 1903 lecture on "The Afro-American Woman: Her Past, Present and Future," given to the Chicago Political Equality League, Wells-Barnett told a mostly white audience that women could accomplish more by combining their reform efforts. She praised white women for their "dignified and courteous" nature and knew they were "incapable of race hatred." She then argued that together black and white women could mold "public sentiment" and "accomplish the reforms that the pulpit and the law have failed to do."[22] One of her audience members, Celia Parker Woolley, a white reformer and Social Gospel Unitarian minister, approached Wells-Barnett after her talk with the idea of opening an interracial center where "white and colored persons could meet and get to know each other better."[23] Wells-Barnett, eagerly hoping to combine white and black women's efforts, agreed to work with Woolley to create such a space, which Woolley would later describe as more of "an idea, than an institution, and that idea is the mitigation of race prejudice."[24]

The first problem became where to establish an interracial facility. The rapid increase in the black population migrating north, as well as an increasing immigrant population, created a city rigidly compartmentalized by race and ethnicity. At the turn of the century, Chicago was the most segregated city in America, with divisions so extreme that Woolley and Wells-Barnett could not find a white landlord willing to rent to them, requiring the group to purchase a house. Woolley and Wells-Barnett agreed that the white women would donate a down payment on the residence and the black women would make the mortgage payments.[25] Wells-Barnett faced some resistance in organizing her part of the bargain, as many black women in Chicago opposed this interracial partnership. Their concern revolved around the equality of power in such groups, as whites dominated the few existing interracial organizations. Wells-Barnett recalled in her autobiography the sustained effort that she and Ferdinand put into winning African American support for the idea, becoming "militant champions in the effort to put the movement over."[26] Once adopted, the plan succeeded and, in 1904, the coalition opened the Frederick Douglass Center, modeled on Jane Addams's Hull-House, offering a space for middle-class women of both races to engage with those they sought to help.[27]

Woolley, although inspired by Wells-Barnett, saw herself in more of an authoritative role than as an equal to her black counterpart.[28] In her autobiography, Wells-Barnett described how soon after the center opened Woolley claimed it as "her" idea and explained its mission as helping "black folks with their problems" rather than interracial cooperation to remediate social issues.[29] This hint of racial superiority in Woolley's comments became overt when she required a white woman run the center, suggesting Mary Plummer as president. Committed to her interracial attempt, Wells-Barnett agreed. As a compromise, Woolley proposed that an African American woman serve as vice-president. Wells-Barnett did not offer herself up for the role, but when no one else came forward, she agreed to serve.

In September of 1904, Wells-Barnett, at forty-two years of age, delivered her fourth and last child, daughter Alfreda. Despite her recent childbirth, Wells-Barnett volunteered at many Frederick Douglass Center's events, organizing educational lectures, classes, and a kindergarten, as well as athletic events and a summer camp.[30] Soon, however, the balance of interracial cooperation became distinctly uneven. Woolley, Wells-Barnett felt, clearly did not like any of her suggestions or criticisms about the facility, escalating the tension in their interactions. One notable exchange occurred when Plummer asked Wells-Barnett to fill in as a guest speaker. With her recent experience likely in mind, she chose to speak on "What It Means to Be a Mother." After explaining to her audience how becoming a parent shaped her efforts at reform, she was appalled when, at the conclusion of her speech, Woolley stood up and, "like a dash of cold water," countered that the "most influential women workers for humanity have not been mothers."[31] Woolley's dismissive comment infuriated Wells-Barnett.

The tension between the two women culminated in 1907, when Plummer, having served two terms as president, stepped down. During the meeting to elect a new leader, members nominated Wells-Barnett for the presidency, a motion she recalled was "greeted with such applause that everybody in the room was sure that I would be elected." Woolley, apparently unwilling to have the only nominee be an African American woman, began actively soliciting the white women in the room to run against Wells-Barnett, eventually finding one willing to do so. Furious at Woolley's manipulation against her, Wells-Barnett stood, "put on my things and left the Douglass Center never to return." Without her, Wells-Barnett noted in her autobiography, the center struggled and closed two years later in 1909.[32]

In addition to lingering feelings of racial superiority, economic differences exacerbated tensions in interracial reform efforts. The Barnetts, considered middle class, partnered with whites often far wealthier than themselves. This divide held true for most black women, who struggled to maintain their middle-class status in organizations with white women who possessed more financial freedom and leisure time, and these differences often led white women to feel that as the primary economic backers of reform efforts they should also be the leaders. As historian Paula Giddings noted, "Blacks were expected to be grateful for the attention" paid to them by white reformers, resulting in an inherent superiority that made working together as equals often difficult.[33] This uneven distribution of power resulted in many black clubwomen avoiding interracial efforts, as they feared losing the autonomy that they enjoyed within their own organizations. These racial and economic reasons, as well as her personality, hindered Wells-Barnett's attempts to establish a thriving interracial women's movement. After years of independent research, writing, and speaking, she struggled to adapt to the shared governance of organizations. She frequently chafed at the formalities and discussions required to make any decision and her desire for action often made her appear impatient and short-tempered. Wells-Barnett's disposition sometimes led to volatile conversations at odds with the equanimity expected within female organizations.[34] After failing to establish an interracial women's group that shared power equally, she returned her focus to her efforts on improving the "moral, civic and social standards" of her race.[35]

Wells-Barnett's temperament offered Booker T. Washington and his supporters a way to minimize her leadership within the national reform movement. The need for Washington to silence Wells-Barnett demonstrated the power she wielded as a leading activist. As she continued to publish about lynchings, she used each incident to disprove Washington's belief that industrial education would end racial violence. Wells-Barnett appeared to thrive on conflict with the Tuskegee president, almost gleefully attacking his points and countering them with her own. In 1904, after several years of public criticism, Washington increased his efforts to undermine Wells-Barnett.[36] His opportunity came when her paper, the *Conservator*, added a new editor. Washington immediately contacted him and suggested that the paper focus on "the progress that the race is making," and not "the weak points that may exist." To make his point explicit, Washington concluded, "Under your wise guidance I am sure that the *Conservator* will be made a power in this direction."[37] Although Washington felt that he had made an ally, the editor, being unorganized, failed to publish the newspaper for weeks at a time. His efforts to silence Wells-Barnett undermined by ineptitude, Washington then sought to quiet Wells-Barnett by challenging her husband's position as an assistant state's attorney. He began pressuring the Republican committee in charge of Barnett's reappointment not to renew his position. Although Ferdinand succeeded in keeping his job despite Washington's efforts, it is clear by examining Washington correspondence that he sought to make life difficult for Wells-Barnett and her husband. Washington and his supporters wrote about trying to "block Barnett and his wife," who they referred to as the "Chicago hyenas."[38]

The Tuskegee president eventually found a way to minimize Wells-Barnett's voice by framing her as an extremist when he publically commented on her "radical stand on behalf of her race."[39] In labeling her a radical, Washington made her an outlier, and his interpretation of her became so accepted that several of her peers, as well as many historians, adopted Washington's assessment of Wells-Barnett's radicalism. While forceful in her beliefs, Wells-Barnett never expressed the desire of a radical to destroy and rebuild society, and in fact remained enduringly optimistic about the power of reform throughout her life.[40] Additionally, both Frederick Douglass and W. E. B. Du Bois shared her ideas about restoring the rights of African Americans through political, economic, and social reform. Nevertheless, Wells-Barnett's personality and gender made accusations of her "radical" stance resonate as her approaches went against the images of benevolent motherhood and feminine morality often employed by female reform groups. Only after she crossed paths with Washington did the idea of a being a radical seem to follow Wells-Barnett, and as one scholar noted, Washington "exercised great influence over black organizations," allowing him the "ability to silence other blacks who criticized him."[41] In short, it is likely that Washington calculated his referral of Wells-Barnett as a radical in order to silence the voice of an aggressive female African American activist and ostracize her from mainstream African American leadership.

The relationship between Washington and W. E. B. Du Bois further exposed the gender politics at play in minimizing Wells-Barnett. Du Bois criticized the Tuskegee president just as loudly as Wells-Barnett and, in 1904, printed an essay, "The Parting of the Ways," disparaging Washington and his policies. Du Bois represented much of what Washington opposed, as he was the first black man to receive a Ph.D. in history from Harvard and supported higher education over an industrial schooling. His recently published *The Souls of Black Folks* (1903), offered an academic exploration of what he described as "double consciousness," a term for understanding how African Americans made conscious and unconscious decisions about their behaviors due to their position in society, directly refuting Washington's ideas on the subject.[42] Du Bois, unlike Wells-Barnett, remained largely unscathed despite his attacks on Washington and continued his activism on a national level. In 1906, Du Bois organized a meeting in Niagara Falls, New York, to create a new black organization without Washington's influence. Unfortunately for reformers such as Wells-Barnett, the Niagara Movement's statement of purpose identified itself as "organized, determined and aggressive action on the part of **men** [emphasis added] who believe in Negro freedom and growth."[43] Although the organization eventually allowed women, it is clear that Du Bois considered racial uplift to be the primary purview of men.[44]

In 1908, racial tensions erupted into a new form of violence: the race riot. In Springfield, Illinois, the hometown of Abraham Lincoln, white Nellie Hallam accused a young black man, George Richardson, of raping her. The police arrested Richardson, who insisted on his innocence. The sheriff, concerned about a mob breaking into the jail, decided to send his prisoner away secretly. He recruited a white restaurateur named Harry Loper to assist in transporting Richardson and another prisoner, Joe James, also charged with the sexual assault of a white female, to another secure location. Shortly after their removal, an angry crowd of whites broke into the prison to find that there were no black men to lynch. Thwarted, the story may have ended except for Kate Howard, a white woman, who passionately urged the white men in the crowd to continue to seek their revenge.

Refocused, the mob connected Loper's earlier presence at the jail with the missing prisoners and descended upon his business, destroying it. The throng then headed to the African American part of town, angry and bent on destruction. Once there, whites attacked any African American unfortunate enough to cross their path, hanging two black men, Scott Burton and William Donegan, as substitutes for their desired victims. The mob then looted and burned black homes and businesses. The destructive rampage ended only when the governor sent in nearly four thousand Illinois militia. After the violence had quieted, it was discovered that ten people were dead, eighty others had sustained injuries, and the crowd had damaged more than two hundred thousand dollars' worth of property, primarily of African Americans. In a later affidavit, Hallam recanted her accusation and admitted that her sexual partner was a white man.[45]

The riot deeply affected Wells-Barnett who felt powerless in the face of such large-scale brutality. She wondered why African Americans had "not yet perfected an organization which was prepared to take hold of this situation."[46] She discussed the Springfield violence in her Sunday school class, expressing her frustration. When her pupils, all young adults, asked her what they could do about such incidents, Wells-Barnett invited them to her house to continue their conversation. The meeting of these young men and women led to the formation of the Negro Fellowship League (NFL), a social group that met weekly to discuss matters affecting African Americans.[47]

After the Springfield race riot of 1908, the Illinois State legislature passed a law requiring the removal of a sheriff from office if he allowed a mob to abduct prisoners from his custody. Intended to prevent the blind eye long turned to white crowds pressuring authorities for prisoners, the 1909 lynching of "Frog" James in Cairo, Illinois, offered the first test of the new regulation. The lynching of James began when authorities discovered the body of a murdered white woman. As Wells-Barnett recalled, the police, "following the usual custom," looked for a black male as the perpetrator, and found a poor, unemployed African American man, "Frog" James, who could not account for his whereabouts during the murder.[48] Wells-Barnett noted the press's unsurprising conclusion of a black murderer, likely alluding to reports in the Cairo newspaper that the black population offered "a constant menace to the town."[49] After authorities arrested James, a mob removed him from the jail, hung him, shot him, and then mutilated his body.[50]

When Wells-Barnett arrived in Cairo, she found that many African Americans believed James guilty of the crime and supported the reinstatement of the sheriff, Frank Davis. Wells-Barnett reacted with surprise, as she assumed that the black community would demand that the sheriff be punished under the new law. Failing to remove the Cairo law enforcement officer from office, Wells-Barnett feared, would result in the statute never being enforced. She began rallying the black community to her view, arguing that even if James committed the crime, they could not overlook the law. Asking local leaders to call together a community meeting, Wells-Barnett spent two hours convincing the local population that Davis failed to use "his great power to protect the victim" from the mob. She urged her audience to defend every "member of the race," and discussed how not demanding action would endanger the "lives of other colored people in Illinois."[51] At the conclusion of her talk, Wells-Barnett called for a resolution to present to the governor against Davis's reinstatement, which "went through without any further objections." She then contacted her husband, who agreed to prepare a legal brief for her to submit with the black community's resolution. When she presented the case to the governor, Wells-Barnett explained, "If this man is sent back [to his job] it will be an encouragement to those who resort to mob violence and will do so at any time, well knowing they will not be called to account for so doing." Allowing him to return to his former position, she concluded, would essentially be governmental "encouragement" of "mob violence." Governor Charles Deneen decided not to reinstate Davis.[52]

The African American Illinois paper the *Springfield Forum* declared of Wells-Barnett's efforts in Cairo that "her voice is ever heard in no uncertain tones for her people and for right whenever the occasion comes and regardless of how acute the crisis."[53] Her work, the paper concluded, "belittles the men to some extent," as "Mrs. Barnett never shrinks nor evades," and "the nation is better off for her having lived in it." The *Chicago Defender*, a newly created black newspaper, offered its own gendered observation of her activities, noting that if a man had her "backbone," lynching "would soon come to a halt."[54] Interestingly, for the first time both papers paired acclaim for Wells-Barnett with criticisms against men for standing aside while she fought these battles. This response became increasingly common as women began using their reform efforts to justify attaining their own political rights, including the right to vote.

Invigorated by her recent victory and gaining positive media responses for her work, Wells-Barnett happily noticed the appearance in several northern newspapers on February 12, 1909, Lincoln's birthday, of an announcement entitled "The Call," seeking to create a national organization focused on racial progress. Such an establishment could address her prior concern about African Americans' inability to offer a unified response to events such as the Springfield race riot. Oswald Garrison Villard, a white journalist and the grandson of abolitionist William Lloyd Garrison, called for a meeting among "believers in democracy" to join together to discuss "the voicing of protests, and the renewal of the struggle for civil and political liberty."[55] Of the sixty respondents, most were either white or male; Wells-Barnett and Mary Church Terrell were the only black women among the roster of volunteers.[56] Initially called the National Negro Committee, the group would soon be renamed the National Association for the Advancement of Colored People (NAACP). Wells-Barnett feared that Washington would attempt to take over this new establishment, a concern ultimately well-founded, as white reformers, such as Villard, the editor of the *New York Evening Post* and the *Nation,* and Mary White Ovington, a prominent white social worker, felt that any new enterprise working on race issues needed his support.[57] Ovington in particular noted, "If you wanted to raise money in New York for anything relating to the Negro, you must have Washington's endorsement."[58] Washington, however, declined his invitation to attend the inaugural meeting, perhaps because several of his critics were among the organization's founders, mitigating some of Wells-Barnett's fears of his influence.

At the conference, Wells-Barnett spoke about the history of lynching and suggested that the group create "a bureau for the investigation and publication of the details" of each death.[59] Previous efforts, she noted, had brought attention to the issue but failed to accomplish any lasting change. A dedicated task force that focused on federal legislation, she felt, could accomplish where previous efforts failed.[60] After several discussions, Wells-Barnett recalled that the members determined that "a committee of forty should be appointed to spend a year in devising ways and means for the establishment of an organization."[61] Although supposedly secret, Wells-Barnett saw the finalized list of forty and felt relief in reading her name and not that of Booker T. Washington. This advance notice only made her shock greater the next day when W. E. B. Du Bois, the only African American on the nominating committee, did not call her name. Shocked, Wells-Barnett claimed that she tried not to make a scene, but simply "put my best face on" and rose to leave. As she walked out, she could not help but notice Mary Ovington with "an air of triumph and a very pleased look on her face."[62] As she departed several members stopped Wells-Barnett, equally stunned, as they also had seen her name on the earlier version of the list. As she prepared to leave, Du Bois called Wells-Barnett back to the meeting. He admitted that he removed her name and claimed Celia Woolley could instead act as her representative. The idea that Woolley would advocate for African American women's interests dismayed Wells-Barnett, as when they ran the Frederick Douglass Center together Woolley repeatedly exhibited her belief in white superiority. Wells-Barnett left the meeting feeling betrayed by Du Bois, her long-time supporter against Washington.

Du Bois's removal of Wells-Barnett from the original document signaled the beginning of a rift between the two black reformers. Previously united against Washington and his policies, Wells-Barnett no longer trusted Du Bois and in her autobiography felt his removal of her from the committee a "deliberate" move intended to "ignore me and my work."[63] Historian Paula Giddings doubted that Du Bois acted alone and proposed Ovington behind the suggestion of adding Woolley instead of Wells-Barnett. Ovington's later comments support this interpretation, as she subsequently claimed that while "fitted for courageous work" and "a great fighter," Wells-Barnett was "not fitted to accept the restraint of organization." She maintained, correctly, that Wells-Barnett liked to "play a lone hand." This behavior, she continued, became an issue for "if you have too many players of lone hands," then "you soon have no game."[64] In addition to Ovington's reasons, scholar Mia Bay noted that Villard's fear of alienating Washington offered another motive for minimizing Wells-Barnett's participation.[65] Regardless of the reason, from 1909 on, Wells-Barnett and Du Bois worked in parallel efforts; he saw himself as an educated and professional reformer aligned with the NAACP, and she an impassioned crusader in Chicago.

Wells-Barnett's initial exclusion from the NAACP remained temporary. The next day, "quite illegally" Ovington later noted, her name was on the list, but she would not remain active in the organization for long.[66] It soon became clear that Ovington and Villard desired to keep the leadership of the association in white hands. Remarks made by Ovington demonstrated that she, like Woolley, made little effort to understand the peculiar problems faced by black women, noting dismissively, "Negro women enjoy organization. They are ambitious for power, often jealous, very sensitive."[67] Villard also proffered a paternalistic rationale in keeping the leadership primarily white, admitting that he "naturally" had "rigged up" the list in advance to better assist "these poor people who have been tricked so often by white men." Those African Americans that questioned his decisions he found "trying" on his patience.[68]

Despite her reservations, Wells-Barnett tried to participate in the organization to the best of her abilities. At the 1910 meeting, she suggested that the NAACP develop its own publication, an idea that the group adopted, creating *The Crisis: A Record of the Darker Races*, to spread news about the organization's work in combating lynching. Her recommendation to issue a national journal was probably not entirely altruistic; Wells-Barnett likely assumed that she would be the logical editorial choice based on her decades of journalistic experience and expertise on lynchings. When the committee instead chose W. E. B. Du Bois to head the magazine, Wells-Barnett recognized that there would not be any leadership opportunities for her within the organization.

The executive committee proceeded to act upon her ideas without her participation, and the situation worsened when the NAACP's leadership began minimizing her past contributions to the anti-lynching movement. In 1911, Ovington wrote a history of the fight against lynching and failed to discuss Wells-Barnett's accomplishments in making racial brutality a national issue. Indeed, Ovington wrote the entire history without even mentioning Wells-Barnett by name. This denigration of her contributions continued when Du Bois began leaving Wells-Barnett out of his reports in *The Crisis*. Even when discussing events that she organized, he would mention everyone in attendance—except her.[69] Du Bois clearly chose to support the NAACP over his and Wells-Barnett's previous anti-Bookerite alliance, leaving her without one of her closest allies.

In the early twentieth century, reform leadership shifted. The standardization of education, created by an increasingly homogeneous curriculum in most universities, professionalized many vocations. One result of this was the emerging perception that reform work was a career, and as such required a college education.[70] This resulted in new organizational leaders, usually well-educated males who replaced female reformers and their moral justifications. This change further minimized Wells-Barnett's opportunities within reform movements, as she lacked a college education and her approaches, formerly praised by race leaders, now appeared to organizers based more on passion than intellectually grounded philosophies. Additionally, Wells-Barnett's personality, which previously endeared her to reformers like Frederick Douglass, led to criticisms from the new generation of activists as she openly voiced her opinions and failed to act deferentially to whites or black men in leadership roles.[71] Wells-Barnett recognized these shifts occurring within reform movements and in a 1910 essay offered a blistering and thinly veiled critique of them. In "The Northern Negro Woman's Social and Moral Condition," Wells-Barnett claimed that organizations only wanted members to play "deaf, dumb and blind" and that white male leaders failed to listen to those with different ideas.[72] She asserted that her experiences as a journalist and a black woman offered her every bit as much of an authentic say in social issues as others with more education.

After her disillusionment with the NAACP, Wells-Barnett became eager to reinsert herself into the black clubwomen's movement and attended the 1910 NACW meeting in Louisville, Kentucky. Once again, a journal's publication became a divisive factor. The Tuskegee Institute published the official periodical of the NACW, the *National Notes*, for free, likely because the editor happened to be Washington's wife, Margaret Murray Washington. She mismanaged the publication by failing to adhere to a consistent schedule, which resulted in erratic printings, and the periodical reaching only a small audience. At the meeting, Wells-Barnett, aware of these issues, suggested the election of a new editor. Before the proposal went to a vote, the president of the NACW, Elizabeth Carter, interceded and ruled Wells-Barnett's motion as out of order. The proposition was sent to the floor for discussion. Due to the group's strong ties to Tuskegee during the past ten years, Wells-Barnett had largely withdrawn from the organization and did not have much support. In trying to remove their publication from Washington's influence, she alienated many members who accused her of trying to take over the editorship.[73] During the ensuing discussion, the women in the audience hissed at Wells-Barnett so loudly that she left the stage.[74]

In 1910, at a Congregational Union dinner, Wells-Barnett found a new focus for her energy when speaker Dr. J. G. K. McClure, the head of the Chicago Theological Seminary, gave a talk on the "White Man's Burden" in which he argued that the black population had the highest rate of criminality in the nation. Wells-Barnett abandoned her prepared speech to follow up on his discussion, openly resenting McClure's implication that African Americans possessed a racial disposition towards committing crime. She countered, "[O]urs is the most neglected group. All the other races in the city are welcomed into the settlements, YWCA's [Young Women's Christian Associations], gymnasiums and every other movement for uplift."[75] Instead, she suggested, to help African Americans succeed, they needed access to the same services offered to all of the other races.[76] Jessie Lawson, a white woman in the audience, approached Wells-Barnett after her talk to confirm that the Young Men's Christian Association (YMCA) did not admit blacks. When Wells-Barnett assured Lawson that she spoke the truth, her husband, the publisher of the *Chicago Daily News* and a major contributor to the YMCA, offered to fund Wells-Barnett's plan to expand the NFL.[77] With a backer in place, Wells-Barnett located a property on 2830 State Street to be a "sort of lighthouse" in the middle of the black south side of Chicago.[78] Even Wells-Barnett could not consider the State Street neighborhood to be a safe location, with six "good time" houses on nearby blocks, but she wanted her center located where patrons most required it, recalling, "I was convinced that they needed State Street as much as State Street needed them."[79] In May 1910, Wells-Barnett opened the "Negro Fellowship League Reading Room and Social Center for men and boys."

Wells-Barnett recounted only one encounter between the community and the NFL, which occurred the first Sunday after the center opened. In the middle of a program, a dozen men in the alley interrupted her discussion with their loud laughter, and she saw through the window that they were shooting craps and drinking beer. Wells-Barnett decided to introduce herself, and while the men declined to shake her white gloved hand or join the meeting, they moved down the street and the reading room experienced no other incidents with the local residents.[80] The NFL soon expanded its services beyond racial discussions, renting lodging out on the second floor, giving food vouchers to a restaurant across the street and starting an employment service that found work for more than one hundred men in its first year.[81] This success at obtaining jobs for their patrons resulted in complaints from a private employment office and the NFL soon obtained a business license for their services.[82]

In the fall of 1910, Wells-Barnett's involvement in the Steve Green legal case increased tensions between her and the NAACP. Green, a tenant farmer in Arkansas, refused to work for his landlord, Will Seidle, after he raised his rent.[83] Angered, Seidle armed himself and confronted Green, shooting and wounding him. In self-defense, Green grabbed his gun and returned fire, killing Seidle. Knowing that the consequence for slaying a white man would be the lynch mob, Green immediately went into hiding. For several weeks, his friends supplied him with food and money until he fled north to Chicago. Just outside the city, authorities arrested Green and arranged to return him to Arkansas. While in custody, Green tried to commit suicide by eating broken glass.[84] His attempt to take his own life made the news, alerting Wells-Barnett to his plight and she mobilized to save Green from the waiting lynch mob.[85] While Green rode on a train back to Arkansas, she utilized her husband's legal expertise to secure a writ of *habeas corpus*. This injunction required a court to determine the legality and the authority by which Arkansas law enforcement held him in custody. Since she filed the writ in Chicago, Wells-Barnett forced the men to return Green to Illinois for the hearing. While lawyers sorted out his legal situation, Green stayed at the NFL.

As his case gained attention, one of the wealthy white founders of the NAACP, Joel Spingarn, donated one hundred dollars to help Green. When the treasurer of the NAACP asked Wells-Barnett if she needed Spingarn's donation to support Green's case, she asked him whether the donor "wishes the money to be used for Steve Green's personal expenses, or whether it is to be used as a contingent fund for the lawyers." In response, Villard suggested to Spingarn that he not fund the legal defense, as black lawyers "usually take advantage of philanthropic interest of this kind to make money for themselves."[86] Spingarn did not care for this response, and he and Wells-Barnett became allies. Although Villard's own words pushed Spingarn to support Wells-Barnett, he blamed her for appropriating a wealthy supporter of the NAACP. Once the court settled the extradition issue, Wells-Barnett used her funds to send Green to Canada. The *Chicago Defender* praised

Wells-Barnett for helping draw attention to Green's plight, with her actions likely saving his life, concluding that she served as the "watchdog of human life and liberty." In contrast, the NAACP's report in *The Crisis* failed to mention Wells-Barnett's name, instead implying that the sole responsibility for assisting Green came from the NAACP. Her old ally Du Bois had again written her out of a story she had nearly single-handedly generated.[87] Despite the NAACP's dismissal of her work, Wells-Barnett proudly recalled her efforts on Steve Green's behalf: "He is one Negro who lives to tell the tale that he was not burned alive according to program."[88]

Although Wells-Barnett recognized that the current administrators of the NAACP would never allow her to assume a leadership role, she also noted that Washington's influence seemed to be waning. President Taft did not lean on Washington as an advisor like his predecessor, resulting in some loss of national prominence, and this combined with an odd incident in March of 1911 caused even his most ardent supporters to question their leader's principles. In New York City, Washington, apparently intoxicated, loitered in front of a building when a white woman walked by. He allegedly called out "Hello, sweetheart" to her, and a nearby white man, observing the greeting and angered by a black man's forwardness towards a white woman, proceeded to chase Washington, catching and severely beating him. In the hospital, after receiving stiches for lacerations to his face and ear, Washington remained mute as to why he had been in the neighborhood or as to the veracity of the eyewitness's version of events.[89]

Despite her biggest adversary's declining influence, in 1911 Wells-Barnett also lost essential support for her own efforts. Julius Rosenwald, a wealthy businessman due to his part ownership of Sears, Roebuck, and Company, announced his plan to raise money for a black YMCA in Chicago. Known as a leading philanthropist, Rosenwald donated millions of his own funds to support African American causes in both the North and the South. Once he heard of Rosenwald's efforts Victor Lawson immediately withdrew his financial support from Wells-Barnett's Negro Fellowship League to join him. Wells-Barnett attempted to convince him that even an African American YMCA would not serve the same population as the NFL, as the YMCA required a membership fee of twelve dollars, an amount many of her clients could not afford.[90] Unable to persuade Lawson, Wells-Barnett founded the newspaper the *Fellowship Herald* in an effort to spread news of her work at the NFL. Over the next few years, her writing would again win her acclaim, with a fellow editor noting of her publication, "It is ably and brilliantly edited" and another praising it as "no doubt, the best paper the Negro has here in Chicago."[91]

Another financial setback occurred in the fall of 1912, when Democrats swept the Illinois elections and the new leadership asked Ferdinand

Barnett, an assistant state's attorney appointed by a Republican more than a decade earlier, to resign. Barnett complied and returned to private legal practice. The political elections of 1912 signified the beginning of a shift in national party ideologies, prompted by the formation of a third political party. When the Republican Party nominated incumbent William Howard Taft as their candidate despite former president Theodore Roosevelt's primary wins, Roosevelt broke away from the Republican Party and created a new coalition, the Progressive Party or Bull Moose Party, named for its robust leader's response to a reporter that he felt as strong as the animal. With his "New Nationalism" platform, Roosevelt focused on social issues such as farm relief, workers' compensation, and women's suffrage. Democratic candidate Woodrow Wilson's candidacy focused on a policy of "New Freedom," aimed to resonate with the Jeffersonian ideal of a smaller government and looser holds on banks and industry. The conservative Republican Taft and Progressive Roosevelt split the vote enough in the presidential election to send Wilson to the White House.

Although the Progressive Party did not survive until the next presidential nomination, the platform would inspire Franklin D. Roosevelt and result in the New Deal, which would solidify a shift in ideologies between the two parties. The Republicans after the Civil War had focused on issues of expansion, education, and social justice. They supported the railroad, western settlements, land grant colleges, and laws protecting African Americans, reflecting their conviction that the government existed to protect and serve its citizens. Yet, by 1930, they began advocating for less governmental intervention and the Democratic Party became the primary supporter of these beliefs. Thus, as the parties' core ideologies evolved, they essentially switched, with Democrats as proponents of policies to assist citizens and Republicans desiring to restrict governmental interference in people's lives.[92]

The 1912 election also placed the issue of women's suffrage at the forefront of politics. Six states, mostly in the West, allowed women to vote. California, as the largest of these states, in permitting women to cast a ballot, allowed female voters to effect the Electoral College and thus the presidential campaign. For the past decade, black women, including Wells-Barnett, had sought to uplift the black race by supporting African American men, the only representatives of the race with access to the ballot. Wells-Barnett's NFL focused primarily on black men and her anti-lynching work had often observed that the continued disenfranchisement of African American men remained a principal motive behind racial violence. In 1913, the women's suffrage movement made progress when Illinois passed the Municipal and Presidential Voting Act, allowing women to vote in local government and presidential elections. The limitation to these types of elections resulted from the wording in the state constitution, which referred to several state offices as chosen by a majority of male voters.[93] Seeing the possibility of women's suffrage on the horizon, Wells-Barnett wasted no time in mobilizing towards this goal.

On January 30, 1913, Wells-Barnett formed the Alpha Suffrage Club, the first black women's voting rights group in Chicago.[94] She made the same argument she had in 1887 for non-partisanship and insisted that the Alpha Suffrage Club women align themselves with the candidate that they felt best embodied the needs of their race, rather than blindly voting along party lines. In addition to mobilizing black women on a local level, Wells-Barnett, also a member of the National American Woman Suffrage Association (NAWSA), sought to support efforts for women's suffrage on a national level, and the Alpha Suffrage Club raised money for several representatives to attend the NAWSA parade in Washington, D.C. Once the delegation arrived, however, the issue of where black women would march in the parade arose.

The suffrage movement's struggle with race began early, when members, primarily composed of middle- and upper-class white northern women, aligned themselves closely with the crusade to abolish slavery. After the Civil War, the Fourteenth Amendment (1868) granted former slaves citizenship with the accompanying inalienable rights afforded by the Constitution and Bill of Rights. The question for suffragists became as to whether citizenship included the right to vote, for if it did then in addition to enfranchising former slaves, the measure would extend the vote to women. For Congress voting was not an absolute right to be enjoyed by all people and the Fifteenth Amendment (1870) granted all men the right to vote, bitterly disappointing suffragists. White women opposed the Fifteenth Amendment, in particular northern abolitionists Susan B. Anthony and Elizabeth Cady Stanton, who discussed their concerns in their weekly women's rights newsletter *The Revolution*. They questioned the government's decision to bestow the vote on previously enslaved men but not educated and moral women. For these reformers, the Fifteenth Amendment was a final "degradation" upon white women, as it would empower black men, the "most hostile" group of men towards women.[95]

After the ratification of the third Reconstruction Amendment, the women's suffrage movement split into two groups. The National Woman Suffrage Association (NWSA), led by reformers Elizabeth Cady Stanton and Susan B. Anthony, sought to pass a national amendment granting women the right to vote. The American Woman Suffrage Association, led by Lucy Stone and Antoinette Brown Blackwell, pursued voting rights on a state-by-state basis. The two groups worked separately until 1890, when they reunited as the National American Woman Suffrage Association under the leadership of Susan B. Anthony. Race remained a divisive issue within the newly unified movement and leaders decided to remain a white organization, asking

African American supporters, including Frederick Douglass, to stop aiding them for fear that southern whites would view NAWSA as an interracial organization and not join. For Anthony and others, the need for southern white women's support to pass a national amendment trumped concerns of racial inequality.

Having earlier discussed the issue of race within the suffrage movement with Anthony, Wells-Barnett hoped that the reinvigorated movement would include African American women. NAWSA planned a march through Washington on March 13, 1913, organized by Alice Paul and Lucy Burns, to coincide with President Woodrow Wilson's inauguration. Intended to draw attention away from the presidential ceremony, the publicity of women from across the nation marching for their rights sought to send a strong message to the newly elected political leader about their demands for suffrage. When Wells-Barnett arrived as part of the delegation of women from Illinois, NAWSA's policy conflicted with several states' interracial delegations. Grace Trout, the white woman selected as the Illinois leader, ultimately decided that "[I]t is unwise to include the colored women" marching with white, informing the others, "I think we should abide by its [NAWSA's] decision."[96]

Wells-Barnett fought Trout's judgment, arguing through tears, "If the Illinois women do not take a stand now in this great democratic parade then the colored women are lost." Trout, affected by her speech, changed her mind and reasserted to NAWSA leadership that the Illinois women would march together. This resulted in another discussion that ultimately forced Trout to inform Wells-Barnett and the other African American women that they would have to march at the end of the parade in the black delegation. Wells-Barnett responded, "I was asked to march with the other women of our state, and I intend to do so or not take part in the parade at all."[97] Despite NAWSA's edict, Wells-Barnett was true to her words. The *Chicago Tribune* sent a reporter along with the sixty-two women and his report described the white women from the Illinois delegation marching down the street when "[s]uddenly from the crowd on the sidewalk Mrs. Barnett walked calmly out to the delegation and assumed her place at the side of Mrs. Squire." The reporter snapped a photo of the three women, which would accompany the story in the paper.[98] In breaking the policy of NAWSA, Wells-Barnett received praise for taking a stand for both her race and gender. The *Chicago Defender* called her a "[m]odern Joan [of] Arc," who "represents the highest type of womanhood in Illinois," and concluded, "The race has no greater leader among the feminine sex than Mrs. Ida B. Wells-Barnett."[99]

In the years following her participation in the 1913 NAWSA march, Wells-Barnett's advocacy for women's suffrage increased. She implemented

Figure 4.1 Wells-Barnett in the 1912 national suffrage parade.
Source: "Illinois Women Participate in Suffrage Parade. This State Was Well Represented in Washington," *The Chicago Daily Tribune*, March 5, 1913

a block system of canvassing to register African American women voters, and the Alpha Suffrage Club membership increased.[100] Yet such advocacy brought about negative responses, with the women encountering sexist language and derision. After one day of registering voters, the women told Wells-Barnett that "men jeered at them and told them they ought to be at home taking care of babies. Others insisted the women were trying to take the place of men and wear the trousers."[101] She told her fellow women to respond to these criticisms by telling hecklers they did this "so that they could help put a colored man in the city council."[102] In having the women answer in this way, Wells-Barnett reassured men that suffragists sought the vote to support male political ambitions, not their own.

In addition to face-to-face dismissals, Wells-Barnett's local suffrage attempts also received mockery in the press. The *Chicago Defender* focused less on the women's efforts and instead discussed their vanity. Registering to vote required each woman to reveal her age, but since they only needed to be twenty-one to register, many of the women tended to underestimate their years on the forms. The paper reprinted several of the women's reported ages alongside with what the paper calculated as their real ages, intending to induce "a fit of laughter" in their readers. Finding humor in their efforts served to undermine the serious political efforts of the women, but the fifty-one year-old Wells-Barnett was not exempt from this conceit, as the *Chicago Defender* listed her reported age as thirty-two.[103] Despite attempts to dismiss the women's work as inconsequential, they proved their importance in the next election after 153,000 black women cast their vote, requiring future candidates to gain the support of African American women in order to win elections.[104]

Race re-emerged as a central issue in national politics when, during President Wilson's first term, Congress proposed discriminatory bills against African Americans at an alarming rate, including those implementing segregation in the government and military, outlawing interracial marriage, and banning the immigration of those with African blood.[105] Legislators proposed these acts knowing that Wilson both believed the separation of the black and white races and needed the support of southern whites in order to work his own political agenda. The Federal government, with Wilson's blessing, began segregating departments and preventing any blacks from being appointed to federal offices.[106] Monroe Trotter, an editor of a Boston paper and one of Wells-Barnett's supporters in the anti-Washington camp, circulated a petition protesting President Wilson's segregation practices. After gaining twenty thousand signatures, he and Wells-Barnett traveled to Washington, D.C. to present their concerns in person, receiving a five-minute audience with the President. Trotter proceeded to deliver a short speech, but both he and Wells-Barnett were disappointed by Wilson's response that his administration had "no policy" on segregation.[107] Although all of the race-based legislation would eventually be defeated, Trotter and Wells-Barnett's visit to the President received criticism from the NAACP for approaching this issue on their own and not as part of the organization. Du Bois printed a pointed editorial in *The Crisis* about "individual sharpshooters" who might think that they are effective, but "[t]here is in the United States but one organization with permanent headquarters, paid officials, active nationwide membership" prepared to fight racial inequality.[108]

In 1913, Wells-Barnett's efforts with the NFL began to suffer due to limited funds; she could no longer afford the rent at 2830 State Street, and moved the organization to a "much smaller and very cramped" place down the street. During this downsizing, municipal court chief justice Harry Olsen, a supporter of Ferdinand Barnett, appointed Wells-Barnett as the first female black probation officer in his Juvenile Court, a position that paid one hundred and fifty dollars a month. She used this salary to continue supporting the NFL, working in court from nine to noon each day and spending her afternoon in the field following up on her eighty-five probationers.[109] She soon combined her roles by having her parolees check in with her at the NFL. She enjoyed the work, proud of the young people she encountered who made changes in their lives. Despite her new full-time job, Wells-Barnett continued to juggle her activism and her family. Charles was now seventeen, Herman fifteen, Ida twelve, and Alfreda nine.[110] She also remained involved in journalism, writing a steady stream of articles and letters focused on any racial injustice she encountered. One 1914 article discussed a newspaper's use of the derogatory terms "boy" and "darkey" to refer to a seventy-year-old African American Civil War veteran. Wells-Barnett defended the man, no stranger herself to disparaging comments. In her own daily life she found such small battles representative of larger inequalities. One incident reflecting this occurred while she was shopping at a Marshall Field's department store, where a clerk called her a "nigger" and refused to help her.[111] In response to this slur, Wells-Barnett gathered up a pair of men's underpants, slung them over her arm, and began to march towards the door until another floor associate offered to assist her.[112]

An important election loomed in 1914 for the Alderman of the Second Ward, the representative for one of the African American sections of Chicago. The Alpha Suffrage Club wanted a black man in the position, and decided to listen to all three African American candidates, choosing only one so as not to divide the black vote among the contenders. After listening to all three men, the club backed Oscar De Priest.[113] Their selection aligned with Wells-Barnett's personal choice. She and De Priest had recently discussed his candidacy, during which he "asked my support and I had told him that I would give it to him with the understanding that if he won he would use his influence to see that Mr. Barnett realized the dream of his life and was elected judge."[114] Recognizing the power of an endorsement by Wells-Barnett, mayoral candidate William Hale Thompson also approached her about supporting him. She accepted once he "convinced her of his sincerity," and agreed that as mayor he would "make the NFL reading room and social center an auxiliary of the city," including giving "city jobs to blacks who came through the NFL's employment agency."[115]

Wells-Barnett spent months supporting her two candidates until unexpected news reached her late in the race that chief municipal court Judge Harry Olson had also decided to run for mayor. Wells-Barnett owed him her current job as a probation officer and he had supported Ferdinand for nearly a decade. Even though Wells-Barnett and her husband believed that Olsen did not stand a chance against Thompson, they agreed that they must support him, and so withdrew from both De Priest's and Thompson's campaigns. As predicted, both De Priest and Thompson won easily, a victory for the Alpha Suffrage Club and their endorsed candidates, but her departure from their campaigns meant that neither of the candidates would honor the political favors that Wells-Barnett negotiated. De Priest's promise of a judgeship for her husband failed to materialize and Thompson claimed he "didn't owe Mrs. Barnett anything because she did not go with them to the end."[116]

Without the political support she had hoped for, Wells-Barnett and the NFL continued to rely on their own resources to fight racial inequality. In

1915, Wells-Barnett, her husband, and the NFL engaged in a lengthy court battle. A week before his parole hearing, the warden accused African American Joseph "Chicken Joe" Campbell of setting a deadly fire in the Joliet Penitentiary, just outside of Chicago. Previously, as a reward for his good conduct, the warden made Campbell a "trusty," and assigned him to be a personal servant to his wife, Odette Allen. When the warden took a trip out of town, the police claimed that Campbell attempted to rape Allen, poured alcohol over her body, and then set a fire to cover up his crime. The coroner determined that a blow to her head knocked Allen unconscious and ruled the cause of death to be a result of fume inhalation. The medical examiner's report did not mention any signs of sexual assault, but the warden's personal physician examined the body and claimed he found evidence of rape, leading the police to arrest Campbell.[117]

Campbell endured more than forty hours of questioning, during which the police engaged in "third degree" tactics. These methods typically included "the use of physical brutality" and "other forms of cruelty, to obtain involuntary confessions or admissions," as well as a refusal to allow the accused access to their legal counsel.[118] After nearly two days of mistreatment, Campbell confessed to the crime, but once he recovered from the abusive interrogation, recanted and avowed his innocence. Wells-Barnett, hearing of his case, traveled to jail to visit him. After their discussion, she wrote in her autobiography, he "told me a straightforward story, every word of which I believed. He also told me how they had tortured him in the effort to make him confess."[119] She began her campaign to help him by bringing public attention to the police's treatment of Campbell, publishing about how the police "sweated and tortured to make him confess to a crime that he may not have committed," leading her to question "Is this justice? Is it humanity? Would we stand to see a dog treated in such fashion without a protest?"[120] The NFL began a fundraising project to support Campbell's legal fees, raising five hundred dollars in six weeks, a notable amount, but likely not enough to offset Ferdinand Barnett's time over the next three years fighting the case in court. At the initial six-week trial, the jury returned a guilty verdict and sentenced Campbell to death. While Barnett appealed, employing the legal system to defend Campbell, Wells-Barnett continued to publicize the case in the Chicago papers. In 1918, the case reached the Illinois Supreme Court, which upheld the original judgment. The governor, sensing the pressure of public sentiment against the death penalty for Campbell, commuted the sentence to life in prison. Wells-Barnett considered this a victory, feeling that she had saved Campbell's life from a system that sought to coerce and convict him.

By 1915, Wells-Barnett, tired of being either ignored or attacked in the pages of *The Crisis*, completely removed herself from the NAACP and turned her focus to another national organization founded by one of her old supporters against Booker T. Washington, Monroe Trotter. Named the National Equal Rights League (NERL), the organization identified itself as a black organization run by and for the benefit of African Americans, a response to the accommodating policies that accompanied interracial associations. In January 1915, Wells-Barnett became the vice president of NERL. A few months later, with Thompson now mayor, Judge Olsen informed Wells-Barnett that he "was not able to keep me in the adult probation office to which he had appointed me."[121] The loss of her job and its income further reduced the NFL's ability to help the community and the employment service fees comprised the League's sole income. In November, news of Booker T. Washington's death surprised many, as in the months before his passing he continued to serve as an activist on a number of issues. Early in November, while in New York, he suffered from kidney pain. His health quickly deteriorated, and a hospitalized Washington told his doctor, "I expect to die and be buried in the South," and demanded to be released in order to return home. His request granted, he returned to Tuskegee on November 14, 1915 and died a few hours later.[122] Washington's passing offered many black activists hope for a shift in African American reform efforts away from the failed conciliatory policies of the past decade.

After 1915, a combination of economic and political factors, including a boll weevil plague and poor weather ruining cotton crops, sent thousands of African Americans north in search of newly emerging industrial jobs in a pattern called the Great Migration. This movement drastically changed the African American population in the North and to Wells-Barnett this demographic shift, especially in Chicago, only added to African American political power. In the North, black men often succeeded in voting, and this ability, combined with the women of Illinois and several other states casting a ballot in their first presidential election in 1916, demonstrated the power of the black constituency.[123] Such influence, Wells-Barnett hoped, would finally create significant progress on issues of lynching and racial inequality. World War I, however, soon subdued her optimism about the changing opportunities for the black race in America.

On April 16, 1917, the United States officially entered World War I, a conflict that sent both white and black troops to fight abroad, ostensibly to protect democratic freedoms. The irony of sending African Americans overseas to fight for the rights of others when theirs were severely repressed at home was not lost on reformers like Wells-Barnett, who used the war as a platform to discuss race in the United States. President Wilson justified America's entry into the conflict in Europe as necessary in order to make the world safe for democracy, a rhetoric many African Americans hoped would be practiced at home as well as abroad. In *The Crisis*, Du

Bois noted of Wilson's encouragement to enlist, "Where he commands one to go I shall go." Other black activists similarly supported the initial war effort, with one claiming that African Americans "have no ordinary interest in the outcome. That which the German power represents today spells death to the aspirations of Negroes and all darker races for equality, freedom, and democracy."[124] This ideology soon faltered as African American troops experienced segregation in quarters and training grounds. Once in Europe, many black regiments received undesirable assignments, primarily as laborers, in conditions so poor that many white officers feared an uprising.[125] These tensions abroad reflected increasing race-based pressures at home and with the shift in African American population, violence began erupting in the North.

Despite the view in the North that segregation existed primarily in the South, three months after America entered the war, a race riot occurred in East St. Louis. Although in the South lynchings attempted to control African American bodies, in the decades prior to World War I racial violence in the Midwest and North sought to remove blacks from their vicinity.[126] This resulted in, among other practices, the creation of "sundown towns," which sociologist James Lowen identified as "any organized jurisdiction" that "kept African Americans or other groups from living in it and was thus 'all-white' on purpose." Thousands of these towns existed in the Midwest, designated by signs, usually at the city limits, warning "Nigger, Don't Let the Sun Go Down on You in [name of town]."[127] The racial dynamics of oppression versus exclusion varied across the North and Midwest, but when African Americans left the South as part of the Great Migration, populations shifted in many areas and it no longer became feasible for whites to keep African Americans out of their municipalities.

The events in East St. Louis offer an example of the consequences resulting from racial tensions in the North.[128] On July 1, 1917, four white men drove a Ford through a black middle-class neighborhood in East St. Louis, shooting guns into several houses and a church. Members of the community responded by arming themselves in case the car returned. When the same car again approached the street, several black men fired shots at the vehicle, which turned away. After hearing reports of African Americans firing guns at white men, the police drove to the neighborhood in a similar vehicle with white detectives in civilian clothes. The armed community members, seeing a Ford car driven by white men, shot into the vehicle, fatally wounding two white police officers. When news of armed blacks shooting and killing police officers spread, the white community formed a mob in the town's main intersection and proceeded to beat any African American unfortunate enough to be passing by.

During the night the violence escalated; whites began shooting African Americans in the streets and the angry crowd also began setting houses in the black neighborhood on fire, with several witnesses reporting mob members throwing African Americans fleeing burning buildings back into the fire. For two days the violence raged, and the resulting death toll is difficult to ascertain, as many bodies were burned beyond recognition or surfaced days later in nearby creeks, unidentifiable.[129] Wells-Barnett determined "150 Negroes had been slaughtered" in the rioting, but the official number was thirty-nine blacks and nine whites.[130] White mobs burned whole sections of the black part of town, displacing almost five thousand African Americans. Many fled the city never to return. Several northern media outlets compared the actions of the white mob's behavior to the ethnic attacks on Jews in Europe. One Jewish leader noted that the Russians could learn a lot about "pogrom making from East St. Louis whites," and that at least the Russians "gave the Jews a chance to run."[131]

Less than forty-eight hours after the violence ended, Wells-Barnett traveled to the town on a fact-finding mission for the NFL, publishing her findings in *The East St. Louis Massacre: The Greatest Outrage of the Century*. Upon her arrival, she noticed that there were no African Americans on the street. Surprised, she walked through the town until arriving at City Hall where she saw several African American women. Approaching them, she discovered that the group was waiting for a military escort back to their homes. Wells-Barnett asked to accompany the women and see the remains of their burned and looted neighborhood for herself. As she talked with the women, she heard of terrible incidents.[132] In her report, Wells-Barnett listed atrocity after atrocity, some from the point of view of African Americans, others from the white militia sent in to end the violence. One of these men, Captain O. C. Smith of the 4th Illinois Infantry, braved rocks and bricks thrown by the white mob during his attempts to end the uprising. Captain Smith later testified that one mob member told him, "I've killed my share of Negroes today. I have killed so many I am tired and somebody else can finish them."[133]

The police did not arrest a single white man for their actions during the riot, but took fifteen African American men into custody, including Dr. LeRoy C. Bundy, "a prominent dentist" charged with "leading the Negroes for defense," resulting in the death of the two police officers. The authorities held Bundy on a forty-eight thousand dollar bail.[134] Wells-Barnett, recognizing how little had changed from the Memphis lynchings of 1892, which also targeted prominent black men despite little evidence, began to fight against the racial inequity in arrests. When a white jury found Bundy guilty and sentenced him to life in prison, she and her husband took up his legal battle, which lasted years. The pair emerged victorious when a judge overturned Bundy's conviction and released him. Despite the positive outcome, this experience drained Ida and Ferdinand both financially and emotionally. Wells-Barnett wrote afterwards how the riot continued to prove that in America having "black skin was a death warrant."[135]

The events in East St. Louis, where whites openly attacked and slaughtered African Americans without any legal repercussions, led Ferdinand Barnett to encourage African Americans at an NFL meeting to "[a]rm yourselves with guns and pistols." Despite his frustrations, Barnett, like his wife, carefully maintained the position of being prepared for defense but not engaging in offense. "Don't buy an arsenal," he advised them, just "enough guns to protect yourself."[136] Barnett's encouragement of African Americans to arm themselves, alongside of Wells-Barnett's demands for a federal investigation into the riot, led the Department of War to open an inquiry on the couple.[137] Their assessment on Wells-Barnett concluded that her pamphlet stirred up "inter-racial antagonism" during a time of war, but they were less successful at scrutinizing Ferdinand, as the agents could not find a single black person willing to admit to having heard Barnett speak about armed defense.[138] Despite this impasse, the attention that the couple received from the government soon intensified after the events of Houston, Texas in the fall of 1917.

Shortly after the United States entered World War I, the military summoned the Twenty-Fourth regiment, an African American unit created during the Civil War, for duty. Instead of fighting overseas, the military sent the men to Texas to guard government property. Historically, the Twenty-Fourth maintained a record for one of the lowest rates of desertion and fewest court marshals, but this changed in August when several incidents culminated in violence. In Houston, the primarily northern black soldiers received repeated abuse from whites, who did not appreciate the influx of hundreds of African Americans into their town, heightening already fraught racial tensions. These hostilities can be seen in the local newspaper such as the August 15, 1917 *Houston Daily Post* that reported, "Willie Shears, an Independence negro, was shot to death at Caldwell Sunday night while resisting a deputy sheriff who attempted to arrest him." The article concluded, "The coroner's verdict says it was a clear case of suicide," suggesting that any attempt by an African American to defy white officers was, essentially, asking to be killed.[139]

A little more than a week later, an incident between white police officers and an African American ignited these simmering racial tensions. Two policemen dragged a black woman, Sara Travers, a mother of five, into the street and proceeded to beat her for refusing to allow them to search her home. They then arrested Travers and placed her in jail on the charge of challenging police officers. When a black soldier, Corporal Charles

Baltimore, learned of the incident, he went to the police station. The conversation turned into a confrontation and police officers struck Baltimore and shot at him, although the shots missed. Officers placed Baltimore under arrest. When he failed to return to the base, a rumor quickly spread of Baltimore's death at the hands of the white officers.[140] When the men of the Twenty-Fourth heard the news, more than one hundred armed soldiers marched to the police station.

With the soldiers inside the building, a mob of nearly a thousand armed whites surrounded the structure. Upon finding himself and his men encircled, Sergeant Vida Henry gave orders to his men to fire into the crowd. An exchange of gunfire ensued. Hours later, with fifteen white and six black casualties, Henry, surrounded by whites, shot himself rather than be taken into custody.[141] The military court-martialed the surviving soldiers, shrouding the process in secrecy and, in December, before the completion of the appeal process, military officers removed thirteen of the soldiers from their cells and "hanged [them] by the neck until they were dead." The killing of black men in active military service without completing due process sparked Wells-Barnett's outrage. According to her, after the soldiers were hung by the neck, "their bodies were thrown into nameless graves." Unsure if the military's actions sought to prevent further unrest or "to placate southern hatred," she found neither an acceptable reason for such treatment.[142]

Wells-Barnett organized the NFL to hold a memorial service for the men to draw attention to their treatment. Du Bois also wrote an editorial in *The Crisis* angrily decrying the deaths of these black men and the government's circumvention of due process. He found such behavior from the military ironic considering the "hundreds of thousands" of whites that regularly murdered African Americans without facing any punishment. This defense, surely appreciated by Wells-Barnett, earned Du Bois a reprimand and almost cost him the editorship of *The Crisis*. Mary Ovington, upset by his tone, began agitating for his replacement.[143] Wells-Barnett encountered issues with her own protest, as "every single pastor refused to let us have the use of the church" to hold her commemoration of the soldiers. She then decided to have buttons emblazoned with the phrase "In Memorial MARTYRED NEGRO SOLDIERS" made to remember the fallen black soldiers. In choosing to proclaim the men martyrs, Wells-Barnett focused on the injustice of their deaths. She wrote, "It seemed to me a terrible thing that our government would take the lives of men who had bared their breasts fighting for the defense of the country."[144] Although the military did not carry out any more secret hangings, the subsequent hearings resulted in sixteen more African American soldiers sentenced to death and another forty-one soldiers sentenced to life imprisonment, with the remaining accused receiving various prison sentences.[145]

While Wells-Barnett protested her government's treatment of the black soldiers in the Twenty-Fourth, she also supported her country, selling Liberty Bonds and raising almost five million dollars among the black clubwomen to support the war effort. She organized Christmas packages for Illinois soldiers serving in the war, among them her stepson. She also continued handing out buttons to whoever wanted one, wearing hers proudly.

Figure 4.2 Ida B. Wells-Barnett, wearing "Martyred Negro Soldiers" button, *c.* 1917–19.
Source: Special Collections Research Center, University of Chicago Library

The pins honoring the soldiers brought Wells-Barnett again to the attention of the government and two white intelligence officers identifying themselves as Secret Service visited her. Wells-Barnett detailed their exchange in her autobiography. The two men warned her that continuing to hand out the buttons would result in her arrest. She asked, "On what charge?" The men answered her by suggesting that they would charge her with treason. Their response, likely meant to intimidate her, did the opposite. She retorted, "I understand treason to mean giving aid and comfort to the enemy in time of war. How can the distribution of this little button do that?" One officer noted that they would drop the matter if "we have to have your assurance that you are not going to distribute any more of them." Wells-Barnett replied, "I can't give you any such promise." She continued that if the men felt her guilty of treason they should do their duty and arrest her.

Having called their bluff, the men declined and instead demanded all of her buttons. When she noted that she did not have anymore, they countered, "Weren't you showing one to a man as we came in?" One can only imagine Wells-Barnett's face as she responded, "[H]e must have taken the button with him." Once again, the men informed her that maligning the government was treason, and Wells-Barnett noted, "[T]he government deserves to be criticized. I think it was a dastardly thing to hang those men as if they were criminals and put them in holes in the ground just as if they had been dead dogs. If it is treason for me to think and say so, then you will have to make the most of it." When the officers told her she should stop as "the rest of your people do not agree with you," she acknowledged that while their statement may be true, "I'd rather go down in history as one lone Negro who dared to tell the government that it had done a dastardly thing than to save my skin by taking back what I have said." The conversation ended with the men suggesting that she consult her lawyer. After they left, Wells-Barnett proudly noted that they had done so without taking any of her buttons.[146]

Notes

1   Ida B. Wells-Barnett, "Lynch Law in America," *The Arena* 23, no. 1, (January 1900): 15–24.
2   Ida B. Wells-Barnett, *Mob Rule in New Orleans: Robert Charles and His Fight to Death, the Story of His Life, Burning Human Beings Alive, Other Lynching Statistics*, Project Gutenburg, 1900, February 8, 2005. http://www.gutenberg.org/files/14976/14976-h/14976-h.htm (accessed March 21, 2016), 6; William Ivy Hair, *Carnival of Fury: Robert Charles and the New Orleans Race Riot of 1900* (Baton Rouge: Louisiana State University Press, 1976), 120.
3   Wells-Barnett, *Mob Rule in New Orleans*, 14.
4   Herbert Shapiro, *White Violence and Black Response: From Reconstruction to Montgomery* (Amherst: University of Massachusetts Press, 1988), 61; Wells-Barnett, *Mob Rule in New Orleans*, 34.
5   Wells-Barnett, *Mob Rule in New Orleans*, 54–55.
6   Wells-Barnett, *Mob Rule in New Orleans*, 65.

7   Wells-Barnett, *Mob Rule in New Orleans*, 66.

8   Quoted in Giddings, *Ida: A Sword among Lions*, 424.

9   Wells-Barnett, *Mob Rule in New Orleans*, 55–56.

10 Wells-Barnett, *Mob Rule in New Orleans*, 68.

11 Hair, 2; James Edward Ford III, "Mob Rule in New Orleans: Anarchy, Governance, and Media Representation," *Biography* 33, no. 1 (2010): 193.

12 See Jane Adams Hull-House Museum, "Jane Addams and Hull-House Museum: About Jane Addams," n.d., http://www.hullhousemuseum.org/about-jane-addams (accessed March 21, 2016).

13 Wells, *Crusade for Justice*, 259.

14 Maurice Hamington, "Public Pragmatism: Jane Addams and Ida B. Wells on Lynching," *The Journal of Speculative Philosophy* 19, no. 2 (2005): 170.

15 Jane Addams, "Respect for Law," in *Lynching and Rape: An Exchange of Views*, ed. Bettina Aptheker (New York: American Institute for Marxist Studies, 1977), 25, 28.

16 Addams, "Respect for Law," 28.

17 Hamington, 172–73.

18 Hamington, 171.

19 Giddings, *Ida: A Sword among Lions*, 429–30.

20 Quoted in Giddings, *Ida: A Sword among Lions*, 434.

21 Giddings, *Ida: A Sword among Lions*, 435, 437. Wells-Barnett also gained a measure of national recognition in 1902 when *Colored American Magazine* named her the foremost authority on lynching and violence. Another reformer, African American John Edward Bruce published *The Blood Red Record: A Review of the Horrible Lynching and Burnings of Negroes by Civilized White Men in the United States, as Taken from the Records*, a pamphlet modeled on Wells-Barnett's *A Red Record*. Schechter, *Ida B. Wells-Barnett and American Reform*, 124.

22 Her reasons consisted of gaining support from white men, which offered a chance to influence the vote and gaining the support of white women, which offered her a chance to combine resources. McMurry, 274; Giddings, *Ida: A Sword among Lions*, 440.

23 Wells, *Crusade for Justice*, 279.

24 Celia Parker Woolley, *Practical Work among the Colored People* (Chicago: Frederick Douglass Center, 1906), 7.

25 It remains so today, more than one hundred years later. See *The Huffington Post*, "Chicago Most Segregated City In America, Despite Significant Improvements In Last Decade," The Huffington Post. January 21, 2012, http://www.huffingtonpost.com/2012/01/31/chicago-most-segregated-c_n_1244098.html (accessed March 30, 2016); Steve Bogira, "Separate, Unequal, and Ignored: Racial Segregation Remains Chicago's Most Fundamental Problem. Why Isn't It an Issue in the Mayor's Race?" *Reader*, February 10, 2011, http://www.chicago reader.com/chicago/chicago-politics-segregation-african-american-black-white-hispanic-latino-population-census-community/Content?oid=3221712 (accessed March 21, 2016).

26 Wells, *Crusade for Justice*, 281.

27 Most successful interracial efforts did not occur until after 1919 in Chicago, after the race riot. Linda Gordon, "Black and White Visions of Welfare: Women's Welfare Activism, 1890–1945," *The Journal of American History* 78, no. 2 (1991), 564.

28 Other African Americans supported Wells-Barnett's perception of Woolley, including newspaper editor Julius Taylor, who claimed Woolley unwilling "to treat us on a plane of equality." McMurry, 275.

29 Wells, *Crusade for Justice*, 281; Giddings, *Ida: A Sword among Lions*, 447.

30 Bay, *To Tell the Truth Freely*, 261. Her husband Ferdinand also volunteered and taught at the center.

31 Wells, *Crusade for Justice*, 282–83.

32 Wells, *Crusade for Justice*, 286–87.

33 Paula Giddings, "Missing in Action Ida B. Wells, the NAACP, and the Historical Record," *Meridians* 1, no. 2 (2001): 10.

34 Bay, *To Tell the Truth Freely*, 262–63.

35 While she had eagerly embraced interracial organizations as a way to leverage the political power of whites on behalf of African Americans, she became disillusioned when control remained in the hands of whites. Schechter, *Ida B. Wells-Barnett and American Reform*, 188.

36 For more on her temper and its consequences see Patricia A. Schechter, "'All the Intensity of My Nature': Ida B. Wells, Anger, and Politics," *Radical History Review* 70 (1998): 48–77.

37 Giddings, *Ida: A Sword among Lions*, 451–52.

38 Schechter, *Ida B. Wells-Barnett and American Reform*, 126.

39 Nicole King, 90.

40 Watkins, 113.

41 Crystal N. Feimster, *Southern Horrors: Women and the Politics of Rape and Lynching* (Cambridge, MA: Harvard University Press, 2009), 120.

42 Giddings, *Ida: A Sword among Lions*, 441.

43 Bay, *To Tell the Truth Freely*, 258.

44 For several years, Wells-Barnett staved off the effects of Washington's attacks through her partnership with Du Bois. In 1906 when her husband announced his candidacy for judge, she placed her energy into his campaign rather than clashing with Washington. After a close race, the *Chicago Chronicle* reported that Barnett, the Republican candidate, had won by 499 votes. Angered at a black man gaining the position, the Democrats demanded a recount, during which they launched an anti-Ferdinand Barnett press campaign. Interestingly enough, after smearing him in the press, the recount found that instead of winning by several hundred votes, Barnett lost the election by a slim margin. As one historian notes, "It is not clear how accurate the recount was" but there were plenty who "wished to see Barnett fail." While difficult, the loss mobilized local African Americans in future elections who adopted the phrase "Remember Barnett" to rally black support for the Republican Party. Giddings, *Ida: A Sword among Lions*, 465–66.

45 Bay, *To Tell the Truth Freely*, 263–64; Giddings, *Ida: A Sword among Lions*, 470–72.

46 Wells, *Crusade for Justice*, 299.

47 Wells, *Crusade for Justice*, 300.

48 Wells, *Crusade for Justice*, 309–10.

49 W. L. Clanahan, "1909: Will James, 'the Froggie', Lynched in Cairo," *New York Age*, November 14, 1909, November 11, 2009, http://www.executedtoday.com/2009/11/11/1909-will-james-the-froggie-lynched-cairo-illinois/ (accessed March 21, 2016).

50 Schechter, *Ida B. Wells-Barnett and American Reform*, 138.

51 Bay, *To Tell the Truth Freely*, 278.

52 Wells, *Crusade for Justice*, 312–17.

53 The *Forum* was a weekly black paper and the only one preserved. Roberta Senechal de la Roche, *In Lincoln's Shadow: The 1908 Race Riot in Springfield, Illinois* (Carbondale: Southern Illinois University Press, 2008), 214.

54 Giddings, *Ida: A Sword among Lions*, 487.

55 Giddings, *Ida: A Sword among Lions*, 472.

56 Giddings, *Ida: A Sword among Lions*, 473.

57 Bay, *To Tell the Truth Freely*, 265.

58 McMurry, 279.

59 Bay, *To Tell the Truth Freely*, 266.

60 Giddings, *Ida: A Sword among Lions*, 474.

61 Wells, *Crusade for Justice*, 323–34.

62 Wells, *Crusade for Justice*, 324–25.

63 Wells, *Crusade for Justice*, 326.

64 Quoted in Giddings, *Ida: A Sword among Lions*, 477–78.

65 Bay, *To Tell the Truth Freely*, 269.

66 McMurry, 282.

67 Schechter, *Ida B. Wells-Barnett and American Reform*, 142.

68 Ovington agreed with Villard's worldview; she kept "forgetting that the Negroes aren't poor people for whom I must kindly do something" but rather have "forceful opinions of their own." McMurry, 281.
69 Giddings, *Ida: A Sword among Lions*, 501.
70 Magali Sarfatti Larson, *The Rise of Professionalism: A Sociological Analysis* (Berkeley: University of California Press, 1977), 152–53.
71 McMurry, 289.
72 Giddings, "Missing in Action Ida B. Wells, the NAACP, and the Historical Record," 11.
73 Giddings, *Ida: A Sword among Lions*, 493–94; McMurry, 286.
74 Wells-Barnett later learned that "Mrs. Washington's friends had construed my activity to mean that I wanted the paper to be taken away from her, and to be elected editor myself." Wells, *Crusade for Justice*, 329.
75 McMurry, 294.
76 In her hometown of Chicago, African Americans remained one of the most underserved populations, an observation supported by Louise deKoven Bowen, a white reformer and supporter of Jane Addam's Hull-House. Bowen noted that while Hull-House helped countless immigrant residents, it overlooked African Americans, who she observed could not gain jobs, an education, or any social mobility. Yet, Bowen found, despite the lack of social support for the African American community, there were surprisingly few black criminals. McMurry, 292.
77 Giddings, *Ida: A Sword among Lions*, 488–89.
78 Bay, *To Tell the Truth Freely*, 282.
79 Wells, *Crusade for Justice*, 304.
80 Giddings, *Ida: A Sword among Lions*, 491.
81 Bay, *To Tell the Truth Freely*, 284.
82 McMurry, 295.
83 Bay, *To Tell the Truth Freely* identifies the landlord as Will Saddler, 284–85.
84 McMurry, 287.
85 Bay, *To Tell the Truth Freely*, 284–85.
86 McMurry, 287.
87 Giddings, *Ida: A Sword among Lions*, 496.
88 Wells, *Crusade for Justice*, 337.
89 Giddings, *Ida: A Sword among Lions*, 497–98.
90 Giddings, *Ida: A Sword among Lions*, 507.
91 McMurry, 296.
92 Arthur Schlesinger, *The Crisis of the Old Order: 1919–1933 (The Age of Roosevelt, Vol. I)* (Boston: Houghton Mifflin, 1957), 26–36.
93 Bay, *To Tell the Truth Freely*, 287.
94 One of the key issues in the suffrage movement was the idea of "No Vote, No Tax" where the Revolutionary War ideology of no taxation without representation became a platform to support women having a political say. Wells, *Crusade for Justice*, 345. Two white women already involved in movement in Chicago, Virginia Brooks and Belle Squire, assisted Wells-Barnett. Giddings, *Ida: A Sword among Lions*, 514.
95 Faye E. Dudden, *Fighting Chance: The Struggle over Woman Suffrage and Black Suffrage in Reconstruction America* (New York: Oxford University Press, 2011), 3, 161–88.
96 Giddings, *Ida: A Sword among Lions*, 515–16.
97 Bay, *To Tell the Truth Freely*, 288; Giddings, *Ida: A Sword among Lions*, 516–17.
98 Giddings, *Ida: A Sword among Lions*, 517. This moment is also portrayed in the Katja von Garnier film *Iron Jawed Angels* (HBO Films, 2004).
99 Editorial, "Illinois Women Participate in Suffrage Parade. This State Was Well Represented in Washington," *The Chicago Daily Tribune*, March 5, 1913. See also Schechter, *Ida B. Wells-Barnett and American Reform*, 201; Giddings, *Ida: A Sword among Lions*, 518.
100 Giddings, *Ida: A Sword among Lions*, 534.

101   Wells, *Crusade for Justice,* 345.
102   Giddings, *Ida: A Sword among Lions,* 535.
103   Giddings, *Ida: A Sword among Lions,* 536.
104   McMurry, 309.
105   Giddings, *Ida: A Sword among Lions,* 519.
106   Henry Blumenthal, "Woodrow Wilson and the Race Question," *The Journal of Negro History* 48, no. 1 (1963), 4–6, 8–9; K. L. Wolgemuth, "Woodrow Wilson and Federal Segregation," *The Journal of Negro History* 44, no. 2 (1959), 158–60.
107   Giddings, *Ida: A Sword among Lions,* 529.
108   Giddings, *Ida: A Sword among Lions,* 530.
109   Bay, *To Tell the Truth Freely,* 286.
110   Wells, *Crusade for Justice,* 335.
111   Giddings, *Ida: A Sword among Lions,* 539.
112   Bay, *To Tell the Truth Freely,* 292.
113   Wanda A. Hendricks, "'Vote for the Advantage of Ourselves and Our Race:' The Election of the First Black Alderman in Chicago," *Illinois Historical Journal,* 87, no. 3 (1994): 182–83.
114   Wells, *Crusade for Justice,* 348.
115   Giddings, *Ida: A Sword among Lions,* 543.
116   This blow affected Wells-Barnett's outlook, noting "we felt that the sun was going to shine on our side of the street, and that we were going to have a friend in court who believed in working for the benefit of our people." Wells, *Crusade for Justice,* 353, 351.
117   Giddings, *Ida: A Sword among Lions,* 549.
118   Edwin R. Keedy, "The Third Degree and Legal Interrogation of Suspects," *University of Pennsylvania Law Review* 85 (1937): 763.
119   Wells, *Crusade for Justice,* 340–41.
120   Bay, *To Tell the Truth Freely,* 290; Giddings, *Ida: A Sword among Lions,* 550.
121   Wells, *Crusade for Justice,* 353.
122   Giddings, *Ida: A Sword among Lions,* 553.
123   Giddings, *Ida: A Sword among Lions,* 557.
124   Arthur E. Barbeau and Florette Henri, *The Unknown Soldiers: Black American Troops in World War I* (Philadelphia: Temple University Press, 1974), 11. See also Eve Darian-Smith, "Re-Reading W. E. B. Du Bois: The Global Dimensions of the US Civil Rights Struggle," *Journal of Global History* 7, no. 3 (2012): 483–505.
125   Barbeau and Henri, 41–42.
126   Lynchings also occurred in the North, but these acts lacked the spectacle aspect and northern mobs only occasionally executed an African American, compared to southern lynch mobs, which targeted African Americans at least eighty percent of the time. Brundage, *Lynching in the New South,* 8.
127   James Lowen, *Sundown Towns: A Hidden Dimension of American Racism* (New York: New Press, 2005), 4, 1.
128   The eastern side of the city was largely industrial factories, which used unskilled immigrant and black labor. Giddings, *Ida: A Sword among Lions,* 559.
129   Giddings, *Ida: A Sword among Lions,* 560–61.
130   Wells, *Crusade for Justice,* 383; Bay, *To Tell the Truth Freely,* 296.
131   Giddings, *Ida: A Sword among Lions,* 561.
132   Giddings, *Ida: A Sword among Lions,* 562–64.
133   Ida B. Wells-Barnett, *The East St. Louis Massacre: The Greatest Outrage of the Century* (Chicago: The Negro Fellowship Herald Press, 1917), 19, also quoted in James Patrick, "The Horror of the East St. Louis Massacre," *Exodus,* February 22, 2000. http://www.usd116.org/profdev/ahtc/lessons/PollockFel10/4chorrorESL.pdf (accessed March 30, 2016).
134   Wells, *Crusade for Justice,* 390; William Edward Burghardt Du Bois, "The Horizon," *The Crisis: A Record of the Darker Races* 15, no. 4 (1918): 196.

135 Quoted in Schechter, *Ida B. Wells-Barnett and American Reform*, 152.
136 Bay, *To Tell the Truth Freely*, 298.
137 McMurry, 315.
138 Bay, *To Tell the Truth Freely*, 299.
139 Edgar A. Schuler, "The Houston Race Riot, 1917," *The Journal of Negro History* 29, no. 3 (1944): 302.
140 Giddings, *Ida: A Sword among Lions*, 567.
141 Giddings, *Ida: A Sword among Lions*, 567–68.
142 Wells, *Crusade for Justice*, 367.
143 Giddings, *Ida: A Sword Among Lions*, 572.
144 Wells, *Crusade for Justice*, 368.
145 Giddings, *Ida: A Sword Among Lions*, 572.
146 Wells, *Crusade for Justice*, 369–70.

CHAPTER 5

THE POLITICAL ARENA, 1918–31

As World War I ended, race became a central issue for the United States both abroad and at home. The Paris Peace Conferences, which began in 1919 to set the terms of the treaties, sought to form new nations and required that the major powers understand how nationality, race, and religion defined peoples and borders. The Peace Conferences also needed to address the racial persecution of Jews carried out in USSR and the Ukraine, as well as how to integrate into society the black Africans brought by France and Germany from their colonies to fight in the conflict.[1] President Wilson, recognizing that these matters rested at the core of reshaping the landscape of Europe, sought American delegates to attend the Peace Conferences with insight into racial identity. In December, Monroe Trotter organized the National Race Conference where two hundred and fifty people from across the nation gathered in Washington, D.C. to vote for representatives.[2] The Universal Negro Improvement Association supported Marcus Garvey and Wells-Barnett as candidates and, in turn, Wells-Barnett supported National Equal Rights League (NERL) founder Monroe Trotter.

Chosen as an alternate, Wells-Barnett's continued outspokenness prevented her from representing the United States at the Peace Conferences.[3] Her growing relationship with Marcus Garvey, a Jamaican activist, placed her at the center of a Military Intelligence Division investigation. The Barnetts met Garvey in 1916, when he came to their home for dinner and spoke at the Negro Fellowship League (NFL).[4] Wells-Barnett shared his ideas about African Americans' need for economic independence and felt he could "solidify the masses of our people and endow them with racial consciousness and racial unity."[5] In 1918, she and Garvey shared a stage, speaking on racial issues at a meeting of Garvey's organization, the Universal Negro

Improvement Association (UNIA). Her continued dialogue on race during the war drew the attention of the Military Intelligence Division (MID), with one of their reports noting, "Ida B. Wells-Barnett is considered a far more dangerous agitator than Marcus Garvey."[6] Unfortunately, the MID did not want race "agitators" at home, let alone abroad, and made it clear that "Ida B. Wells-Barnett's presence in Paris during the Peace Conference would not be welcomed by the government."[7] Her selection as an alternate required her to pay her own way, a difficulty that she might have overcome, except the government refused to issue her a passport.[8]

During 1919, Marcus Garvey became increasingly radical in his stance on race in America. He created a "back to Africa" movement to relocate American blacks to their "own land," a migration he argued would free them from white domination. Wells-Barnett did not support his new idea, noting in her autobiography that he was "drunk with power." In order to assist in returning blacks to Africa, Garvey started an African American-owned shipping company, the Black Star Line. He funded this venture by advertising stock in the company in African American periodicals, promising that the "Black Star Line will turn over large profits and dividends."[9] Garvey, more preoccupied with the ideology behind his business than the day-to-day running of it, hired inexperienced managers and soon the Black Star Line was in complete financial collapse. In addition to losing his company and the money of his investors, in 1922 the Federal Bureau of Investigation (FBI) charged Garvey with mail fraud. The UNIA had been on the Federal government's watch list for years due to Garvey's encouragement of African Americans to embrace their own power and fight white oppression. After trying to find a reason to remove Garvey from the United States, an investigation into the process of selling the Black Star Line's stock through the mail led authorities to conclude that Garvey committed fraud. A jury sentenced him to five years in prison and, upon his release, the government deported Garvey back to Jamaica.[10]

In her autobiography, Wells-Barnett claimed that she warned Garvey that the Black Star Line "require[d] more thought and preparation before it should be launched," and "[p]erhaps if Mr. Garvey had listened to my advice he need not have undergone the humiliations which afterward became his."[11] During his time in prison, even open-minded reformers like Wells-Barnett distanced themselves from Garvey's ideologies, which developed a radical bent. He praised the Ku Klux Klan, claiming that he held the same ideas about the black race's power and purity as the white supremacist organization did about its own race. Perhaps unaware of the history and violence of the Klan, he could have misunderstood their activities. Regardless, Garvey, Wells-Barnett wrote, "made an impression on this country as no Negro before him had ever done."[12]

During World War I, black and white American soldiers fought side by side in the trenches of Europe, and many African American soldiers received egalitarian treatment for the first time abroad. Upon their return, black veterans grew impatient with the racism that they continued to experience; their comrades died for their country, yet the United States remained a place where whites could publically murder African Americans without punishment. For whites, World War I resulted in increased concern over the possibility of returning African American soldiers demanding equal rights. In the South, lynchers began targeting black soldiers in order to send a message that the place of African Americans in southern society remained unchanged.[13] The NAACP's investigation into the lynching of Bud Johnson on July 31, 1919, revealed that whites targeted him due to his status as a soldier.[14] Johnson received permission to return home from World War I to care for his ill father, but upon his arrival in Florida, he learned of his father's death and bills from the funeral expenses. "Whites" wanted Johnson to pay off his debt by giving up his father's farm, but he refused. In response, a mob of two hundred and fifty people gathered, with an eyewitness account claiming that members shouted, "[G]et ropes, get coal oil and gasoline and let us burn this Negro up... He is saucy. He thinks he is a soldier." Johnson's lynching resulted in part from fears that he returned from combat with an "uppity" attitude and felt entitled to deference or other signs of equality. In response to an increase in southern lynchings, the NAACP intensified its efforts to pass anti-lynching legislation in Congress.[15]

Increased racial tensions after World War I existed across the nation, not just the South. In an editorial for *The Crisis*, Du Bois noted, "This country of ours, despite all its better souls have done and dreamed, is yet a shameful land... It disfranchises its own citizens... It encourages ignorance." His concluding remarks—"We return. We return from fighting. We return fighting"—rallied African Americans to continue the battle at home for social change.[16] In the North, the struggle to deal with the shifting racial dynamics brought on by the Great Migration continued, and statements such as the one appearing in the newly formed newspaper the *Chicago Whip,* that "the compromising peace-at-any-price Negro is rapidly passing into the scrap heap of yesterday," only bolstered northerners' apprehensions.

The number of African Americans in Chicago had tripled in the last decade, yet this population remained restricted to the South side of Chicago in the designated Black wards, or legislative districts. The fifty wards that divided the city worked to prevent African Americans from expanding outside black-dominated districts, as any attempt to move outside black neighborhoods resulted in violence, and any effort to integrate housing resulted in residential bombings. The Chicago police recorded twenty-six bombings from July 1917 to July 1919.[17] Of those incidents, the authorities made only two arrests and neither resulted in an indictment.[18] In 1919, the Barnetts moved to the edge of the dividing line for their neighborhood when they bought a house at 3624 Grand Boulevard. Their relocation into this borderland resulted in the *Chicago Post*'s lamentation that "colored people" now lived in homes on "Grand boulevard and on South Park, Calumet and Prairie avenues."[19] While white papers feared this encroachment of non-whites, black Chicago newspapers wanted justice for the continued bombings. When one explosion killed a little girl, demands increased. Wells-Barnett sought protection for black community members from this terroristic violence, but the mayor refused to grant her an audience. She attempted to discuss the issue with the Chief of Police, who dismissively told Wells-Barnett that he could not spare his officers to "protect the homes of colored people."[20] Frustrated by the authorities, Wells-Barnett endeavored to create public pressure for action, publishing a letter in the *Chicago Tribune* asking for justice "before it is too late." In her plea, she mentioned fearing that the racial tension signified by the bombings would explode in a "bloody" event similar to East St. Louis.[21] Unfortunately, she was right.

As temperatures soared in July, the segregated beaches along Lake Michigan became crowded. On Sunday, July 29, 1919, a group of black teenaged boys made a raft and happily drifted in the water on the designated beach for African Americans. As they floated closer to the white beach, a white man on the shore began throwing rocks at them, striking one child, Eugene Williams, in the head. Williams lost consciousness and despite efforts by his friends to save him, drowned.[22] When the police arrived and bystanders pointed out the stone-thrower, the white police officers refused to arrest the man. When a black officer arrived and attempted to apprehend him, a white officer prevented him from taking the offender into custody. Soon after the incident, a group of African Americans in a nearby neighborhood headed towards the beach, seeking answers. On their way, they encountered a white police officer on the street. Angry, they chased the officer until a white, Irish gang came to his aid. The two groups fought all night, leaving twenty-seven African Americans dead and countless others wounded and beaten.[23]

When the newspaper reported on the beach incident and subsequent hostility, Wells-Barnett recognized that the story could spark another round of violence and, indeed, rioting soon ensued. Wells-Barnett went to her local chapter of the NERL and organized a Protective Association composed of local leaders and ministers.[24] She recalled, "This organization met daily while the trouble was in progress, and a committee was appointed to wait on Mayor Thompson and the chief of police asking protection for our people."[25] The rioting occurred primarily in the frontiers between segregated neighborhoods, placing the Barnett family in the middle of the action. In response to the almost continuous reports of attacks against African

Americans, the community organized a blockade of black men along State Street. This Wells-Barnett referred to as the "von Hindenberg [sic] line," an allusion to the precautionary stronghold created during World War I by the Germans that held against attack until the end of the war. Despite the line of defense, on Monday, two days after the drowning, the Protective Association heard reports of "hoodlums over in the Stockyards district" heading to State Street "to annihilate Negro citizens." They did not arrive; instead the white mob became sidetracked and attacked black stockyard workers, beating and stabbing them, with at least four men dying in the altercation.[26] The Barnetts, who believed in self-defense, owned guns, but although the violence occurred "a stone's throw from our house," it never threatened their home.[27]

The rioting lasted for five days, injuring more than five hundred people and leaving twenty-three African Americans and fifteen whites dead.[28] Mary Byron Clarke, a black woman who lived near the Barnetts on Grand Boulevard, called the police when a mob threatened her home. When the police arrived, rather than disperse the mob, they knocked down her door and arrested her and her husband.[29] As Wells-Barnett learned of these incidents of violence, she offered her response in an interview for the *Chicago Daily News,* noting how America praised black soldiers for killing Germans who violated democracy, and yet white authorities viewed African Americans as the guilty party even as "white Huns" wanted to take their lives and destroy their homes.[30] Such talk again brought Wells-Barnett to the attention of the MID, but this inquiry agreed with her observation that the government failed "to safeguard the interests of blacks" and did not pursue any charges.[31]

Wells-Barnett became involved in the legal cases of the rioters, a continuation of her efforts to guarantee justice for African Americans within the courtroom. She contacted Thomas Maclay Hoyne, the state's attorney, who assured her that "punishment" would be "meted out to the rioters." Wells-Barnett testified before the grand jury, telling them of the violence she witnessed as well as repeating evidence from those too afraid to appear. Soon the mood of the hearings changed when Edward J. Brundage, the Attorney General of Illinois, joined the prosecution. Brundage's assignment upset Wells-Barnett, who believed him to be racially biased. A few years earlier he had prosecuted rioters in East St. Louis, sending fifteen black men to prison with substantial sentences while no whites served time. Wells-Barnett felt that the African American men Brundage prosecuted were only guilty of "protecting themselves from attacks by the white rioters." Fearful that Brundage would repeat the past and refocus the Chicago investigation on African Americans, she began giving public interviews, telling reporters that "the colored people did not want Mr. Brundage to take charge" as "we had a state's attorney perfectly capable of doing the work," explaining Brundage's poor record in this type of situation. To Wells-Barnett's relief, the Grand Jury had noticed the racial inequality developing in the prosecution, and refused to move the proceedings forward until the attorneys also charged white men. Wells-Barnett recalled the Grand Jury's determination that "colored men couldn't have created a riot by themselves."[32]

With the Grand Jury's recognition of the racial inequality in the prosecution, Wells-Barnett redoubled her efforts to remove Brundage from the legal team, meeting with the Protective Association to ask that they add their voice to those pressuring for state's attorney Hoyne to be the sole prosecutor. The association refused to support her, and in fact chose to endorse Brundage's continuation in the matter. Shocked and angered, Wells-Barnett stood and laid her membership card down on the table. She informed the representatives that she would not "be guilty of belonging to an organization that would do such a treacherous thing as to ask the white man who had put fifteen of our people in prison to take hold and do the same sort of thing here." She left the meeting "with tears streaming down" her face as she thought of the black men who would be prosecuted by Brundage for defending themselves and their families while the white men who had attacked their homes received little or no legal punishment.[33]

While Wells-Barnett focused on bringing those responsible for the violence to justice in the state judicial system, the NAACP opened its own investigation into the riot. The NAACP sent Walter White, the twenty-six year-old assistant of national secretary James Weldon Johnson, to report on the incident for the NAACP.[34] White, one of the first black field officers of the organization, became a key investigator in racial violence for the NAACP, for although an African American, he could physically pass as a white man with his blue eyes and light skin. White recalled in his autobiography one instance of his mistaken racial identity after a lynching in Florida, when he encountered three white children walking to school who eagerly told him about attending a lynching. One, "the eldest, a ruddy-cheeked girl of nine or ten, asked if I was going to the place, where 'the niggers' had been killed." When White replied that he might the girl launched "animatedly, almost as joyously as though the memory were of Christmas morning or the circus," with her younger companions interjecting about "the fun we had burning the niggers."[35]

When White arrived in Chicago, he began interviewing people, including local leaders. Wells-Barnett, having criticized the NAACP for its unwillingness to engage in protests against lynchings, grew angry when she learned that White had arranged to meet with her husband to discuss the issue she had been publically fighting for months. Wells-Barnett interrupted the appointment and confronted White, who noted in his own autobiography that she proceeded to berate the NAACP and "every organization in Chicago because they have not come into her organization and allowed her to dictate to them." He reported to Mary Ovington, "She is a troublemaker and is causing complications by starting a fund of her own to defend riot victims."[36] Indeed, the national headquarters had closed the Chicago NAACP office rather than allow the possibility that Wells-Barnett might influence the organization. From Wells-Barnett's perspective, the association had once again swooped in to usurp her, while in White's mind, her refusal to subvert her work to his, as part of a national organization, made her a "troublemaker." Walter White's conflict with Wells-Barnett may have had more to do with her gender than her ideas, as one of his biographers identified White's dislike of strong women and difficulty working with them throughout his career, an issue he had with Ovington, a white woman, as well.[37] Regardless, the NAACP's investigation, as Wells-Barnett predicted, resulted in no discernable changes. The Chicago race riot became one of the twenty-five uprisings in the summer of 1919, earning the season the designation of "Red Summer," in reference to the blood of both races shed in violence across the nation.

After the riot, support for Wells-Barnett's Negro Fellowship Reading Room suffered. The NFL, Wells-Barnett recalled in her autobiography, was a "burden" growing "heavier each day." Since she had lost her probation officer job, the profits from the employment service remained the only income supporting the organization. After the state opened a free office nearby, even that meager income dropped and "there was not always enough left to pay the rent."[38] In addition, the growth of a similar organization, the Urban League, pulled supporters from the NFL. Founded in New York in 1911 by an interracial coalition, the Urban League sought to help the influx of African Americans to northern cities by assisting newly transplanted residents in locating jobs and housing.[39] Wells-Barnett's dislike for the organization, although it shared similar goals as the NFL, stemmed from the fact that it drew upon Booker T. Washington's idea of industrial education. In 1915, the well-funded Urban League expanded to Chicago, and as other local reformers, including Jane Addams, began supporting the organization, the NFL, already having lost some patrons to the YMCA, could not survive the direct competition.[40] In 1919, The Urban League placed more than fourteen thousand African Americans in industrial jobs.[41] Despite this success rate, Wells-Barnett remained concerned that the Tuskegee influence meant that the leaders focused only on placing African Americans in trade jobs.[42] Years later Wells-Barnett remained bitter about the Urban League's expansion into Chicago, noting, "It seemed that the Urban League was brought to Chicago to supplant the activities of the Negro Fellowship League."[43]

Wells-Barnett attempted to keep the NFL afloat by finding new avenues of support, and considered incorporating the establishment into the outreach work of African American churches. A coalition of black ministries agreed to support the NFL if she stepped down as president. Wells-Barnett, desperate to save her decade-long work, agreed to these terms, as "the church had money. They knew I had the vision."[44] Soon after this arrangement, members of the church leadership demeaned the working class and urban poor that the NFL primarily served, referring to one of the officers as a "ragpicker."[45] Wells-Barnett knew her patrons were not middle class, and defended the man to the church administration explaining, "The leader of my Bible class is a rag picker. I see him every time I go downtown on the streetcar with a large bag of dirty rags on his back" and he "ought to be given credit rather than disparagement." Already concerned about the church leaders' attitude towards her and those she helped, she withdrew the offer to merge the NFL into the religious configuration after she went to pick up the payment for the six months of back rent she owed and the chairman was "afraid to trust me with the check." At this, Wells-Barnett admitted, "I lost control of myself and told him that I wouldn't go on with the deal."[46]

In November 1919, a week before Thanksgiving, Wells-Barnett arrived at the NFL to find an empty building, everything confiscated by the landlord to cover unpaid rent.[47] Wells-Barnett recalled in her autobiography,

> All I can say of that ten years I spent on State Street is that no human being ever came inside the doors asking for food who [sic] was not given a card to a restaurant across the way. No one sought a night's lodging in vain, for after his case was investigated, a card to the Douglass Hotel was given him.

She concluded that the NFL fulfilled its goal of helping the black man "at the hour of his greatest need" and "the race would get the benefit of our action."[48]

Despite her sadness over the closing of the NFL, Wells-Barnett spent the fall embroiled in the legal proceedings from another race riot, this one in Elaine, Arkansas, resulting from an attempt to unionize black sharecroppers. The Progressive Farmers and Household Union had visited Elaine earlier in the summer and urged local African Americans to demand a fair price for their crops. The current system, useful in keeping black labor in place, allowed white property owners to charge high rates for use of the land and tools, and then buy cotton for less than market price. The union found a lawyer for the sharecroppers to help them sue for their share of the current crop, and on September 30, 1919, armed white men arrived at an organizational union meeting held at a church. Recognizing the inherent danger in attempting to unite against white landowners, armed guards stood outside the building, and when the white gang arrived, a firefight broke out, killing two white men, including the deputy sheriff. As news spread of armed African Americans shooting and killing white men, thousands traveled to Elaine to help put down what the local white paper termed a "negro uprising." The Governor of Arkansas sent five hundred troops to prevent violence from breaking out, but upon their arrival, the soldiers supported the white mob, turning their military grade weapons, including machine guns, on African Americans.[49]

Immediately after the event, Walter White traveled to Arkansas on behalf of the NAACP to investigate, posing as a white newspaper reporter. A lack of funds delayed Wells-Barnett's own inquiry until January 1920. She did publish a letter in the *Chicago Defender* refuting the southern white paper's characterization of the events as an uprising by blacks, which justified the ensuing violence as necessary to protect whites. Wells-Barnett countered that "the riot had been precipitated by the refusal of colored men to sell their cotton below the market price." As with the other race riots, authorities arrested "scores" of African Americans and "herded" them into prison. In order to secure a release from jail, each African American needed a white employer to "vouch for him as being a 'good nigger.'" This oath primarily occurred only after an African American agreed to work for the white employer for low wages.[50] White's investigation, published by the Associated Press and in the *Chicago Defender,* told how the police subjected the accused to physical torture, including "electricity," beatings, and other punishments until they "confess they had a conspiracy to kill white folks."[51] As White concluded his investigation, he nearly encountered a lynch mob himself. When he boarded the train to depart from Elaine, the conductor asked him why he was leaving when the "fun" was about to start. Inquiring as to what he meant, the conductor explained to White that the locals had discovered a "yellow nigger" had been in town passing for white and a mob intended to lynch him.[52]

At the first trial of the Elaine rioters, a dozen African American men, represented by white lawyers in front of an all-white jury, received twelve guilty verdicts in less than eight minutes. All were sentenced to the electric chair.[53] Hearing of this, Wells-Barnett began a fundraising campaign for new legal counsel to appeal the death sentences. In response to her requests, Wells-Barnett reported, "Many people all over the country sent in contributions to assist in securing legal talent." She also received a letter from one of the twelve men offering thanks and remarking that her efforts were "the first word or offer of help they had from their own people."[54] In addition to supporting the legal fight of the accused black men, Wells-Barnett pledged to help the refugees flooding north into Chicago as thousands of African Americans left Arkansas. She approached Oscar De Priest, the Chicago politician she had briefly campaigned for in the 1914 election. In 1917, De Priest lost his city council seat after authorities charged him with "conspiracy to protect gambling."[55] The charges dropped, he regrouped and, in 1918, founded the People's Movement, a grassroots black political group that supported black candidates who could "not be bought at any price."[56]

Wells-Barnett spoke at a meeting to more than one thousand members of De Priest's People's Movement, suggesting that local African Americans "use our influence to bring thousands more away from Arkansas, which needed Negro labor," a resolution that unanimously passed. A letter from the NAACP soon undermined her feeling of success in rallying support for the plight of southern blacks. The correspondence contained an objection to Wells-Barnett raising money for the legal defense of the convicted men and informed her that the NAACP was "already doing all the work necessary in the matter" and she should "turn over to the NAACP all money" she had received. Wells-Barnett refused, feeling that people had entrusted their donations to support the legal defense to her, and in good conscious, she could not turn them over. Instead, she published a letter in the *Chicago Defender* asking those who had donated permission to use the money for her own investigation, which would also "find out just what the NAACP had done." When she felt that enough donors had consented, she boarded a train in January 1920.[57]

Upon arriving in Elaine, Wells-Barnett immediately traveled to the jail to interview the accused men. Like Walter White, she found that the prisoners "were beaten, given electric shocks, and in every possible way terrorized in an effort to force them to confess that their organization was a conspiracy for the purpose of murdering white people and confiscating their property."[58] After hours of interviews, Wells-Barnett grew impatient with the men, telling them, "You have talked and sung and prayed about dying" and "God knows that you are innocent of the offense for which you expect to be electrocuted," so she demanded, "why don't you pray to live and ask to be freed?"[59] Before leaving town, Wells-Barnett also stopped in to meet the newly appointed African American lawyer for the men, Scipio Africanus Jones, who credited her efforts in the northern presses with raising awareness about the men's plight. Jones, Well-Barnett noted, believed that the publicity she created not only resulted in a successful appeal date, but had also raised enough money to continue the legal proceedings ahead of them.[60]

Wells-Barnett published the results of her investigation in her last pamphlet, *The Arkansas Race Riot* (1920). Like her first works on lynching, Wells-Barnett countered the white newspaper's version of events that claimed that local African Americans plotted to kill whites and take their land. In the tract, she noted her determination to lay the facts "before the world" in order to gain "public sympathy" so "the whole country will say let those men go free!"[61] Her report also included an estimate of the number of fatalities due to the violence, which agreed with Walter White's assessment that the African American death toll approached two hundred. Many whites buried or burned the bodies of their black victims to avoid any legal responsibility for their actions, preventing an exact count of African American deaths. In contrast to the hundreds killed and harmed, only five white men died during the riots, and this disparity in statistics supported Wells-Barnett's contention that African Americans were the victims of armed white men and not vice versa.[62]

As in all of her writings, Wells-Barnett humanized the victims of racial violence. In the publication, she recounted the multiple effects that this violence had on not only those arrested, but also their wives and children. She narrated how one woman hid with her children for days during the rioting, only to find her husband imprisoned and her home locked and empty. When she asked her white landlord what happened, he informed her that she would not get her property back, nor would he pay her for the last year's crops, and that if she did not leave, he would kill her. Another black woman recounted how white men beat, "kicked," and "pistol-whipped" her for attempting to join the union efforts.[63] As Wells-Barnett's pamphlet, published in May 1920, continued to solicit support and donations, she again upset the leadership within the NAACP, who feared that her tactics could upend their own efforts. Mary Ovington had set the association to assisting those accused of instigating the riot, but did so by approaching members of Congress. She desired that these efforts remain out of the public eye, claiming that the NAACP's name must "not be used in connection with the defense of the prisoners."[64] This official position, also supported by Secretary James Weldon Johnson, maintained that publicity would hurt the prisoners' chances of release.

Although Wells-Barnett and the NAACP offered disparate approaches to the defense of the accused Arkansas rioters, both claimed victory. The NAACP's legal team, led by Boston attorney Moorfield Storey, appealed the case to the Arkansas Supreme Court, who denied the petition. The NAACP's legal team then submitted a writ of habeas corpus, since the violent interrogation tactics of twelve men deprived them of due process, against E. H. Dempsey, the warden of the prison system. This action delayed the executions and allowed Storey to file for a writ of *habeas corpus* in federal court. The case, heard by the Supreme Court in 1923, overturned the convictions for the men in the first important civil rights victory involving criminal law since the inception of the NAACP. The Justices found little legality within the original trial proceeding.[65] Although Wells-Barnett often felt the NAACP's tactics too indirect, their ability to procure a legal defense and successfully overturn the verdict saved black lives. Through her grass-roots agitation, Wells-Barnett brought attention to the cause, but could not muster this level of legal expertise. This high-profile Supreme Court legal victory both strengthened the mission of the NAACP and attracted more support and donations, making the organization a powerful tool for African Americans to agitate for civil liberties.[66] In her autobiography, Wells-Barnett insisted that if she had not resuscitated the prisoners' minds and souls during her visit, the reversal of the verdict would have hardly mattered. She concluded her chapter on the Elaine riot with a vignette, set a year after the court's decision, when a black man knocked on her door. In responding to her query, he told her, "I am one of them twelve men that you came down to Arkansas about last year." The man, now free, had moved to Chicago and "he felt indebted for my efforts," Wells-Barnett wrote, and relayed how her telling them to "quit talking about dying" changed everything. "We never talked about dying anymore," he told her. "[E]very last one of us is out and enjoying his freedom."[67]

In 1920, conditions deteriorated in Chicago. An economic recession led to massive layoffs and, as the first to suffer from job cuts, by the end of the year nearly twenty thousand African Americans were jobless.[68] At the same time, Wells-Barnett clearly struggled to find her place in society. Her NFL had closed and she remained unwelcome at NACW. The reports of constant violence clearly wore on her, and her physical health mirrored her mental exhaustion. On December 15, 1920, Provident Hospital admitted Wells-Barnett for gallstones, but complications kept her in the hospital for five weeks.[69] The *Chicago Defender* reported that she remained too sick to receive visitors until Christmas Day when the "Barnett family attended en masse." After her release, she remained bed-ridden at home until March.[70] In her autobiography, Wells-Barnett admitted that her recovery took the better part of a year, during which she contemplated her life. Rather pessimistically, she concluded that she had nothing to show for her years of activism. Such thoughts did not deter her, as it might others; instead, she regrouped, setting new goals.[71] Sometime during her year of recovery, a small fire destroyed her personal letters and papers, most of them unpublished and lost to history.[72]

After her illness, Wells-Barnett promised herself that she would "make some preparation of a personal nature for the future."[73] At fifty-seven years of age, her siblings were all now married with children and remained largely scattered across the nation; Lily and Alfred lived in California and George resided in Kansas. Wells-Barnett remained distant, both geographically and emotionally, from these three siblings, although George's son Jack set off during a teenage rebellion to Chicago to visit his aunt, whom he had heard of but never met. Only Annie remained nearby, now married in Chicago, but the two sisters often fought and went long periods without speaking to each other.[74] Within her own family, Wells-Barnett's children had begun their adult lives. Charles dropped out of high school and worked as a mechanic and chauffeur, eventually marrying. Herman graduated from college and practiced law with Ferdinand, and although married with children, his sister Alfreda noted, Herman "loved betting on the horses."[75] Ida Jr. worked as a secretary in her father's law office and never married. Wells-Barnett wanted Alfreda, the youngest, to go to law school and be a lawyer, but instead she became a social worker.

On August 18, 1920, three-quarters of the states ratified the Nineteenth Amendment, giving all women the right to vote. The amendment surely influenced Wells-Barnett's decision on her future actions. Since 1883, she had viewed the legal system as a way to create equality. She fought against lynching because whites used it as a social control mechanism and circumvented the legal process. She created the NFL specifically to help her race by helping black men, as they were the only ones with any access to political power. With the Nineteenth Amendment, Wells-Barnett now had the same rights as whites and black men and no longer needed to work with interracial groups or male leaders. When she returned to the public sphere in 1922, her focus became gaining political power for black women, culminating in her own run for political office.

One of Wells-Barnett's new goals appears to have been putting her differences with the NAACP aside in order to support their efforts to pass a federal anti-lynching bill. The measure sought to make a mob of five or more, gathered for "depriving any person of his life without authority of law," a federal offense. The bill set a five-year minimum jail sentence for anyone participating in a lynching.[76] Put forward by Leonidas C. Dyer, a Republican from a black majority district in St. Louis, Missouri, and known as the Dyer Anti-Lynching Bill, the measure sought to punish states who failed to protect mob victims.[77] In 1922, after passing in the House of Representatives, the Dyer Bill was before the Senate. The NAACP actively worked to push the proposal forward, organizing public demonstrations, including pickets, and the vote received national attention. Despite these efforts, the Senate did not pass the bill. Over the next few years, the NAACP repeatedly attempted to reintroduce the regulation, but the 1922 effort became the closest that the measure ever came to becoming legislation.[78]

Wells-Barnett joined the NAACP's attempts to help pass the Dyer Bill, yet the leadership in the organization continued to minimize her contributions. In the fall of 1922, NAACP officer James Weldon Johnson attended the annual NACW meeting to regroup for the Dyer's Bill reintroduction.

With Wells-Barnett in the audience, Addie Waites Hunton, who also worked with the NAACP, introduced Johnson, and both speakers proceeded to ignore her contributions to the anti-lynching movement, disregarding the fact that she created the national conversation about lynching in the first place, which had directly led to the establishment of a national organization devoted to ending the practice. Hunton spoke instead of the impact of John Mitchell, Jr., giving him credit for spreading knowledge about lynchings.[79] Mitchell, the editor of the *Richmond Planet*, published many articles about lynchings in the 1880s, bringing attention to the violence with observations such as "Southern white folks have gone to roasting Negroes, we presume the next step will be to eat them."[80] He, however, did not seek to explain or end lynchings. In contrast, Wells-Barnett exposed the reality behind lynchings and received national attention for doing so.[81] Hunton, a progressive reformer who worked for the YMCA in New York and traveled with black troops during World War I, did not have an obvious reason for leaving Wells-Barnett out of her speech. The only reason for doing so would be her acceptance of the NAACP's own narrative about the history of the anti-lynching movement, which failed to include the former "Princess of the Press."[82] In her autobiography, Wells-Barnett sarcastically clarified that Hunton "was gracious enough" to mention her once in an offhand remark as having "done some work against lynching."[83]

Wells-Barnett, full of ideas but without any organization through which to implement them, attempted to incite new momentum at the 1924 NACW meeting when she announced her candidacy for president. Wells-Barnett, who members had hissed off the stage at the 1910 meeting, had not been involved in NACW since. In contrast, her opponent Mary McLeod Bethune had been steadily active in the organization since 1912, and had just completed a term as vice president from 1922 to 1924.[84] As historian Paula Giddings remarked, "What was she thinking? Certainly it wasn't the prospect that she could actually win."[85] It is likely that Wells-Barnett knew that she could not win against Mary McLeod Bethune, but perhaps victory was not her goal. Although Wells-Barnett had little chance of prevailing, her run for the presidency was not out of character. Wells-Barnett saw herself as an activist at heart, and when efforts stopped moving forward, she did what she always did, and threw herself in the middle. Even if her effort failed, Wells-Barnett preferred any action to passivity as a method for inciting change. By putting herself forward as a candidate, she gained a platform for her ideas and for discussing a transformation in the focus of the NACW. She felt that the group remained too concerned about portraying an image of black respectability and the strategies they used, similar to the NAACP of lobbying for peaceful change, had repeatedly failed.[86] Wells-Barnett had little patience for policies that echoed Washington's accommodationist approach, and rather than asking for whites' help, she felt that her race needed to demand change. Now that black women had the vote, she saw NACW as having the potential to organize and engage black women in political issues.

When the results of the election were announced, Wells-Barnett received only forty-two votes to Bethune's six hundred and fifty eight.[87] Upon hearing the results, Wells-Barnett made a motion to make the vote for Bethune unanimous, which passed.[88] Due to her gracious action, she received positive media attention. The *Chicago Defender* newspaper reported, "No greater scene was enacted" at the conference, than when "Mrs. Ida B. Wells-Barnett walked to the center of the platform and put her arms around Mrs. Bethune."[89] Although the organization likely saw Bethune as a moderate candidate compared to Wells-Barnett, it soon became apparent that the new president harbored a similar desire to shift NACW's prevailing ideology. Bethune suggested that the organization change their slogan from "Lifting as We Climb" to "Not for Ourselves, but for Others," a motto focused on helping all members of society regardless of race, class, or gender.[90]

Her presidential run and graceful deference to Bethune brought Wells-Barnett's name back into circulation among black women and allowed her re-entry into local clubwomen efforts. She became active in several local organizations, including the American Rose Art Club, the Chicago Association of Club Women, and the Cook County Federation of Club Women.[91] She also regained the presidency of the Ida B. Wells Club. When two southern black women, Mary Booze and Mamie Williams, both at the NACW convention, approached Wells-Barnett about working with the Chicago chapter of the National League of Republican Colored Women (NLRCW), to mobilize other African American women to vote for Republican candidates.[92] Wells-Barnett, thrilled to engage black women politically through an organization, agreed. Such work was needed, for as historian Catherine E. Rymph noted, in the decade after receiving the vote, many black women "remained skeptical" about the act of voting, and clubs such as the NLRCW sought to educate them about how political change could alleviate social issues.[93]

In 1926, Wells-Barnett also formed the Women's Forum, a group focused on weekly social programs.[94] She used this organization to introduce women to social injustices beyond racial violence, most notably advocating for the unionization of Chicago's Pullman Company employees into the Brotherhood of Sleeping Car Porters (BSCP). In 1925, the Pullman Company was the largest employer of African Americans in the United States. Most worked as porters and maids, serving more than thirty-five million travelers each year.[95] The unionization effort occurred in Chicago, where the Pullman Company had their headquarters. Although they consistently underpaid their black workers, the motivation to organize also stemmed from the dehumanizing working conditions. The company instructed all passengers to call the male African American porters "George," after George Pullman, the founder of the railroad company.[96] Considering African Americans interchangeable reflected a stereotypical cultural portrayal of black men. The Pullman Company played on the image of the "Uncle Tom," derived from Harriet Beecher Stowe's famous novel *Uncle Tom's Cabin*, which stereotyped subservient black men as "good" slaves who were "obedient," "loyal," and "non-complaining."[97] It is evident that the Pullman Company wanted this connection between African American males and servitude, as George Pullman openly discussed his decision to exclusively hire black men in order to keep the idea of slavery alive for his white passengers.[98]

The pay hierarchy within the railroad workers reflected the racial inequities of the Pullman Company's beliefs. White conductors earned roughly one hundred and fifty dollars a month, compared to the black porters who earned seventy-two dollars and fifty cents a month. Even African American men who worked in the meatpacking factories in Chicago earned a monthly salary of eighty-eight dollars a month.[99] Despite the pay disparity, many porters felt that the job offered them status. By working for the rich, they could receive tips, and often had a measure of health insurance. Eventually these fringe benefits failed to compensate for the pay disparity as the wages for skilled black laborers continued to rise and railroad salaries remained stagnant. When the porters attempted to unionize, the Pullman Company responded with every resource available to them to stop these efforts—even placing spies on trains to report on the activities of their employees in order to fire anyone with union sympathies.[100]

Chicago's black clubwomen became the first to advocate for the African American porters, led by Wells-Barnett, who one historian identified as "the most important figure in assisting the union."[101] Her efforts began after she invited the head of the Brotherhood of Sleeping Car Porters, A. Phillip Randolph, to speak in her home. Always critical of the portrayal of events in the press, which opposed the unionization effort, Wells-Barnett wanted to hear from the organizer himself. After Wells-Barnett heard his perspective, she had Randolph address the Women's Forum, and after his speech, the members endorsed the unionization effort.[102] The Brotherhood, through reformers such as Wells-Barnett, created a network of support so successful that the Pullman Company had to spend thousands of dollars to influence the black press and black ministers against the attempt.[103]

Wells-Barnett saw the issue of unionization as larger than labor or economics. For her, the interconnectedness of race, gender, and class in preventing social change required activists to tackle all three issues.[104] Wells-Barnett's efforts to garner public support helped tip the scales towards support for the unionization, and beyond raising awareness among black clubwomen, she wrote about the porters' efforts in the *Chicago Defender*. In 1927, the Pullman Company discontinued its policy of addressing porters as "George" and in light of this progress, more African Americans desired to join the Brotherhood of Sleeping Car Porters union.[105] This concession, however, remained the high point of the effort for many years, as the Brotherhood of Sleeping Car Porters' unionization efforts would not succeed until 1935.

After months of heavy rains in April 1927, several levees holding back the Mississippi River gave way and the Delta valley experienced the greatest flood in history. The water overflowed along the river from Mississippi to Ohio, leading the Arkansas River and Red River to flood as well, engulfing areas of Oklahoma, Texas, and Louisiana. The deluge affected towns as far as sixty miles away from the river and resulted in more than two hundred and fifty deaths. The flooding displaced more than 700,000 people in the Mississippi Delta, where seventy-five percent of the population was African American.[106] Blacks in this region supplied ninety-five percent of the local workforce, primarily as plantation labor. With their employees displaced by the natural disaster, white landowners pressured the American Red Cross to temporarily house, not relocate, the evacuees. As a result, African American refugees faced few options. One National Guard soldier explained the process of returning the displaced workers, noting that as soon as a planter's property dried out, he arrived at the camp and "picked out his niggers."[107]

Wells-Barnett's involvement in the treatment of African Americans in the refugee camps began after a runaway evacuee came to Chicago to see her, hoping she could help the situation. She never named her informant, who explained how authorities forced "unclaimed" African Americans to repair the levees in dangerous conditions, supervised by armed guards who would shoot anyone trying to flee. He demonstrated their commitment to this violence by revealing a recent gunshot wound in his leg, suffered when he escaped. Spurred to action, Wells-Barnett wrote in the *Chicago Defender* of the plight of these African Americans, demanding an investigation into practices at the camps. Such an inquiry, she noted, must come from the outside, as "black ministers in Greenville were being paid off to ensure investigators and the public that the refugees weren't being ill-treated."[108] Indeed, despite claims of good treatment, it appeared that the black refugees lived in mud, worked at gunpoint, and could only travel with a pass. If any man declined to return to work, either on the plantation or on repairing the levee, camp leaders would retaliate by refusing "to issue rations to black women and children." Enraged, Wells-Barnett wrote a series of letters to Herbert Hoover, the secretary of commerce and in charge of federal flood relief, which she also published in the *Chicago Defender*. These missives openly decried this treatment and again led to recognition of Wells-Barnett as "an uncompromising fighter" for the rights of African Americans.[109]

As she undertook these efforts, the Ida B. Wells Woman's Club held a celebratory event in her honor, where attendees categorized Wells-Barnett as the "mother of our clubs" and speakers discussed the many lives she had affected.[110] Despite this tribute, aimed at recognizing her for her efforts, an event soon made Wells-Barnett and other African Americans painfully aware of the inequalities they still faced. The American Citizenship Federation, an interracial group Wells-Barnett identified as seeking to foster "patriotism in our country" planned to hold a fundraiser at the Drake Hotel.[111] The owner of the *Chicago Defender*, Robert S. Abbott, an African American, received an invitation to the event and sent his acceptance, but an issue soon arose as the committee had chosen a segregated hotel. The organizers immediately asked Abbott to rescind his acceptance, since they could not guarantee his admission. Wells-Barnett recalled in her autobiography, "It so happened that the very next day" the American Citizenship Federation planned a lunch for the black clubwomen in order to ask for money to support their efforts. Rather blithely she claimed to have made a last minute decision to attend the event and sat peacefully through "the most beautiful address by a gentleman who outlined the plans for the truer American organization of our country," followed by the appeal for pledges of money. With business done, Wells-Barnett rose and asked the speaker to verify that the organization had indeed asked Abbott to withdraw his acceptance of their invitation based on the policies of the Drake Hotel. Upon confirmation of this, Wells-Barnett wrote an article in the *Chicago Defender* explaining how the organization excluded its African American members. She then cut out clippings of her article and sent it to each individual on the board of directors. A few days later, the *Chicago Tribune* reported that the "two-million-dollar drive had been called off."[112]

While she took on issues of inequality, Wells-Barnett, who had committed herself to mobilizing African Americans to organize for political change on their own behalf, found that many black women remained unsure of whether to continue to align themselves with previous organizations or break away and form new ones.[113] In 1927, likely in preparation for the 1928 elections, she founded the Third Ward Women's Political Club.[114] Her vision, unique among all previous political clubs, was not just to educate and encourage black women to vote, but to train African American women to run for office themselves.[115] In her address at the club's founding, Wells-Barnett spoke about enacting change through "women uniting politically and supporting women for office."[116] Unfortunately for Wells-Barnett, Prohibition gangsters controlled most of Chicago's politics, and used their considerable money and influence to run their own candidates.

Black Republicans, buoyed by the increased population of African Americans brought north by massive migrations, dominated the vote in the Second and Third Wards of Chicago. This block of voters, including Wells-Barnett's Alpha Suffrage Club, had earlier supported William Hale Thompson in his winning bid for mayor, a position he held until 1923. Wells-Barnett lost much of her respect for him in the wake of the Chicago Riot of 1919, after he ignored her attempts to meet with him and de-escalate racial tensions. In 1927, Thompson was again in the race for mayor, supported by his primary campaign contributor, the infamous Al Capone, one of the leaders of organized crime in Chicago. Capone made millions bootlegging alcohol, illegal in the United States after the passage of the Twenty-first Amendment in 1920.[117] The mobster donated at least a hundred thousand dollars, and likely upward of a quarter of a million dollars to support Thompson's mayoral race.[118] During the campaign, at least twenty-five thousand mob members served in more than thirteen hundred Chicago organizations, and the involvement of gangs, each supporting their own candidate in return for a blind eye turned to their activities, resulted in violence permeating the political scene.[119] Opponents of Thompson arranged for authorities to storm the Second Ward on Election Day and arrest more than a thousand people to prevent them from voting. The assassination of three candidates for office from the Second Ward, two black and one white, the bombings of the homes of Thompson's advisors, and the shooting of two of Senator Charles Deneen's staff, all likely committed by gangsters, further ensured that political control remained in certain hands.[120] A win by Thompson, many believed, would give his mobster supporters "free reign to plunder the city."[121]

Wells-Barnett viewed the corrupt politicians, the gambling, and the illegal drinking in the Second Ward as preventing social progress. She noted how "vice lords" affected the future of many African Americans and that locals needed a "crusade" against this type of exploitation.[122] Once again favoring a direct approach, Wells-Barnett nominated herself as a candidate to attend the 1928 Republican National Convention.[123] Voters would choose two delegates from the five on the ballot. Wells-Barnett, the only woman to run, declared herself an independent. She ran against Oscar De Priest, removed from his City Council seat years earlier due to his connections to gambling and organized crime, and Daniel Jackson, who also had mob connections.[124]

Wells-Barnett, unable to beat either of these well-connected and well-funded candidates, shifted her focus from representing the Republican Party at the national level to increasing her efforts at the local level. In 1928, she became a National Organizer for the Colored Women of Illinois and traveled all over the state to campaign for Hoover on behalf of the Illinois

Republican National Committee. She sent out mass mailings, organized rallies, and gave speeches drawing as many as a thousand people. She wrote her own pamphlet, "Why I Am for Hoover," and credited her efforts with raising the number of Illinois black women registered to vote by "nearly 50 percent."[125] It seemed that she quickly ran into trouble with the higher-ups in the organization, for despite her success in garnering pledges to vote for Hoover, her name did not appear on the organization's list of "outstanding women." The leadership refused to reimburse her for her expenses, including printing copies of her speech and pledge cards. Records from private meetings suggested that they viewed Wells-Barnett and her tactics with distain, with one organizer dismissively saying, "You know how Mrs. Barnett would act."[126] The leaders also chose not to forward a letter that Wells-Barnett wrote to Hoover, noting, "Thank heaven he may never see it."[127] These responses insinuated that while she remained useful to the organization's leadership, perhaps her reputation of being outspoken had preceded her, or that the upper levels of administration found her grassroots approaches undiplomatic. Although Wells-Barnett's efforts on his behalf paid off when Hoover won the presidential election, he disappointed her early on in his term when he refused to push the South to end segregation or confront the nationwide issue of racial inequality.[128]

Although Wells-Barnett's recent work kept her name in circulation in regional efforts, she remained out of the national spotlight and continued to be passed over for recognition. She did not make white journalist Ida Tarbell's annual list of the "most prominent women in America," although Tarbell included fellow black female leader Mary McLeod Bethune. A memorial plaque for Susan B. Anthony included Mary Church Terrell, but no other black women.[129] Wells-Barnett felt her own exclusions during a 1927 conversation. She recalled:

> A young woman recently asked me to tell her of my connection with the lynching agitation which was started in 1892. She said she was at a YWCA vesper service when the subject for discussion was Joan of Arc, and each person was asked to tell of someone they knew who had traits of character resembling this French heroine and martyr. She was the only colored girl present, and not wishing to lag behind the others, she named me. She was then asked to tell why she thought I deserved such mention. She said, "Mrs. Barnett, I couldn't tell why I thought so. I have heard you mentioned so often by that name, so I gave it. I was dreadfully embarrassed. Won't you please tell me what it was you did, so the next time I am asked such a question I can give an intelligent answer?"

Wells-Barnett resignedly noted that at twenty-five years old, "the happenings about which she inquired took place before she was born" and "there was no record" for her generation to learn about "how the agitation against the lynching evil began." Now removed from the NAACP and NACW, these exclusions resulted in the minimization of her accomplishments as those in power reframed the movement for social progress on their own terms. As a result of this realization, Wells-Barnett decided "for the first time in my life" to write about herself and in 1928 began work on her autobiography.[130]

The 1929 stock market crash hurt the national and local economy, and the Barnetts' financial status mirrored that of the country at large. Wells-Barnett did not currently work for a salary and the family could no longer afford domestic help. In 1929, with only Ida Jr. living at home, Wells-Barnett and her husband sold their large house on Grand Boulevard and moved to a smaller apartment.[131] Their economic circumstances suffered further when Wells-Barnett announced her intention to run for a seat in the Illinois State Senate, believing that black women voters possessed enough political power to elect an African American woman after seeing that voters sent Ruth Hanna McCormick to Washington, D.C.

A white woman, Ruth married Joseph Medill McCormick, who served as an Illinois state representative and one-term senator. He lost his bid for re-nomination in 1924, and during his last week in the Senate died from a pill overdose, which authorities ruled a suicide.[132] In 1927, his widow Ruth challenged six Republican candidates to win a seat in the United States House of Representatives. In 1930, she announced her plan to run for Senate, the first serious attempt by a woman to do so. She ran as an outsider, someone not influenced by the machinations of Chicago politics, a policy reflected in her slogan, "No favors and no bunk." Voters found her a refreshing change from the corruption of politics and she won the primary against incumbent Charles Deneen, who had previously defeated her husband.[133] As a white woman, McCormick brought Mary Church Terrell, who she had met during her husband's time in Washington, D.C., to Illinois in order to organize African American women on her behalf. This decision angered many black clubwomen who disliked McCormick for selecting an outsider, and among the dissenters was Wells-Barnett, who expressed disappointment in McCormick's choice. Mary Church Terrell's autobiography recalled that the black Chicago women threatened not to vote for McCormick unless Terrell's role changed.[134] In response to this discontent, McCormick shifted Terrell's focus to outside of Chicago.[135] Despite her landslide win against Deneen in the Republican primary, McCormick lost the Senate seat to Democrat J. Hamilton Lewis in the fall of 1930.

McCormick's announcement of her political run and the 1929 election of Oscar De Priest, the first African American in Congress in the twentieth century, inspired several black women to enter the race for the state legislature. In June of 1929, the Third Ward Women's Political Club announced that they would offer a "Race woman candidate" and ultimately endorsed

Mary C. Clark. Soon another African American woman joined the race, lawyer Georgia Jones-Ellis.[136] For several months, the two women canvassed for votes against two black male candidates, lawyer Warren B. Douglas and incumbent Adelbert H. Roberts, who in 1925 had become the first black man elected to the state legislature.[137] In January, with an April primary looming, Wells-Barnett announced that she would also run for the seat, but failed to complete her paperwork until February, leaving only a month for her to actively campaign. This left the African American women of the South Side of Chicago with three black women candidates, a dilemma that could easily result in a split vote and none of the women succeeding. Wells-Barnett's campaign, her efforts hampered by a lack of funds, consisted of a paid announcement in the paper and some flyers. None of the political candidates she supported in the past advocated on her behalf, leaving Wells-Barnett to conclude that they remained "stubborn about helping women," but more likely this resulted from her timing, since most local groups and political parties endorsed candidates early.[138]

Why Wells-Barnett chose to run is unclear. She believed that African American women should be in politics, and likely felt that the possibility for success existed in light of white women's and black men's recent achievements. Yet her decision to run against two other black women candidates at the last minute seems incompatible with her desire for black female representation.[139] Even more confusing is the financial strain that her campaign placed on the family's resources. During 1930, Wells-Barnett kept a brief accounting of expenses, which revealed her fear that she would be unable to afford a winter coat for Ida Jr.[140] In the primary election, Wells-Barnett received only 752 votes of the more than ten thousand cast. The two men garnered the highest votes, with Roberts edging out Douglas by 787 votes, more than anyone cast for Wells-Barnett.[141] Voters would not elect any woman to the State Senate for another twenty years.[142]

Wells-Barnett appeared to take the defeat in her stride. Although she complained about her lack of support, she felt that the campaign offered lessons about black women and politics.[143] The necessity for African American women to engage in politics, run for office, and use this influence to enact social change became evident shortly after Wells-Barnett's loss. On May 24, 1930, the *Chicago Defender* published a commentary titled, "Are Our Women as Bad as This?" and, for Wells-Barnett, the article must have seemed a reprint from decades earlier, as the author argued that "Nigger women" were sexually "easy" and that "no such animal" as a "respectable Colored woman" existed.[144] Although the paper printed several rebuttals against the piece in subsequent weeks, its appearance suggested that the negative racial stereotypes of black women remained culturally prevalent. This type of article, similar to many published at the height of lynchings in the 1890s, may have been a response to the recent increase in southern racial violence.

During the 1920s, the number of lynchings declined from fifty-nine in 1921 to ten in 1929.[145] Although the Dyer Bill failed to pass and become law, the debate over its necessity elevated lynching to a national issue and several states instituted penalties. The economic hardship of the Great Depression reversed the downward trend, and the number of lynchings rose again in 1929 and 1930, prompting another wave of anti-lynching activism, this time led by southern white women. The Association of Southern Women for the Prevention of Lynching (ASWPL), founded by Jessie Daniel Ames, supported Wells-Barnett's assertions from the 1890s about the motives behind lynchings. The ASWPL argued that the rhetoric of black men's desire to rape white women was a thinly veiled justification for white men to maintain sexual control over women.[146] This wave of protest against lynchings, after decades of effort, would be the last. During the 1930s, lynchings would decrease before declining significantly in the 1940s.[147] A new generation's cultural attitudes, combined with the labor shifts resulting from the Great Migration, as well as the after-effects of the Great Depression, gradually changed southern society.

After her loss in the State Senate primary election in 1930, Wells-Barnett became involved in efforts to block John J. Parker's congressional confirmation for appointment to the United States Supreme Court. Parker, a white judge from North Carolina, openly expressed the desire to prevent African Americans from gaining political power, indicating in speeches how "the negro in politics is a source of evil and danger for both races."[148] While the NAACP protested against Parker, Wells-Barnett helped organize the Illinois Women's Republican Club against the nomination, and the combined pressure, quantified by the thousands of petitions and telegrams, resulted in the rejection of Parker's nomination. Wells-Barnett, who regretted her earlier support of Hoover, wrote of her pleasure in teaching him "a lesson" by agitating against his nominee, and her pride in demonstrating the growing influence of African Americans in politics.[149]

On the local level, Wells-Barnett became involved in another case involving the treatment of African Americans by authorities. In early 1930, the police arrested a fifteen-year-old African American girl, Frances Jordan, based on the testimony of a gardener who claimed to have witnessed Jordan strike a school official. Jordon, a minor, once in custody suffered violent threats from the police, including assurances that they would shoot her. Locked up for two days and not allowed contact with her family or a lawyer, authorities also forced Jordon to undergo an examination for venereal disease, which likely included a pelvic exam. Adding further insult, the government billed her three dollars to cover the cost of the invasive screening. Wells-Barnett and her husband, once they learned of Jordan's treatment, publicized her experiences in the *Chicago Defender*. Wells-Barnett feared that if a public outcry did not materialize, the Juvenile Court might sentence

Jordan to the State Training School for Girls. Despite its official name, most locals referred to the government-run institution by its location, the town of Geneva. A segregated facility, Geneva represented the increased involvement in social welfare representative of post-Progressive Era United States, with social workers, doctors, and psychiatrists on staff to support those labeled as "hysterical," "Lesbian," "feebleminded," or delinquent.[150] Based on the percentages of the population, African American girls were overrepresented and the court sent nearly all of them to the facility for "immoral" reasons.[151] The police forcing Jordan to undergo a venereal disease test prior to her court appearance suggests that local authorities had already determined that she fell into this category. During Jordan's court case, Wells-Barnett and her clubwomen publicized the conditions of the Geneva, even meeting with the Governor about the situation at the State Training School for Girls.[152] Wells-Barnett's investigation revealed that white patients received special privileges and confirmed that African American girls performed "servant's work."[153] Other accounts suggested that white workers often employed aggressive tactics against the girls, overwhelmingly using force against African American youths, but not whites.[154] In addition, overcrowding led to worsening conditions. Wells-Barnett noted how one hundred and four girls were living in the space intended for thirty-two.[155]

Throughout her inquiry into the condition of Geneva, Wells-Barnett remained active in Chicago, presiding over the Ida B. Wells Club, chairing several events, and continuing to write her autobiography.[156] In March 1931, a sixty-eight year-old Wells-Barnett returned home from a shopping trip feeling poorly. She took to her bed for the remainder of the day, and when Ferdinand stopped to kiss her goodbye the next morning, he noticed her fevered forehead. After becoming incoherent, Wells-Barnett was admitted to the hospital and slipped into a coma.[157] Three days later, on March 25, without regaining consciousness, she died of uremic poisoning due to kidney failure. Her passing stunned Ferdinand who lived five more years without her, before his death in 1936.[158] At her funeral, the church overflowed and many waited outside, "shivering in the biting March wind" to pass by her coffin.[159]

The *Chicago Defender* reported on the "simple dignity and a solemnity" of her funeral as befitting the "passing of a great woman."[160] Without "fanfare or trumpets," people grieved her with "earnest, sincere words."[161] Her minister spoke of her "untiring" and "almost hopeless war against civil oppression." Her old ally turned rival W. E. B. Du Bois eulogized her in *The Crisis*, crediting her for pioneering an anti-lynching crusade that woke "the conscience of the nation." Yet this brief recognition of her influence was all Du Bois cared to muster, as even in her obituary he could not resist claiming how after her initial efforts, anti-lynching reforms were "taken up on a much larger scale by the NAACP and carried to greater success." Black clubwomen offered the most accurate interpretation of her life. Clubwoman and activist Irene McCoy Gaines recalled, "It was her special mission to interpret and express the wrongs and sufferings of an oppressed race."[162] Another Chicago clubwoman wrote to NACW president Sallie Stewart that despite Wells-Barnett's strained relationship with the organization, her death meant that a "strong forceful woman has gone." In response, NACW's *National Notes* printed perhaps the most accurate eulogy of her life, recalling, "She was often criticized, misjudged and misunderstood because she fought for justice and civil righteousness," yet she always had the "vision to see the RIGHT." [163]

NOTES

1   Keith L. Nelson, "The 'Black Horror on the Rhine': Race as a Factor in Post-World War I Diplomacy," *The Journal of Modern History* 42, no. 4 (1970): 610; Alan Sharp, *The Versailles Settlement: Peacemaking after the First World War, 1919–1923*, second edition (New York: Palgrave Macmillan, 2008), 141.

2   Giddings, *Ida: A Sword among Lions*, 586.

3   Writing about the decision in her autobiography, Wells-Barnett simply stated that she declined the offer, saying that her years in "fighting the race's battles" had made her "financially unable" to make the trip. Giddings, *Ida: A Sword among Lions*, 587.

4   McMurry, 322.

5   Wells, *Crusade for Justice*, 381.

6   Giddings, *Ida: A Sword among Lions*, 590.

7   Mark Ellis, *Race, War, and Surveillance: African Americans and the United States Government during World War I* (Bloomington: Indiana University Press, 2001), 193.

8   Giddings, *Ida: A Sword among Lions*, 587.

9   E. David Cronon, *Black Moses: The Story of Marcus Garvey and the Universal Negro Improvement Association* (Madison: University of Wisconsin Press, 1969), 52.

10 Jonathan P. Eburne, "Garveyism and Its Involutions," *African American Review* 47, no. 1 (2004): 14–15.

11 Wells, *Crusade for Justice*, 381–82.

12 Wells, *Crusade for Justice*, 380–81.

13 George C. Rable, "The South and the Politics of Antilynching Legislation, 1920–1940," *The Journal of Southern History* 51, no. 2 (1985): 208.

14 Another example is that of Charles Kelly, a black veteran of World War I. Driving his father, the Reverend Ranse Kelly, to church one Sunday in 1919, he met another car in the road, driven by a white youth. Apparently, Kelly "did not turn out of the road soon enough to suit the boy so he went home and got his father, two brothers and sister." They found Kelly and at that point "the father of the white boy, Hugh Sams, drew his gun and asked Kelly why he did not turn out of the road. Kelly tried to run, whereupon he was shot in the back and killed." As a former soldier, Kelly offered an inviting target. NAACP Collection, Group I, Series C, Box 354, Subject File: Lynching, Fayette Georgia, 1919.

15 Rable, 203.

16 William Edward Burghardt Du Bois, "Returning Soldiers," *The Crisis: A Record of the Darker Races*, 18, no. 1 (1919): 13–14.

17 McMurry, 325.

18 Giddings, *Ida: A Sword among Lions*, 595.

19 Giddings, *Ida: A Sword among Lions*, 594.
20 Giddings, *Ida: A Sword among Lions*, 595.
21 Bay, *To Tell the Truth Freely*, 305.
22 Giddings, *Ida: A Sword among Lions*, 596; Bay, *To Tell the Truth Freely*, 305.
23 Giddings, Ida: *A Sword among Lions*, 596.
24 McMurry, 326.
25 Wells, *Crusade for Justice*, 405–6.
26 Giddings, *Ida: A Sword among Lions*, 597.
27 Bay, *To Tell the Truth Freely*, 305–6.
28 Schechter, *Ida B. Wells-Barnett and American Reform*, 155.
29 Giddings, *Ida: A Sword among Lions*, 598.
30 Giddings, *Ida: A Sword among Lions*, 598.
31 Giddings, *Ida: A Sword among Lions*, 598.
32 Wells, *Crusade for Justice*, 407–8.
33 Wells, *Crusade for Justice*, 407–8.
34 Giddings, *Ida: A Sword among Lions*, 602.
35 Walter White, *Rope & Faggot: A Biography of Judge Lynch* (Notre Dame: University of Notre Dame Press, 2002), 3.
36 Bay, *To Tell the Truth Freely*, 306; Giddings, *Ida: A Sword among Lions*, 602.
37 Kenneth Robert Janken, *White: The Biography of Walter White, Mr. NAACP* (New York: The New Press, 2003), xv.
38 Wells, *Crusade for Justice*, 408.
39 Touré F. Reed, *Not Alms but Opportunity: The Urban League & the Politics of Racial Uplift, 1910-1950* (Chapel Hill: University of North Carolina Press, 2008), 11–12.
40 Wells-Barnett's dislike of the organization began earlier when the organizer met with her about the new group and made her feel belittled. Wells, *Crusade for Justice*, 372–73.
41 Reed, 70.
42 Giddings, *Ida: A Sword among Lions*, 618.
43 McMurry, 329.
44 Wells, *Crusade for Justice*, 356.
45 McMurry, 328.
46 Wells, *Crusade for Justice*, 357–58.
47 Giddings, *Ida: A Sword among Lions*, 620.
48 Wells, *Crusade for Justice*, 333.
49 Giddings, *Ida: A Sword among Lions*, 605; Bay, *To Tell the Truth Freely*, 305–6.
50 Bay, *To Tell the Truth Freely*, 308.
51 Wells, *Crusade for Justice*, 398–99.
52 Giddings, *Ida: A Sword among Lions*, 605.
53 Giddings, *Ida: A Sword among Lions*, 606.
54 Wells, *Crusade for Justice*, 398–99.
55 Mark H. Haller, "Policy Gambling, Entertainment, and the Emergence of Black Politics: Chicago from 1900 to 1940," *Journal of Social History* 24, no. 4 (1991): 724.
56 Anne Meis Knupfer, "*Toward a Tenderer Humanity and a Nobler Womanhood:" African-American Women's Clubs in Chicago, 1890 to 1920* (New York: New York University Press, 1996), 54.
57 Wells, *Crusade for Justice*, 400–1.
58 Wells, *Crusade for Justice*, 402.
59 Wells, *Crusade for Justice*, 402–3.
60 Giddings, *Ida: A Sword among Lions*, 611.
61 Giddings, *Ida: A Sword among Lions*, 612.
62 Bay, *To Tell the Truth Freely*, 307–8.
63 Giddings, *Ida: A Sword among Lions*, 612.
64 Giddings, *Ida: A Sword among Lions*, 609.

65 Moore et al. v. Dempsey, Keeper of Arkansas State Penitentiary. (1923) 261 U.S. 86; John S. Waterman and Edward E. Overton, "The Aftermath of Moore v. Dempsey," *Washington University Law Review* 18, no. 2 (1993): 117–26; William B. Hixson Jr., *Moorfield Storey and the Abolitionist Tradition* (New York: Oxford University Press, 1972), chapter three; White Walter, *A Man Called White: The Autobiography of Walter White* (Bloomington: Indiana University Press, 1948), 52–53.

66 Mark V. Tushnet, *The NAACP's Legal Strategy against Segregated Education, 1925–1950* (Chapel Hill: University of North Carolina Press, 2005), 1.

67 Wells, *Crusade for Justice*, 404.

68 Giddings, *Ida: A Sword among Lions*, 616.

69 Giddings, *Ida: A Sword among Lions*, 620.

70 McMurry, 329.

71 Wells, *Crusade for Justice*, 414.

72 Duster, ed., *Crusade for Justice*, xxvii.

73 Wells, *Crusade for Justice*, 414.

74 Giddings, *Ida: A Sword among Lions*, 621.

75 Giddings, *Ida: A Sword among Lions*, 622.

76 Rable, 203.

77 Claudine L. Ferrell, *Nightmare and Dream: Antilynching in Congress, 1917–1922* (New York: Garland Publishing, Inc., 1986), 306.

78 Giddings, *Ida: A Sword among Lions*, 626.

79 Giddings, *Ida: A Sword among Lions*, 628.

80 Elsa Barkley Brown, "Negotiating and Transforming the Public Sphere: African American Political Life in the Transition from Slavery to Freedom." *Public Culture* 7 (1994): 139.

81 Joy Weatherley Williams, "John Mitchell, Jr., and the Richmond Planet," *The Library of Virginia*, n.d., http://www.lva.virginia.gov/exhibits/mitchell/ajax.htm (accessed March 21, 2016) and "Lynch Law Must Go!" http://www.lva.virginia.gov/exhibits/mitchell/lynch1.htm.

82 See Susan Chandler, "Addie Hunton and the Construction of an African American Female Peace Perspective," *Affilia* 20 (Fall 2005): 270–83.

83 Giddings, *Ida: A Sword among Lions*, 628.

84 Joyce Ann Hanson, *Mary McLeod Bethune and Black Women's Political Activism* (Columbia: University of Missouri Press, 2003), 105–6.

85 Giddings, *Ida: A Sword among Lions*, 632.

86 Bay, *To Tell the Truth Freely*, 319.

87 Giddings, *Ida: A Sword among Lions*, 632.

88 Giddings, *Ida: A Sword among Lions*, 632.

89 Schechter, *Ida B. Wells-Barnett and American Reform*, 232.

90 Hanson, 105.

91 Duster, ed., *Crusade for Justice*, xxix.

92 Catherine E. Rymph, *Republican Women: Feminism and Conservatism from Suffrage through the Rise of the New Right* (Chapel Hill: University of North Carolina Press, 2006), 52–53.

93 Rymph, 55.

94 Schechter, *Ida B. Wells-Barnett and American Reform*, 315.

95 Beth Tompkins Bates, *Pullman Porters and the Rise of Protest Politics in Black America, 1925–1945* (Chapel Hill: University of North Carolina Press, 2001), 18.

96 Giddings, *Ida: A Sword among Lions*, 635.

97 David Pilgrim, "The Tom Caricature," *Ferris State University Jim Crow Museum of Racist Memorabilia*, December 2012, http://www.ferris.edu/news/jimcrow/tom/ (accessed March 21, 2016).

98 Larry Tye, *Rising from the Rails: Pullman Porters and the Making of the Black Middle Class* (New York: Henry Holt & Company, Inc., 2004), 3.

99 Giddings, *Ida: A Sword among Lions*, 635.

100 Giddings, *Ida: A Sword among Lions*, 635–36.
101 Bates, *Pullman Porters and the Rise of Protest Politics in Black America*, 66.
102 Bates, *Pullman Porters and the Rise of Protest Politics in Black America*, 72.
103 Beth Tompkins Bates, "A New Crowd Challenges the Agenda of the Old Guard in the NAACP, 1933–1941," *The American Historical Review* 102, no. 2 (1997): 347.
104 Deborah Grey White, *Too Heavy a Load: Black Women in Defense of Themselves, 1894–1994* (New York: W. W. Norton & Company, 1999), 73.
105 Giddings, *Ida: A Sword among Lions*, 641.
106 Robyn Spencer, "Contested Terrain: The Mississippi Flood of 1927 and the Struggle to Control Black Labor," *The Journal of Negro History* 79, no. 2 (1994): 170–71.
107 Spencer, 173.
108 Giddings, *Ida: A Sword among Lions*, 642–43.
109 Schechter, *Ida B. Wells-Barnett and American Reform*, 237.
110 Schechter, *Ida B. Wells-Barnett and American Reform*, 238.
111 Wells, *Crusade for Justice*, 415–16.
112 Wells, *Crusade for Justice*, 417–18.
113 Giddings, *Ida: A Sword among Lions*, 645.
114 Giddings, *Ida: A Sword among Lions*, 644.
115 Giddings, *Ida: A Sword among Lions*, 644.
116 Schechter, *Ida B. Wells-Barnett and American Reform*, 239.
117 Mark H. Haller, "Policy Gambling, Entertainment, and the Emergence of Black Politics: Chicago from 1900 to 1940," *Journal of Social History* 24, no. 4 (1991): 720–21.
118 Giddings, *Ida: A Sword among Lions*, 644.
119 Gus Russo, *The Outfit: The Role of Chicago's Underworld in the Shaping of Modern America* (New York: Bloomsbury Press, 2002), 12.
120 Giddings, *Ida: A Sword among Lions*, 647.
121 Russo, 19.
122 Giddings, *Ida: A Sword among Lions*, 648.
123 Bay, *To Tell the Truth Freely*, 322.
124 Haller, 725.
125 Schechter, *Ida B. Wells-Barnett and American Reform*, 239.
126 McMurry, 334–35.
127 Schechter, *Ida B. Wells-Barnett and American Reform*, 239.
128 Bay, *To Tell the Truth Freely*, 322–23.
129 Schechter, *Ida B. Wells-Barnett and American Reform*, 237.
130 Wells, *Crusade for Justice*, 3–4.
131 Duster, ed., *Crusade for Justice*, xxx.
132 Kristie Miller, "Ruth Hanna McCormick and the Senatorial Election of 1930," *Illinois Historical Journal* 81, no. 3 (1988): 193–94.
133 Miller, 195.
134 Schechter, *Ida B. Wells-Barnett and American Reform*, 241.
135 Giddings, *Ida: A Sword among Lions*, 652.
136 Schechter, *Ida B. Wells-Barnett and American Reform*, 242.
137 Erma Brooks Williams, *Political Empowerment of Illinois' African-American State Lawmakers from 1877 to 2005* (Lanham: University Press of America, 2008), 7, 8.
138 Schechter, *Ida B. Wells-Barnett and American Reform*, 243.
139 She did consider withdrawing after learning that her son Herman stole money to pay for his gambling debts, but determined that it was "too late to withdraw." Giddings, *Ida: A Sword among Lions*, 653–54.
140 The campaign expenses took any extra money the family had. She carefully notes the five dollars spent to print petitions for her name to appear on the ballot and the seventy-five dollars to print campaign materials. Bay, *To Tell the Truth Freely*, 324.

141 Giddings, *Ida: A Sword among Lions*, 654.
142 Schechter, *Ida B. Wells-Barnett and American Reform*, 240.
143 Giddings, *Ida: A Sword among Lions*, 654.
144 Schechter, *Ida B. Wells-Barnett and American Reform*, 244.
145 Phillip Dray, *At the Hands of Persons Unknown: The Lynching of Black America* (New York: Random House, 2002), 254, 336.
146 See Jacquelyn Dowd Hall, *Revolt against Chivalry: Jessie Daniel Ames and the Women's Campaign against Lynching* (New York: Columbia University Press, 1993), xxi. The rhetoric about the fear of rape, Ames argued, "regulated white women's behavior" and rested upon the idea of white male protection. This chivalrous code dictated the relationships between white men and women and African Americans.
147 Brundage, *Lynching in the New South*, 209, 252.
148 Bay, *To Tell the Truth Freely*, 325.
149 Giddings, *Ida: A Sword among Lions*, 655.
150 Anne Meis Knupfer, " 'To Become Good, Self-Supporting Women': The State Industrial School for Delinquent Girls at Geneva, Illinois, 1900–1935," *Journal of the History of Sexuality* 9, no. 4 (2000): 421.
151 Knupfer, 422.
152 Schechter, *Ida B. Wells-Barnett and American Reform*, 314.
153 Schechter, *Ida B. Wells-Barnett and American Reform*, 228.
154 Knupfer, 436.
155 Schechter, *Ida B. Wells-Barnett and American Reform*, 228.
156 Giddings, *Ida: A Sword among Lions*, 655.
157 Giddings, *Ida: A Sword among Lions*, 657.
158 Bay, *To Tell the Truth Freely*, 325; Schechter, *Ida B. Wells-Barnett and American Reform*, 248.
159 McMurry, 336.
160 McMurry, 336.
161 Schechter, *Ida B. Wells-Barnett and American Reform*, 249.
162 McMurry, 337.
163 Giddings, *Ida: A Sword among Lions*, 658; emphasis in original.

CONCLUSION
AN ELUSIVE LEGACY

When Ida B. Wells-Barnett began penning her autobiography in 1928, she became the first black female political activist to write a full-length account of their life.[1] After her encounter with the young black woman who was only vaguely aware of her accomplishments, Wells-Barnett recognized that most African Americans lacked any knowledge "of authentic race history" and hoped that the story of her life would teach new generations about the struggles of the past. Unfortunately, her autobiography, *Crusade for Justice*, remained unfinished at the time of her death. Unpublished for decades, Wells-Barnett's goal to change the dominant narrative of history to include African Americans' struggles against the retrenchment of white supremacy not only remained unfulfilled, but this racial narrative suffered further setbacks when southern states began systematically rewriting the South's past.[2]

The 1915 film *Birth of a Nation*, D. W. Griffith's adaptation of Thomas Dixon's novel *The Clansman*, became the first box office blockbuster. Watched by more than fifty million people in theaters, the production earned the equivalent of 1.8 billion dollars.[3] Although based on a fictional account, the film depicted its events as historical truth, portraying Reconstruction as a time when white southerners endured "Negro Rule," by "vicious" and "obscene" African Americans.[4] One of the film's plotlines centers on a savage black man's attempt to rape a young white woman, with the Ku Klux Klan riding in to rescue her from certain assault. The film closed with images of the Ku Klux Klan as the triumphant "liberators" of whites from black rule, responsible for restoring white supremacy to the South.[5] This powerful imagery of the South, "reborn from the ride of the white-robed Knights of Christ" who freed the white race from African Americans, influenced audiences across the nation.[6]

As whites accepted the story of *Birth of a Nation* as a true historical account, newly written textbooks adopted a similar narrative, further crediting this portrayal. Charles A. and Mary R. Beard's 1921 text, *History of the United States*, noted,

> Slavery was no crime; it was an actual benefit to the slaves. The beneficial effects of slavery were proved, they [the slave owners] said, by the fact that the slaves were happier, more comfortable, and more intelligent than their ancestors in Africa, and it was believed that they were better off in bondage than they would be if they were free.[7]

Schoolbooks across the nation described Reconstruction as a time when African Americans, inferior and incapable of caring for themselves, nearly brought society to ruin. The Dunning School, a group of white historians publishing on Reconstruction, named for the Columbia University Professor William Archibald Dunning, validated these textbook interpretations. This group of scholars, some of the first professional historians, "rewrote the history" of the Civil War and Reconstruction, and the public accepted this narrative, as it reflected the ideology about African Americans spread in the press during the past decades.[8] As historian Francis B. Simkins noted, "Sometimes Southern historians forget that what is often important to Southerners is not what actually happened but what is believed to have happened."[9]

Depictions such as those in *Birth of a Nation*, textbooks, and historical publications created the all-encompassing narrative that Wells-Barnett sought to counter with her autobiography. Her version of history focused on the "storm and stress" within the South after the Civil War and the attempts to subjugate African Americans by the "Ku Klux Klan, ballot-box stuffing," and the "wholesale murders of Negroes who tried to exercise their new-found rights as free men and citizens." In doing so, Wells sought to give her readers an "authentic" story of her race, demonstrating their agency and efforts to keep their political and social freedoms, including her own varied successes in fighting for racial justice.[10] Yet, her version of events failed to have the impact she desired as it remained unpublished until 1970, when her daughter released *Crusade for Justice: The Autobiography of Ida B. Wells*.

For nearly her entire life, Wells-Barnett used her pen to agitate for change and continued to do so in the telling of her own history.[11] Autobiographies are complex acts of self-creation and essentially a self-reconstructing process, as people often reshape conversations and events.[12] Wells-Barnett's autobiography is no exception and readers must consider the work critically, yet the constructed nature of her manuscript allows scholars to understand how she viewed herself and her own accomplishments. The first third of her autobiography examines her childhood, moving into a discussion of her anti-lynching campaign, trips to England, and work in the early clubwomen movement. The last third focuses on her work in Illinois, an introspective attempt to garner meaning from her successes and failures.[13] Despite telling her personal story, Wells-Barnett's autobiography lacks emotional depth. She shared her frustrations, yet the reader learns little about her feelings beyond her activism. Her marriage, for example, remains largely unexplored. She drops this major life event into the narrative without any prior discussion of a courtship, nor is it accompanied by any discussion of love, passion, or joy. She simply informs the reader of her nuptials, noting, "On June 27 1895 I was married in the city of Chicago to Attorney F. L. Barnett."[14] Indeed, without her Memphis diary, scholars would have little insight into the turmoil that Wells faced while struggling with societal expectations as a southern young black woman. Instead, she chose to separate much of her adult personal life from her efforts at reform, leaving scholars with little insight into anything outside the scope of her public work.

As Wells-Barnett wrote her autobiography, her impact and successes had already been minimized. After the NAACP leadership of Ovington and Du Bois wrote the history of the anti-lynching movement omitting Wells, many other reformers continued the practice of writing her out of the historical narrative. Wells-Barnett noted in the daybook she sporadically kept during the last year of her life, that she read the new book from Carter G. Woodson for the January 13, 1930 "meeting of the local Negro History club." Known as the father of black history, Woodson's history of her race contained "no mention of anti-lynching contribution."[15] Others followed Woodson's example. Walter White did not mention her in his book on lynching, *Rope & Faggot: A Biography of Judge Lynch* (1928).[16] Neither did Arthur Raper in his 1933 examination of racial violence, *The Tragedy of Lynching*.[17] In contrast, her peers, including W. E. B. Du Bois, Booker T. Washington, James Addams, and Mary Church Terrell, received detailed mentions in most treatises on social reform.

For decades, Wells's work remained on the periphery of historical knowledge, despite her press coverage nearly rivaling Frederick Douglass's during the 1890s.[18] In the past decades, historians have examined Wells's actions, ideologies, and words, but when scholars do recognize Wells, it is often only for her anti-lynching campaign. Her activism, however, needs to be understood as a continuous and lifelong effort. Her fight against lynching grew out of her legal battles to halt segregation and would springboard her into advocating for education, jobs, and legal equality. As one historian noted,

"Her destination sometimes changed" but what remained consistent for her entire life was "her desire to protect."[19]

In 1997, Jacqueline Jones Royster edited a short volume, *Southern Horrors and Other Writings: The Anti-Lynching Campaign of Ida B. Wells, 1892–1900*, intended to bring Wells's work into the college classroom. Primarily focusing on her anti-lynching efforts during the height of her popularity, Royster introduced a generation to *Southern Horrors, A Red Record*, and *Mob Rule in New Orleans*. Other scholars began exploring Wells-Barnett and her world, with Linda O. McMurry writing one of the first book-length treatments of Wells with her 1998 work, *To Keep the Waters Troubled: The Life of Ida B. Wells*, finding "very few events of any significance to African Americans happened" during Wells's lifetime "without the involvement of this remarkable woman."[20] Patricia A. Schechter in *Ida B. Wells-Barnett and American Reform, 1880–1930* (2001), sought to understand the ideology driving Wells-Barnett's activism in order to "understand more fully the history of women, racism, and reform in the United States." She does so by using a concept she terms "visionary pragmatism," defined as "a distinctive blend of religious and political commitments."[21] As Tommy J. Curry has demonstrated, the framework of "visionary pragmatism," is a "severe misinterpretation" of Wells's ideology, a result of imposing current-day ideas on the past.[22] Historian Mia Bay also found that Schechter's approach resulted in the oversimplification of complex social forces.[23] Although her religious beliefs shaped Wells-Barnett, who regularly attended church and found moral guidance in the Bible, these ideas appear only to support her innate understanding of social wrongs.

Five years later, in 2007, James West Davidson's *"They Say:" Ida B. Wells and the Reconstruction of Race*, focused on Wells's early experiences during Reconstruction in the South. Ending in 1892, before her anti-lynching crusade, Davidson concentrated on the effect that Wells's forceful removal from the train and her social life in Memphis had on her worldview. Although the study loses some impact by ending before her ideas matured or she provoked social change, it offers previously overlooked details into her early life and experiences. In 2009, Paula Giddings published a nearly eight-hundred-page book on Wells, the most extensive work to date devoted to her. In *Ida: A Sword among Lions, Ida B. Wells and the Campaign against Lynching*, Giddings contextualized Wells within the framework of the Progressive Era and compared her struggles with those of other members of the black middle class. Mia Bay's 2009 book *To Tell the Truth Freely: The Life of Ida B. Wells* focused on Wells's failure to maintain a national role as a reformer after 1909. Bay found that her gender rendered Wells an "unlikely successor to Douglass in an era when men predominated not just in politics, but in all organizations and movements."[24]

Wells was a driven, flawed, and dynamic individual. As a young woman on a train in 1883, she recognized that the color of her skin would affect every aspect of her life, and she chose to fight this discrimination in the legal system, in the press, in her city, in her country, and internationally. Her relationships and feuds with leaders of her time, including T. Thomas Fortune, Frederick Douglass, Booker T. Washington, and W. E. B. Du Bois demonstrate the complicated gender dynamics for women reformers during the late nineteenth and early twentieth centuries. At first, Wells needed men like Fortune and Douglass to support her right to be in the public sphere. With the professionalization of reform efforts, her position as a female lacking in education enabled elite reformers to push her aside. Undaunted, she regrouped and refocused on African American women gaining political power in order to enact social reforms.

Wells recognized with startling clarity the power dynamics of her world, which allowed her to attack injustice differently than white men, white women, or African American men. Unfortunately, not a well-behaved woman by the social dictates of her world, her personality made it easier for others to justify positioning her on the margins of history. As Mary Church Terrell noted, "Colored women know all too well if they make themselves conspicuous or objectionable...they are courting disaster and ruin," and every day Ida B. Wells risked misfortune.[25] Her conflicts with Frances Willard and Jane Addams demonstrated her frustration with white elite women, who could not seem to understand the realities that black women faced. Willard harbored her own prejudices and concerns about African Americans voting, while Addams, like many other white women, simply could not see all the institutional barriers in black women's paths. Her relationships with black women remained fraught as well, resulting in a tense relationship with other black female reformers and the organizations that they guided.

Wells wore many hats in her life, at times focusing on gender issues, at others race concerns, and others class problems, but she fought every day against injustice. Without any political power of her own for much of her life, Wells worked to restore the voting rights of black men. When granted suffrage, she sought to organize African American women. Nearly every one of Wells's efforts in Chicago sought to assist the poor, a rather unpopular idea during her lifetime. As someone who spent her early life in a constant financial struggle, Wells, unlike many others who believed in Social Darwinism, knew that class and morality were not connected. She felt that the poor deserved help, and grew frustrated when other organizations overlooked poverty-stricken urban African Americans. As a result, she worked for more than a decade to create a space to help black men in the Frederick Douglass Reading Room and later the Negro Fellowship League. In seeking to help the poorest of her people, she expanded the idea of racial uplift to apply to all blacks, not just financially stable ones. Her own economic status prevented her from enjoying both the leisure and the social capital of better-off black women such as Mary Church Terrell or white women like Mary Ovington, and while this made her more sympathetic to lower-class African Americans, it created an insurmountable gulf between Wells-Barnett and upper-class reformers.

These differences, along with her temperament, alienated those of her own world. By all accounts, she could be a difficult woman to work with; her worldview left little room for dissent and she publically voiced her concerns and criticisms. Yet to explain this oversight by claiming that her difficult personality prevented her from gaining the recognition she deserved during her lifetime, fails to consider the cultural realities and biases of her world. Her race, gender, and class played an enormous role in her detractors' ability to marginalize her. As a black, middle-class female, she lacked the social capital to create her own legacy.

In the past few years, our culture has sporadically celebrated Wells, such as when the United States Post Office commemorated her on a stamp for Black History Month in 1990 or when Chicagoans named a public housing project after her.[26] Yet more work must be done in order for her to gain a place in history.[27] Wells's life illuminates issues of race, gender, class, religion, politics, region, and reform, and her story is interwoven into the history of the United States as it confronted the challenges of a modern world. She, and those who fought alongside her, helped crack the foundations of white supremacy. The truths she exposed resonated with the Civil Rights Movement and reverberate in modern times as concerns about race, black masculinity, police authority, and legal equality continue to circulate. Without an understanding of the past, and knowledge of black reformers such as Wells, citizens lose sight of the long history of these inequalities. Undoubtedly, the best way to honor Ida B. Wells is to follow her example and interrogate the structures of our society; examine the racial, gender, class and other disparities that permeate our culture; and instead of accepting injustice, confront it. As she encouraged her audiences to do, remember: it is the duty of each generation to "turn the Light of Truth" on wrongs and attempt to right them.[28]

Notes

1 Giddings, "Missing in Action Ida B. Wells, the NAACP, and the Historical Record," 2.
2 In the early twentieth century, the emergence of industrialization and mass culture also offered white southerners a public space in which to reiterate their justifications for dominance over African Americans. Advertisement campaigns for many domestic products, including baking supplies, appliances, food, and cleaning supplies, such as Aunt Jemima, Cream of Wheat, Czar baking powder, and others, called on nostalgic southern images of "good darkies" to reinforce

the idealized racial roles of southern antebellum slavery while connecting blackness with racial inferiority. See M. M. Manring, *Slave in a Box: The Strange Career of Aunt Jemima* (Charlottesville: University Press of Virginia, 1998), and Marilyn Kern-Foxworth, *Aunt Jemima, Uncle Ben, and Rastus: Blacks in Advertising, Yesterday, Today, and Tomorrow* (Westport: Praeger, 1994).

3 Wyn Craig Wade, *The Fiery Cross: The Ku Klux Klan in America* (New York: Simon and Schuster, 2005), 120; Richard Corliss, "D.W. Griffith's The Birth of a Nation 100 Years Later: Still Great, Still Shameful," *Time*, 2015, http://time.com/3729807/d-w-griffiths-the-birth-of-a-nation-10/ (accessed March 21, 2016); Craig D'ooge, "'The Birth of a Nation' Symposium on Classic Film Discusses Inaccuracies and Virtues," *Library of Congress Information Bulletin*, June 27, 1994, http://www.loc.gov/loc/lcib/94/9413/nation.html (accessed March 21, 2016).

4 White southerner Katherine Du Pre Lumpkin recalled as a child seeing *Birth of a Nation* several times and that her fellow members of the audience "sighed and shivered, and now and then shouted or wept in their intensity" at the images of the noble southern men and women. Katharine Du Pre Lumpkin, *The Making of a Southerner* (Athens: University of Georgia Press, 1991), 200.

5 Wade, *The Fiery Cross*, 131–32.

6 Michael Rogin, "'The Sword Became a Flashing Vision:' D. W. Griffith's The Birth of a Nation," *Representations* 9, Winter (1985): 150. Indeed, by the early twentieth century as they faced increased immigration, many white northerners sympathized with southerners, understanding the desire to prevent non-whites from gaining political and economic power.

7 Lawrence D. Reddick, "Racial Attitudes in American History Textbooks of the South," *The Journal of Negro History* 19, no. 3 (1934): 231.

8 Glenda Gilmore, "Which Southerners? Which Southern Historians? A Century of Teaching Southern History at Yale," *The Yale Review*, January (2011): 60. See also John David Smith and J. Vincent Lowery, ed., *The Dunning School Historians, Race, and the Meaning of Reconstruction* (Lexington: University Press of Kentucky, 2013).

9 Francis B. Simkins, "Tolerating the South's Past," *Journal of Southern History* 21, no. 1 (1955): 14.

10 Wells, *Crusade for Justice*, 3–4.

11 James Edward Ford III, 192. See also James Olney, "Autobiographical Traditions Black and White," in *Located Lives: Place and Idea in Southern Autobiography*, ed. Bill J. Berry (Athens: University of Georgia Press, 1990).

12 James Olney explores how authors throughout time have used memory to create narratives in *Memory and Narrative: The Weave of Life Writing* (Chicago: University of Chicago Press, 2001). Paul John Eakin argues that the act of living affects one's identity, and that the self and the life story are symbiotic in their connection in *How Our Lives Become Stories: Making Selves* (New York: Cornell University Press, 2001). Linda Anderson uses feminist, psychoanalytic, and poststructuralist approaches to understand life stories in *Autobiography* (New York: Routledge, 2001). Sidonie Smith and Julia Watson examine the components of autobiographical texts, including memory, experience, and identity. In doing so, they argue that the author uses the autobiography as a means to establish their identity and find their voice. Sidonie Smith and Julia Watson, *Reading Autobiography: A Guide for Interpreting Life Narratives* (Minneapolis: University of Minnesota Press, 2002).

13 Schechter, *Ida B. Wells-Barnett and American Reform*, 10–11.

14 Wells, *Crusade for Justice*, 239.

15 Decosta-Willis, ed., *The Memphis Diary of Ida B. Wells*, 168.

16 Giddings, *Ida: A Sword among Lions*, 656.

17 Giddings, *Ida: A Sword among Lions*, 6–7.

18 McMurry, xiv.

19 McMurry, 338.

20 She also notes "When I began this study, I had no idea how much I would discover" and that an examination of Wells-Barnett's life could fill five volumes. McMurry, ix. McMurry offered

readers a well-researched examination of her entire life. She argues that as an activist Wells had to choose between her race and her gender. This approach is perhaps an oversimplification of the identities that Wells adopted at various times.

21 Schechter, *Ida B. Wells-Barnett and American Reform*, preface, 9.

22 Tommy J. Curry, "The Fortune of Wells: Ida B. Wells-Barnett's Use of T. Thomas Fortune's Philosophy of Social Agitation as a Prolegomenon to Militant Civil Rights Activism," *Transactions of the Charles S. Peirce Society* 48, no. 4 (2012): 460.

23 Mia Bay, "The Improbable Ida B. Wells," *Reviews in American History* 30, no. 3 (2002): 441.

24 Bay, *To Tell the Truth Freely*, 191–92.

25 Quoted in Patricia A. Schechter, " 'All the Intensity of My Nature': Ida B. Wells, Anger, and Politics," *Radical History Review* 70 (1998): 50.

26 In Chicago, an effort is underway to place a twenty-foot tall sculpture to commemorate her legacy. Ida B. Wells Commemorative Art Committee, "Ida B. Wells Monument," 2015, http://www.idabwellsmonument.org/ (accessed March 3, 2016).

27 *The Ida Initiative* is an online project working to create an online space for teaching and engaging with her work. University of Tennessee, School of Journalism & Electronic Media, "The Ida Initiative," *Ida B. & Beyond Conference*, September 16, 2013, https://theidainitiative.wordpress.com/ (accessed March 21, 2016).

28 "Miss Ida B. Wells, A Lecture," *Washington Bee*, October 22, 1892.

Documents

T. THOMAS FORTUNE ON "THE NEGRO AND THE NATION"

HEADNOTE:

Fortune, the most famous black journalist of his day, was an early mentor and defender of Wells. Born a slave, he identified the key issues affecting African Americans' progress in the South after Reconstruction, including the loss of the vote, unequal education, and racial violence, all areas where Wells would focus her efforts. In 1884, Fortune published this analysis of the loss of civil rights in the South, arguing that for the United States to progress as a whole, inequity must end.

EXCERPT:

The war of the Rebellion settled only one question: It forever settled the question of chattel slavery[3] in this country. It forever choked the life out of the infamy of the Constitutional right of one man to rob another, by purchase of his person, or of his honest share of the produce of his own labor. But this was the only question permanently and irrevocably settled. Nor was this *the* all-absorbing question involved. The right of a State to secede from the so-called *Union* remains where it was when the treasonable shot upon Fort Sumter aroused the people to all the horrors of internecine war. And the measure of protection which the National government owes the individual members of States, a right imposed upon it by the adoption of the XIVth Amendment[4] to the Constitution, remains still to be affirmed.

It was not sufficient that the Federal government should expend its blood and treasure to unfetter the limbs of four millions of people. There can be a slavery more odious, more galling, than mere chattel slavery. It has been declared to be an act of charity to enforce ignorance upon the slave, since to inform his intelligence would simply be to make his unnatural lot all the more unbearable. Instance the miserable existence of Æsop, the great black moralist. But this is just what the manumission of the black people of this country has accomplished. They are more absolutely under the control of the Southern whites; they are more systematically robbed of their labor; they are more poorly housed, clothed and fed, than under the slave régime; and they enjoy, practically, less of the protection of the laws of the State or of the Federal government. When they appeal to the Federal government they are told by the Supreme Court to go to the State authorities—as if they would have appealed to the one had the other given them that protection to which their sovereign citizenship entitles them!

...The newspapers of the country, voicing the sentiments of the people, literally hiss into silence any man who has the courage to protest against the prevailing tendency to lawlessness[6] and bare-faced usurpation; while parties have ceased to deal with the question for other than purposes of political capital. Even this fruitful mine is well-nigh exhausted. A few more years, and the usurper and the man of violence will be left in undisputed possession of his blood-stained inheritance. No man will attempt to deter him from sowing broadcast the seeds of revolution and death. Brave men are powerless to combat this organized brigandage, complaint of which, in derision, has been termed "waving the bloody shirt."

You may rob and maltreat a slave and ask him what he is going to do about it, and he can make no reply. He is bound hand and foot; he is effectually gagged. Despair is his only refuge. He knows it is useless to appeal from tyranny unto the designers and apologists of tyranny. Ignominious death alone can bring him relief. This was the case of thousands of men doomed by the institution of slavery. *But such is not the case with free men.* You cannot oppress and murder freemen as you would slaves: you cannot so insult them with the question, "What are you going to do about it?" When you ask free men that question you appeal to men who, though sunk to the verge of despair, yet are capable of uprising and ripping hip and thigh those who deemed them incapable of so rising above their condition. The history of mankind is fruitful of such uprisings of races and classes reduced to a condition of absolute despair. The American negro is no better and no worse than the Haytian revolutionists headed by Toussaint l'Overture, Christophe and the bloody Dessalaines...

To tell a man he is free when he has neither money nor the opportunity to make it, is simply to mock him. To tell him he has no master when he cannot live except by permission of the man who, under favorable conditions, monopolizes all the land, is to deal in the most tantalizing contradiction of terms. But this is just what the United States did for the black man. And yet because he has not grown learned and wealthy in twenty years, because he does not own broad acres and a large bank account, people are not wanting who declare he has no capacity, that he is improvident by nature and mendacious from inclination.

FOOTNOTES:

[3] Neither slavery nor involuntary servitude, except as a punishment for crime, whereof the party shall have been duly convicted, shall exist within the United States, or any place subject to their jurisdiction.—Art. XIII. Sec. 1 of the Constitution.

[4] All persons born or naturalized in the United States, and subject to the jurisdiction thereof, are citizens of the United States and of the State in which they reside. No State shall make or enforce any law which shall abridge the privileges or immunities of citizens of the United States; *nor shall any State deprive any person of life, liberty, or property without due process of law, nor deny to any person within its jurisdiction the equal protection of the laws*—XIVth Amendment, Section 1.

[6]While I write these lines, the daily newspapers furnish the following paragraph. It is but one of the waifs that are to be found in the newspapers day by day. There is always some circumstance which justifies the murder and exculpates the murderer. The black always deserves his fate. I give the paragraph:

"SPEAR, MITCHELL Co., N.C., March 19, 1884.—Col. J.M. English, a farmer and prominent citizen living at Plumtree, Mitchell County, N.C., shot and killed a mulatto named Jack Mathis at that place Saturday, March 1. There had been difficulty between them for several months.

"Mathis last summer worked in one of Col. English's mica mines. Evidence pointed to him being implicated in the systematic stealing of mica from the mine. Still it was not direct enough to convict him, but he was discharged by English. Mathis was also a tenant of one of English's houses and lots. In resentment he damaged the property by destroying fences, tearing off weather boards from the house, and injuring the fruit trees. For this Col. English prosecuted the negro, and on Feb. 9, before a local Justice, ex-Sheriff Wiseman, he got a judgment for $100. On the date stated, during a casual meeting, hot words grew into an altercation, and Col. English shot the negro. Mathis was a powerful man. English is a cripple, being lame in a leg from a wound received in the Mexican war.

A trial was had before a preliminary court recently, Col. S.C. Vance appearing for Col. English. After a hearing of all the testimony the court reached a decision of justifiable homicide and English was released. The locality of the shooting is in the mountains of western North Carolina, and not far from the Flat Rock mica mine, the scene of the brutal midnight murder, Feb. 17, of Burleson, Miller, and Horton by Rae and Anderson, two revenue officers, who took this means to gain possession of the mica mine."

My knowledge of such affairs in the South is, that the black and the white have an altercation over some trivial thing, and the white to end the argument shoots the black man down. The negro is always a *"powerful fellow"* and the white man a "weak sickly man." The law and public opinion always side with the white man.

SOURCE

Timothy Thomas Fortune, *Black and White: Land, Labor, and Politics in the South* (New York: Fords, Howard, & Hulbert), 1884. Excerpt from Chapter Three: The Negro and the Nation, pp. 14–18.

IDA B. WELLS-BARNETT'S *A RED RECORD:*
TABULATED STATISTICS AND ALLEGED CAUSES OF LYNCHINGS IN THE UNITED STATES. CHAPTERS 1, 8, 10

HEADNOTE:

As a follow-up to her first pamphlet and in-depth study of lynching, *Southern Horrors* (1892), Wells published *A Red Record* in 1895. Wells continued to use Frederick Douglass's letter as a preface to her work, and having made lynching an international topic of reform, focused on the lack of civilization exhibited by whites, especially with the rise of spectacle lynchings. These passages focus on three chapters. The first section sets the context for Wells's arguments, while the eighth part discusses her issues with Temperance leader Frances Willard, and the tenth segment implores readers to act to end lynchings.

EXCERPT:

PREFACE

HON. FREDERICK DOUGLASS'S LETTER

DEAR MISS WELLS:

Let me give you thanks for your faithful paper on the lynch abomination now generally practiced against colored people in the South. There has been no word equal to it in convincing power. I have spoken, but my word is feeble in comparison. You give us what you know and testify from actual knowledge. You have dealt with the facts with cool, painstaking fidelity, and left those naked and uncontradicted facts to speak for themselves.

Brave woman! you have done your people and mine a service which can neither be weighed nor measured. If the American conscience were only half alive, if the American church and clergy were only half Christianized, if American moral sensibility were not hardened by persistent infliction of outrage and crime against colored people, a scream of horror, shame, and indignation would rise to Heaven wherever your pamphlet shall be read.

But alas! even crime has power to reproduce itself and create conditions favorable to its own existence. It sometimes seems we are deserted by earth and Heaven—yet we must still think, speak and work, and trust in the power of a merciful God for final deliverance.

Very truly and gratefully yours,

FREDERICK DOUGLASS

Cedar Hill, Anacostia, D.C.

1 THE CASE STATED

Beginning with the emancipation of the Negro, the inevitable result of unbridled power exercised for two and a half centuries, by the white man over the Negro, began to show itself in acts of conscienceless outlawry. During the slave regime, the Southern white man owned the Negro body and soul. It was to his interest to dwarf the soul and preserve the body. Vested with unlimited power over his slave, to subject him to any and all kinds of physical punishment, the white man was still restrained from such punishment as tended to injure the slave by abating his physical powers and thereby reducing his financial worth. While slaves were scourged mercilessly, and in countless cases inhumanly treated in other respects, still the white owner rarely permitted his anger to go so far as to take a life, which would entail upon him a loss of several hundred dollars. The slave was rarely killed, he was too valuable; it was easier and quite as effective, for discipline or revenge, to sell him "Down South."

But Emancipation came and the vested interests of the white man in the Negro's body were lost. The white man had no right to scourge the emancipated Negro, still less has he a right to kill him. But the Southern white people had been educated so long in that school of practice, in which might makes right, that they disdained to draw strict lines of action in dealing with the Negro. In slave times the Negro was kept subservient and submissive by the frequency and severity of the scourging, but, with freedom, a new system of intimidation came into vogue; the Negro was not only whipped and scourged; he was killed.

Not all nor nearly all of the murders done by white men, during the past thirty years in the South, have come to light, but the statistics as gathered and preserved by white men, and which have not been questioned, show that during these years more than ten thousand Negroes have been killed in cold blood, without the formality of judicial trial and legal execution. And yet, as evidence of the absolute impunity with which the white man dares to kill a Negro, the same record shows that during all these years, and for all these murders only three white men have been tried, convicted, and executed. As no white man has been lynched for the murder of colored people, these three executions are the only instances of the death penalty being visited upon white men for murdering Negroes.

Naturally enough the commission of these crimes began to tell upon the public conscience, and the Southern white man, as a tribute to the nineteenth-century civilization, was in a manner compelled to give excuses for his barbarism. His excuses have adapted themselves to the emergency, and are aptly outlined by that greatest of all Negroes, Frederick Douglass, in an article of recent date, in which he shows that there have been three distinct eras of Southern barbarism, to account for which three distinct excuses have been made.

The first excuse given to the civilized world for the murder of unoffending Negroes was the necessity of the white man to repress and stamp out alleged "race riots." For years immediately succeeding the war there was an appalling slaughter of colored people, and the wires usually conveyed to northern people and the world the intelligence, first, that an insurrection was being planned by Negroes, which, a few hours later, would prove to have been vigorously resisted by white men, and controlled with a resulting loss of several killed and wounded. It was always a remarkable feature in these insurrections and riots that only Negroes were killed during the rioting, and that all the white men escaped unharmed.

From 1865 to 1872, hundreds of colored men and women were mercilessly murdered and the almost invariable reason assigned was that they met their death by being alleged participants in an insurrection or riot. But this story at last wore itself out. No insurrection ever materialized; no Negro rioter was ever apprehended and proven guilty, and no dynamite ever recorded the black man's protest against oppression and wrong. It was too much to ask thoughtful people to believe this transparent story, and the southern white people at last made up their minds that some other excuse must be had...

But it was a bootless strife for colored people. The government which had made the Negro a citizen found itself unable to protect him. It gave him the right to vote, but denied him the protection which should have maintained that right. Scourged from his home; hunted through the swamps; hung by midnight raiders, and openly murdered in the light of day, the Negro clung to his right of franchise with a heroism which would have wrung admiration from the hearts of savages. He believed that in that small white ballot there was a subtle something which stood for manhood as well as citizenship, and thousands of brave black men went to their graves, exemplifying the one by dying for the other.

The white man's victory soon became complete by fraud, violence, intimidation and murder. The franchise vouchsafed to the Negro grew to be a "barren ideality," and regardless of numbers, the colored people found themselves voiceless in the councils of those whose duty it was to rule. With no longer the fear of "Negro Domination" before their eyes, the white man's second excuse became valueless. With the Southern governments all subverted and the Negro actually eliminated from all participation in state and national elections, there could be no longer an excuse for killing Negroes to prevent "Negro Domination."

Brutality still continued; Negroes were whipped, scourged, exiled, shot and hung whenever and wherever it pleased the white man so to treat them, and as the civilized world with increasing persistency held the white people of the South to account for its outlawry, the murderers invented the third excuse—that Negroes had to be killed to avenge their assaults upon women. There could be framed no possible excuse more harmful to the Negro and more unanswerable if true in its sufficiency for the white man...

A word as to the charge itself. In considering the third reason assigned by the Southern white people for the butchery of blacks, the question must be asked, what the white man means when he charges the black man with rape. Does he mean the crime which the statutes of the civilized states describe as such? Not by any means. With the Southern white man, any mesalliance existing between a white woman and a colored man is a sufficient foundation for the charge of rape. The Southern white man says that it is impossible for a voluntary alliance to exist between a white woman and a colored man, and therefore, the fact of an alliance is a proof of force. In numerous instances where colored men have have [sic] been lynched on the charge of rape, it was positively known at the time of lynching, and indisputably proven after the victim's death, that the relationship sustained between the man and woman was voluntary and clandestine, and that in no court of law could even the charge of assault have been successfully maintained...

8 MISS WILLARD'S ATTITUDE

No class of American citizens stands in greater need of the humane and thoughtful consideration of all sections of our country than do the colored people, nor does any class exceed us in the measure of grateful regard for acts of kindly interest in our behalf. It is, therefore, to us, a matter of keen regret that a Christian organization, so large and influential as the Woman's Christian Temperance Union, should refuse to give its sympathy and support to our oppressed people who ask no further favor than the promotion of public sentiment which shall guarantee to every person accused of crime the safeguard of a fair and impartial trial, and protection from butchery by brutal mobs. Accustomed as we are to the indifference and apathy of Christian people, we would bear this instance of ill fortune in silence, had not Miss Willard gone out of her way to antagonize the cause so dear to our hearts by including in her Annual Address to the W.C.T.U. Convention at Cleveland, November 5, 1894, a studied, unjust and wholly unwarranted attack upon our work.

In her address Miss Willard said:

The zeal for her race of Miss Ida B. Wells, a bright young colored woman, has, it seems to me, clouded her perception as to who were her friends and well-wishers in all high-minded and legitimate efforts to banish the abomination of lynching and torture from the land of the free and the home of the brave. It is my firm belief that in the statements made by Miss Wells concerning white women having taken the initiative in nameless acts between the races she has put an imputation upon half the white race in this country that is unjust, and, save in the rarest exceptional instances, wholly without foundation. This is the unanimous opinion of the most disinterested and observant leaders of opinion whom I have consulted on the subject, and I do not fear to say that the laudable efforts she is making are greatly handicapped by statements of this kind, nor to urge her as a friend and well-wisher to banish from her vocabulary all such allusions as a source of weakness to the cause she has at heart.

This paragraph, brief as it is, contains two statements which have not the slightest foundation in fact. At no time, nor in any place, have I made statements "concerning white women having taken the initiative in nameless acts between the races." Further, at no time, or place nor under any circumstance, have I directly or inferentially "put an imputation upon half the white race in this country" and I challenge this "friend and well-wisher" to give proof of the truth of her charge. Miss Willard protests against lynching in one paragraph and then, in the next, deliberately misrepresents my position in order that she may criticise a movement, whose only purpose is to protect our oppressed race from vindictive slander and Lynch Law.

What I have said and what I now repeat—in answer to her first charge—is, that colored men have been lynched for assault upon women, when the facts were plain that the relationship between the victim lynched and the alleged victim of his assault was voluntary, clandestine and illicit. For that very reason we maintain, that, in every section of our land, the accused should have a fair, impartial trial, so that a man who is colored shall not be hanged for an offense, which, if he were white, would not be adjudged a crime…

10 THE REMEDY

Therefore, we demand a fair trial by law for those accused of crime, and punishment by law after honest conviction. No maudlin sympathy for criminals is solicited, but we do ask that the law shall punish all alike. We earnestly desire those that control the forces which make public sentiment to join with us in the demand. Surely the humanitarian spirit of this country which reaches out to denounce the treatment of the Russian Jews, the Armenian Christians, the laboring poor of Europe, the Siberian exiles and the native women of India—will not longer [sic] refuse to lift its voice on this subject. If it were known that the cannibals or the savage Indians had burned three human beings alive in the past two years, the whole of Christendom would be roused, to devise ways and means to put a stop to it. Can you remain silent and inactive when such things are done in our own community and country? Is your duty to humanity in the United States less binding?

What can you do, reader, to prevent lynching, to thwart anarchy and promote law and order throughout our land?

1st. You can help disseminate the facts contained in this book by bringing them to the knowledge of every one with whom you come in contact, to the end that public sentiment may be revolutionized. Let the facts speak for themselves, with you as a medium.

2d. You can be instrumental in having churches, missionary societies, Y.M.C.A.'s, W.C.T.U.'s and all Christian and moral forces in connection with your religious and social life, pass resolutions of condemnation and protest every time a lynching takes place; and see that they are sent to the place where these outrages occur.

3d. Bring to the intelligent consideration of Southern people the refusal of capital to invest where lawlessness and mob violence hold sway. Many labor organizations have declared by resolution that they would avoid lynch infested localities as they would the pestilence when seeking new homes. If the South wishes to build up its waste places quickly, there is no better way than to uphold the majesty of the law by enforcing obedience to the same, and meting out the same punishment to all classes of criminals, white as well as black. "Equality before the law," must become a fact as well as a theory before America is truly the "land of the free and the home of the brave."

4th. Think and act on independent lines in this behalf, remembering that after all, it is the white man's civilization and the white man's government which are on trial. This crusade will determine whether that civilization can maintain itself by itself, or whether anarchy shall prevail; Whether this Nation shall write itself down a success at self government, or in deepest humiliation admit its failure complete; whether the precepts and theories of Christianity are professed and practiced by American white people as

Golden Rules of thought and action, or adopted as a system of morals to be preached to, heathen until they attain to the intelligence which needs the system of Lynch Law.

5th. Congressman Blair offered a resolution in the House of Representatives, August, 1894. The organized life of the country can speedily make this a law by sending resolutions to Congress indorsing Mr. Blair's bill and asking Congress to create the commission. In no better way can the question be settled, and the Negro does not fear the issue.

Source

Ida B. Wells-Barnett, *A Red Record: Tabulated Statistics and Alleged Causes of Lynchings in the United States* (Chicago: Donohue & Henneberry, 1895), chapters 1, 8, 10. Excerpts.

JOSEPHINE ST. PIERRE RUFFIN'S "ADDRESS TO THE FIRST NATIONAL CONFERENCE OF COLORED WOMEN"

HEADNOTE:

Josephine St. Pierre Ruffin was a member of the Ida B. Wells Testimonial Reception Committee, founded the Women's New Era Club in 1894, and edited the corresponding magazine, *Women's Era*. In 1896, her organization joined with Mary Church Terrell's National Federation of African-American Women. The following is her address to the congregation at the 1896 first national meeting of the National Association of Colored Women. Ida B. Wells sat in the audience and heard Ruffin describe her goals for the organization and the pressing issues facing African American women.

EXCERPT:

It is with especial joy and pride that I welcome you all to this, our first conference. It is only recently that women have waked up to the importance of meeting in council, and great as has been the advantage of women generally, and important as it is and has been that they should confer, the necessity has not been nearly so great, matters at stake not nearly so vital, as that we, bearing peculiar blunders, suffering under especial hardships, enduring peculiar privations, should meet for a "good talk" among ourselves. Although rather hastily called, you as well as I can testify how long and how earnestly a conference has been thought of and hoped for and even prepared for. These women's clubs, which have sprung up all over the country, built and run upon broad, strong lines, have all been a preparation, small conferences in themselves, and their spontaneous birth and enthusiastic support have been little less than inspirational on the part of our women and a general preparation for a large union such as it is hopes this conference will lead to. Five years ago we had no colored women's clubs outside of those formed for special work; to-day, with little over a month's notice, we are able to call representatives from more than twenty clubs. It is a good showing, it stands for much, it shows that we are truly American women, with all the adaptability, readiness to seize and possess our opportunities, willingness to do our part for good as other American women.

The reasons why we should confer are so apparent that it would seem hardly necessary to enumerate them, and yet there is none of them but demand our serious consideration. In the first place we need to feel the cheer and inspiration of meeting each other, we need to gain the courage and fresh life that comes from the mingling of congenial souls, of those working for the same ends. Next, we need to talk over not only those things which are of vital importance to us as women, but also the things that are of especial interest to us as colored women, the training of our children, openings for our boys and girls, how they can be prepared for occupations and occupations may be found or opened for them, what we especially can do in the moral education of the race with which we are identified, our mental elevation and physical development, the home training it is necessary to give our children in order to prepare them to meet the peculiar conditions in which they shall find themselves, how to make the most of our own, to some extent, limited opportunities, these are some of our own peculiar questions to be discussed. Besides these are the general questions of the day, which we cannot afford to be indifferent to: temperance, morality, the higher education, hygienic and domestic questions. If these things need the serious consideration of women more advantageously placed by reason of all the aid to right thinking and living with which they are surrounded, surely we, with everything to pull us back, to hinder us in developing, need to take every opportunity and means for the thoughtful consideration which shall lead to wise action.

I have left the strongest reasons for our conferring together until the last. All over America there is to be found a large and growing class of earnest, intelligent, progressive colored women, women who, if not leading full useful lives, are only waiting for the opportunity to do so, many of them warped and cramped for lack of opportunity, not only to do more but be more; and yet, if an estimate of the colored women of America is called for, the inevitable reply, glibly given, is, "For the most part ignorant and immoral, some exceptions, of course, but these don't count." Now, for the sake of the thousands of self-sacrificing young women teaching and preaching in lonely southern backwoods for the noble army of mothers who have given birth to these girls, mothers whose intelligence is only limited by their opportunity to get at books, for the sake of the fine cultured women who have carried off the honors in school here and often abroad, for the sake of our own dignity, the dignity of our race, and the future good name of our children, it is "mete, right and our bounden duty" to stand forth and declare ourselves and principles, to teach an ignorant and suspicious world that our aims and interests are identical with those of all good aspiring women. Too long have we been silent under unjust and unholy charges; we cannot expect to have them removed until we disprove them through ourselves. It is not enough to try to disprove unjust charges through individual effort, that never goes any further. Year after year southern women have protested against the admission of colored women into any national organization on the ground of the immorality of these women, and because all refutation has only been tried by individual work the charge has never been crushed, as it could and should have been at the first. Now with an army of organized women standing for purity and mental worth, we in ourselves deny the charge and open the eyes of the world to a state of affairs to which they have been blind, often willfully so, and the very fact that the charges, audaciously and flippantly made, as they often are, are of so humiliating and delicate a nature, serves to protect the accuser by driving the helpless accused into mortified silence. It is to break this silence, not by noisy protestations of what we are not, but by a dignified showing of what we are and hope to become that we are impelled to take this step, to make of this gathering an object lesson to the world. For many and apparent reasons, it is especially fitting that the women of the race take the lead in this movement, but for all this we recognize the necessity of the sympathy of our husbands, brothers and fathers.

Our woman's movement is woman's movement in that it is led and directed by women for the good of women and men, for the benefit of all humanity, which is more than any one branch or section of it. We want, we ask the active interest of our men, and, too, we are not drawing the color line; we are women, American women, as intensely interested in all that pertains to us as such as all other American women; we are not alienating or withdrawing, we are only coming to the front, willing to join any others in the same work and cordially inviting and welcoming any others to join us.

If there is any one thing I would especially enjoin upon this conference it is union and earnestness. The questions that are to come before us are of too much import to be weakened by my trivialities or personalities. If any differences arise let them be quickly settled, with the feeling that we are all workers to the same end, to elevate and dignify colored American womanhood. This conference will not be what I expect if it does not show the wisdom, indeed the absolute necessity of a national organization of our women. Every year new questions coming up will prove it to us. This hurried, almost informal convention does not begin to meet our needs, it is only a beginning, made here in dear old Boston, where the scales of justice and generosity hang evenly balanced, and where the people "dare be true" to their best instincts and stand ready to lend aid and sympathy to worthy strugglers. It is hoped and believed that from this will spring an organization that will in truth bring in a new era to the colored women of America.

SOURCE

Josephine St. Pierre Ruffin, "Address to the First National Conference of Colored Women," *Woman's Era* 2 (August 1895): 13–15.

BOOKER T. WASHINGTON, "THE ATLANTA EXPOSITION ADDRESS"

HEADNOTE:

This address, commonly referred to as the "Atlanta Compromise Speech" unveiled Washington's plan for advancing the African American race through industrial labor. Washington argued that industrial education and hard work would solve the "Negro problem" of the South. For many reformers, including Ida B. Wells and William Edward Burghardt Du Bois, Washington's approach ignored the context of poverty, disenfranchisement, and racial violence. Despite this criticism, Washington's points were popular with whites who also desired to maintain the current status quo. This speech catapulted Washington to national attention and poised him to be the next national leader of the African American reform movement.

EXCERPT:

When I arose to speak, there was considerable cheering, especially from the coloured people. As I remember it now, the thing that was uppermost in my mind was the desire to say something that would cement the friendship of the races and bring about hearty cooperation between them. So far as my outward surroundings were concerned, the only thing that I recall distinctly now is that when I got up, I saw thousands of eyes looking intently into my face. The following is the address which I delivered: Mr. President and Gentlemen of the Board of Directors and Citizens...

Ignorant and inexperienced, it is not strange that in the first years of our new life we began at the top instead of at the bottom; that a seat in Congress or the state legislature was more sought than real estate or industrial skill; that the political convention or stump speaking had more attractions than starting a dairy farm or truck garden...

To those of my race who depend on bettering their condition in a foreign land or who underestimate the importance of cultivating friendly relations with the Southern white man, who is their next-door neighbour, I would say: "Cast down your bucket where you are"—cast it down in making friends in every manly way of the people of all races by whom we are surrounded.

Cast it down in agriculture, mechanics, in commerce, in domestic service, and in the professions. And in this connection it is well to bear in mind that whatever other sins the South may be called to bear, when it comes to business, pure and simple, it is in the South that the Negro is given a man's chance in the commercial world, and in nothing is this Exposition more eloquent than in emphasizing this chance. Our greatest danger is that in the great leap from slavery to freedom we may overlook the fact that the masses of us are to live by the productions of our hands, and fail to keep in mind that we shall prosper in proportion as we learn to dignify and glorify common labour and put brains and skill into the common occupations of life; shall prosper in proportion as we learn to draw the line between the superficial and the substantial, the ornamental gewgaws [sic] of life and the useful. No race can prosper till it learns that there is as much dignity in tilling a field as in writing a poem. It is at the bottom of life we must begin, and not at the top. Nor should we permit our grievances to overshadow our opportunities...

The wisest among my race understand that the agitation of questions of social equality is the extremest folly, and that progress in the enjoyment of all the privileges that will come to us must be the result of severe and constant struggle rather than of artificial forcing. No race that has anything to contribute to the markets of the world is long in any degree ostracized [sic]. It is important and right that all privileges of the law be ours, but it is vastly more important that we be prepared for the exercises of these privileges. The opportunity to earn a dollar in a factory just now is worth infinitely more than the opportunity to spend a dollar in an opera-house.

In conclusion, may I repeat that nothing in thirty years has given us more hope and encouragement, and drawn us so near to you of the white race, as this opportunity offered by the Exposition; and here bending, as it were, over the altar that represents the results of the struggles of your race and mine, both starting practically empty-handed three decades ago, I pledge that in your effort to work out the great and intricate problem which God has laid at the doors of the South, you shall have at all times the patient, sympathetic help of my race; only let this be constantly in mind, that, while from representations in these buildings of the product of field, of forest, of mine, of factory, letters, and art, much good will come, yet far above and beyond material benefits will be that higher good, that, let us pray God, will come, in a blotting out of sectional differences and racial animosities and suspicions, in a determination to administer absolute justice, in a willing obedience among all classes to the mandates of law. This, this, [sic] coupled with our material prosperity, will bring into our beloved South a new heaven and a new earth...

SOURCE

Booker T. Washington, *Up from Slavery: An Autobiography* (Garden City: Doubleday & Company, Inc.), 1901. Excerpt from Chapter XIV on The Atlanta Exposition Address, pp. 760–64.

WILLIAM EDWARD BURGHARDT DU BOIS, "OF MR. BOOKER T. WASHINGTON AND OTHERS" FROM *THE SOULS OF BLACK FOLK*

INTRODUCTORY REMARKS:

Du Bois's *The Souls of Black Folk,* examined the post-Civil War South, including some autobiographical details along with discussions on the development of racist policies and their effects on African Americans. Most famously Du Bois claimed, "[T]he problem of the Twentieth Century is the problem of the color-line" (p. 5). In this excerpt, Du Bois discusses Booker T. Washington's approach to racial reform, which he felt harmed the progress of African Americans.

EXCERPT:

Mr. Washington represents in Negro thought the old attitude of adjustment and submission; but adjustment at such a peculiar time as to make his programme unique. This is an age of unusual economic development, and Mr. Washington's programme naturally takes an economic cast, becoming a gospel of Work and Money to such an extent as apparently almost completely to overshadow the higher aims of life. Moreover, this is an age when the more advanced races are coming in closer contact with the less developed races, and the race-feeling is therefore intensified; and Mr. Washington's programme practically accepts the alleged inferiority of the Negro races. Again, in our own land, the reaction from the sentiment of war time has given impetus to race-prejudice against Negroes, and Mr. Washington withdraws many of the high demands of Negroes as men and American citizens. In other periods of intensified prejudice all the Negro's tendency to self-assertion has been called forth; at this period a policy of submission is advocated. In the history of nearly all other races and peoples the doctrine preached at such crises has been that manly self-respect is worth more than lands and houses, and that a people who voluntarily surrender such respect, or cease striving for it, are not worth civilizing.

In answer to this, it has been claimed that the Negro can survive only through submission. Mr. Washington distinctly asks that black people give up, at least for the present, three things,—

First, political power,

Second, insistence on civil rights,

Third, higher education of Negro youth,—and concentrate all their energies on industrial education, and accumulation of wealth, and the conciliation of the South. This policy has been courageously and insistently advocated for over fifteen years, and has been triumphant for perhaps ten years. As a result of this tender of the palm-branch, what has been the return? In these years there have occurred:

1. The disfranchisement of the Negro.
2. The legal creation of a distinct status of civil inferiority for the Negro.
3. The steady withdrawal of aid from institutions for the higher training of the Negro.

These movements are not, to be sure, direct results of Mr. Washington's teachings; but his propaganda has, without a shadow of doubt, helped their speedier accomplishment. The question then comes: Is it possible, and probable, that nine millions of men can make effective progress in economic lines if they are deprived of political rights, made a servile caste, and allowed only the most meagre chance for developing their exceptional men? If history and reason give any distinct answer to these questions, it is an emphatic NO. And Mr. Washington thus faces the triple paradox of his career:

1. He is striving nobly to make Negro artisans business men and property-owners; but it is utterly impossible, under modern competitive methods, for workingmen and property-owners to defend their rights and exist without the right of suffrage.
2. He insists on thrift and self-respect, but at the same time counsels a silent submission to civic inferiority such as is bound to sap the manhood of any race in the long run.
3. He advocates common-school and industrial training, and depreciates institutions of higher learning; but neither the Negro common-schools,

nor Tuskegee itself, could remain open a day were it not for teachers trained in Negro colleges, or trained by their graduates.

This triple paradox in Mr. Washington's position is the object of criticism by two classes of colored Americans. One class is spiritually descended from Toussaint the Savior, through Gabriel, Vesey, and Turner, and they represent the attitude of revolt and revenge; they hate the white South blindly and distrust the white race generally, and so far as they agree on definite action, think that the Negro's only hope lies in emigration beyond the borders of the United States. And yet, by the irony of fate, nothing has more effectually made this programme seem hopeless than the recent course of the United States toward weaker and darker peoples in the West Indies, Hawaii, and the Philippines,—for where in the world may we go and be safe from lying and brute force?

The other class of Negroes who cannot agree with Mr. Washington has hitherto said little aloud. They deprecate the sight of scattered counsels, of internal disagreement; and especially they dislike making their just criticism of a useful and earnest man an excuse for a general discharge of venom from small-minded opponents. Nevertheless, the questions involved are so fundamental and serious that it is difficult to see how men like the Grimkes, Kelly Miller, J. W. E. Bowen, and other representatives of this group, can much longer be silent. Such men feel in conscience bound to ask of this nation three things:

1. The right to vote.
2. Civic equality.
3. The education of youth according to ability. They acknowledge Mr. Washington's invaluable service in counselling patience and courtesy in such demands; they do not ask that ignorant black men vote when ignorant whites are debarred, or that any reasonable restrictions in the suffrage should not be applied; they know that the low social level of the mass of the race is responsible for much discrimination against it, but they also know, and the nation knows, that relentless color-prejudice is more often a cause than a result of the Negro's degradation; they seek the abatement of this relic of barbarism, and not its systematic encouragement and pampering by all agencies of social power from the Associated Press to the Church of Christ. They advocate, with Mr. Washington, a broad system of Negro common schools supplemented by thorough industrial training; but they are surprised that a man of Mr. Washington's insight cannot see that no such educational system ever has rested or can rest on any other basis than that of the well-equipped college and university, and they insist that

there is a demand for a few such institutions throughout the South to train the best of the Negro youth as teachers, professional men, and leaders.

This group of men honor Mr. Washington for his attitude of conciliation toward the white South; they accept the "Atlanta Compromise" in its broadest interpretation; they recognize, with him, many signs of promise, many men of high purpose and fair judgment, in this section; they know that no easy task has been laid upon a region already tottering under heavy burdens. But, nevertheless, they insist that the way to truth and right lies in straightforward honesty, not in indiscriminate flattery; in praising those of the South who do well and criticising uncompromisingly those who do ill; in taking advantage of the opportunities at hand and urging their fellows to do the same, but at the same time in remembering that only a firm adherence to their higher ideals and aspirations will ever keep those ideals within the realm of possibility. They do not expect that the free right to vote, to enjoy civic rights, and to be educated, will come in a moment; they do not expect to see the bias and prejudices of years disappear at the blast of a trumpet; but they are absolutely certain that the way for a people to gain their reasonable rights is not by voluntarily throwing them away and insisting that they do not want them; that the way for a people to gain respect is not by continually belittling and ridiculing themselves; that, on the contrary, Negroes must insist continually, in season and out of season, that voting is necessary to modern manhood, that color discrimination is barbarism, and that black boys need education as well as white boys.

Source

William Edward Burghardt Du Bois, *The Souls of Black Folk* (Chicago: Project Bartleby), 1903. Excerpt from Chapter Three: Of Mr. Booker T. Washington and Others, pp. 30–33.

MARY CHURCH TERRELL, "THE PROGRESS OF COLORED WOMEN" SPEECH GIVEN AT THE 1898 NATIONAL AMERICAN WOMEN'S SUFFRAGE ASSOCIATION

HEADNOTE:

In this speech, Terrell discusses the limitations of race and gender imposed upon African Americans and women by society. Delivered to commemorate the fiftieth anniversary of the founding of the suffrage movement at Seneca Falls, New York in 1848, Terrell reminds her audience of white and black women of the racial work African American women have done and what remains to be achieved. She also praised Booker T. Washington and his policies as well as the temperance movement. By 1898, the separation of Wells and Terrell's ideologies is clear, and although the two women would work together in founding the National Association for the Advancement of Colored People (NAACP), their legacies could not be more different. Terrell's leadership was largely lauded in contrast to Wells, who was dismissed from the mainstream movement and forgotten in many narratives. Terrell's approaches to activism and her conciliatory manner received, like Washington, a more favorable response.

EXCERPT:

Fifty years ago a meeting such as this, planned, conducted and addressed by women would have been an impossibility. Less than forty years ago, few sane men would have predicted that either a slave or one of his descendants would in this century at least, address such an audience in the Nation's

Capital at the invitation of women representing the highest, broadest, best type of womanhood, that can be found anywhere in the world. Thus to me this semi-centennial of the National American Woman Suffrage Association is a double jubilee, rejoicing as I do, not only in the prospective enfranchisement of my sex but in the emancipation of my race.

When Ernestine Rose, Lucretia Mott, Elizabeth Cady Stanton, Lucy Stone and Susan B. Anthony began that agitation by which colleges were opened to women and the numerous reforms inaugurated for the amelioration of their condition along all lines, their sisters who groaned in bondage had little reason to hope that these blessings would ever brighten their crushed and blighted lives, for during those days of oppression and despair, colored women were not only refused admittance to institutions of learning, but the law of the States in which the majority lived made it a crime to teach them to read. Not only could they possess no property, but even their bodies were not their own. Nothing, in short, that could degrade or brutalize the womanhood of the race was lacking in that system from which colored women then had little hope of escape. So gloomy were their prospects, so fatal the laws, so pernicious the customs, only fifty years ago. But, from the day their fetters were broken and their minds released from the darkness of ignorance to which for more than two hundred years they had been doomed, from the day they could stand erect in the dignity of womanhood, no longer bond but free, till tonight, colored women have forged steadily ahead in the acquisition of knowledge and in the cultivation of those virtues which make for good...

Consider if you will, the almost insurmountable obstacles which have confronted colored women in their efforts to educate and cultivate themselves since their emancipation, and I dare assert, not boastfully, but with pardonable pride, I hope, that the progress they have made and the work they have accomplished, will bear a favorable comparison at least with that of their more fortunate sisters, from whom the opportunity of acquiring knowledge and the means of self-culture have never been entirely withheld. For, not only are colored women with ambition and aspiration handicapped on account of their sex, but they are everywhere baffled and mocked on account of their race. Desperately and continuously they are forced to fight that opposition, born of a cruel, unreasonable prejudice which neither their merit nor their necessity seems able to subdue. Not only because they are women, but because they are colored women, are discouragement and disappointment meeting them at every turn. Avocations opened and opportunities offered to their more favored sisters have been and are tonight closed and barred against them. While those of the dominant race have a variety of trades and pursuits from which they may choose, the woman through whose veins one drop of African blood is known to flow is limited to a pitiful few. So overcrowded are the avocations in which colored women may engage and so poor is the pay in consequence, that only the barest livelihood can be eked out by the rank and file. And yet, in spite of the opposition encountered, the obstacles opposed to their acquisition of knowledge and their accumulation of property, the progress made by colored women along these lines has never been surpassed by that of any people in the history of the world...

With tireless energy and eager zeal, colored women have, since their emancipation, been continuously prosecuting the work of educating and elevating their race, as though upon themselves alone devolved the accomplishment of this great task. Of the teachers engaged in instructing colored youth, it is perhaps no exaggeration to say that fully ninety per cent are women. In the back-woods, remote from the civilization and comforts of the city and town, on the plantations reeking with ignorance and vice, our colored women may be found battling with evils which such conditions always entail. Many a heroine, of whom the world will never hear, has thus sacrificed her life to her race amid surroundings and in the face of privations which only martyrs can tolerate and bear. Shirking responsibility has never been a fault with which colored women might be truthfully charged. Indefatigably and conscientiously, in public work of all kinds they engage, that they may benefit and elevate their race. The result of this labor has been prodigious indeed. By banding themselves together in the interest of education and morality, by adopting the most practical and useful means to this end, colored women have in thirty short years become a great power for good.

Through the National Association of Colored Women, which was formed by the union of two large organizations in July, 1896, and which is now the only national body among colored women, much good has been done in the past, and more will be accomplished in the future, we hope. Believing that it is only through the home that a people can become really good and truly great, the National Association of Colored Women has entered that sacred domain. Homes, more homes, better homes, purer homes is the text upon which our have been and will be preached. Through mothers' meetings, which are a special feature of the work planned by the Association, much useful information in everything pertaining to the home will be disseminated. We would have heart-to-heart talks with our women, that we may strike at the root of evils, many of which lie, alas, at the fireside. If the women of the dominant race with all the centuries of education, culture and refinement back of them, with all their wealth of opportunity ever present with them—if these women feel the need of a Mothers' Congress that they may be enlightened as to the best methods of rearing children and conducting their homes, how much more do our women, from whom shackles have but yesterday fallen, need information on the same vital subjects? And so throughout the country we are working vigorously and conscientiously to establish Mothers' Congresses in every community in which our women may be found.

Under the direction of the Tuskegee, Alabama branch of the National Association, the work of bringing the light of knowledge and the gospel of cleanliness to their benighted sisters on the plantations has been conducted with signal success. Their efforts have thus far been confined to four estates, comprising thousand [sic] of acres of land, on which live hundreds of colored people, yet in the darkness of ignorance and the grip of sin, miles away from churches and schools. Under the evil influences of plantation owners, and through no fault of their own, the condition of the colored people is, in some sections to-day no better than it was at the close of the war...

By the Tuskegee club and many others all over the country, object lessons are given in the best way to sweep, dust, cook, wash and iron, together with other information concerning household affairs. Talks on social purity and the proper method of rearing children are made for the benefit of those mothers, who in many instances fall short of their duty, not because they are vicious and depraved, but because they are ignorant and poor...

Questions affecting or legal status as a race are also constantly agitated by our women. In Louisiana and Tennessee, colored women have several times petitioned the legislatures of their respective States to repeal the obnoxious "Jim Crow Car" laws, nor will any stone be left unturned until this iniquitous and unjust enactment against respectable American citizens be forever wiped from the statutes of the South. Against the barbarous Convict Lease System of Georgia, of which negroes, especially the female prisoners, are the principal victims, colored women are waging a ceaseless war. By two lecturers, each of whom, under the Woman's Christian Temperance Union has been National Superintendent of work among colored people, the cause of temperance has for many years been eloquently espoused...

And so, lifting as we climb, onward and upward we go, struggling and striving, and hoping that the buds and blossoms of our desires will burst into glorious fruition ere long. With courage, born of success achieved in the past, with a keen sense of the responsibility which we shall continue to assume, we look forward to a future large with promise and hope. Seeking no favors because of our color, nor patronage because of our needs, we knock at the bar of justice, asking an equal chance.

SOURCE

Mary Church Terrell, "The Progress of Colored Women," Address to the National American Women's Suffrage Association, Washington, D.C. February 18, 1898. Excerpts.

IDA B. WELLS-BARNETT, *MOB RULE IN NEW ORLEANS* 1900

INTRODUCTORY REMARKS:

In *Mob Rule in New Orleans,* Wells-Barnett explores the varying discrepancies in the press about Robert Charles's lynching and the violence leading up to his death. She demonstrates how the media's characterization of Charles as a thief emerged as justification for the violence whites committed against him. Wells-Barnett included long excerpts of white press clippings, revealing whites' anger that Robert Charles dared to fight back against white authority. Quoting from press accounts effectively made her arguments about white prejudices and brutality for her. Wells-Barnett also included the mayor's call for Charles's body to further support her long-held point that prominent men and members of the community participated in lynchings.

EXCERPT:

Shot An Officer

The bloodiest week which New Orleans has known since the massacre of the Italians in 1892 was ushered in Monday, July 24, by the inexcusable and unprovoked assault upon two colored men by police officers of New Orleans. Fortified by the assurance born of long experience in the New Orleans service, three policemen, Sergeant Aucoin, Officer Mora and Officer Cantrelle, observing two colored men sitting on doorsteps on Dryades street, between Washington Avenue and 6th Streets, determined, without a shadow of authority, to arrest them. One of the colored men was named Robert Charles, the other was a lad of nineteen named Leonard Pierce. The colored men had left their homes, a few blocks distant, about an hour prior, and had been sitting upon the doorsteps for a short time talking together. They had not broken the peace in any way whatever, no warrant was in the policemen's hands justifying their arrest, and no crime had been committed of which they were the suspects. The policemen, however, secure in the firm belief that they could do anything to a Negro that they wished, approached the two men, and in less than three minutes from the time they accosted them attempted to put both colored men under arrest. The younger of the two men, Pierce, submitted to arrest, for the officer, Cantrelle, who accosted him, put his gun in the young man's face ready to blow his brains out if he moved. The other colored man, Charles, was made the victim of a savage attack by Officer Mora, who used a billet and then drew a gun and tried to kill Charles. Charles drew his gun nearly as quickly as the policeman, and began a duel in the street, in which both participants were shot. The policeman got the worst of the duel, and fell helpless to the sidewalk. Charles made his escape. Cantrelle took Pierce, his captive, to the police station, to which place Mora, the wounded officer, was also taken, and a man hunt at once instituted for Charles, the wounded fugitive.

In any law-abiding community Charles would have been justified in delivering himself up immediately to the properly constituted authorities and asking a trial by a jury of his peers. He could have been certain that in resisting an unwarranted arrest he had a right to defend his life, even to the point of taking one in that defense, but Charles knew that his arrest in New Orleans, even for defending his life, meant nothing short of a long term in the penitentiary, and still more probable death by lynching at the hands of a cowardly mob. He very bravely determined to protect his life as long as he had breath in his body and strength to draw a hair trigger on his would-be murderers. How well he was justified in that belief is well shown by the newspaper accounts which were given of this transaction. Without a single line of evidence to justify the assertion, the New Orleans daily papers at once declared that both Pierce and Charles were desperadoes, that they were contemplating a burglary and that they began the assault upon the policemen. It is interesting to note how the two leading papers of New Orleans, the *Picayune* and the *Times-Democrat*, exert themselves to justify the policemen in the absolutely unprovoked attack upon the two colored men. As these two papers did all in their power to give an excuse for the action of the policemen, it is interesting to note their versions. The *Times-Democrat* of Tuesday morning, the twenty-fifth, says:

Two blacks, who are desperate men, and no doubt will be proven burglars, made it interesting and dangerous for three bluecoats on Dryades street, between Washington Avenue and Sixth Street, the Negroes using pistols first and dropping Patrolman Mora. But the desperate darkies did not go free, for the taller of the two, Robinson, is badly wounded and under cover, while Leonard Pierce is in jail.

For a long time that particular neighborhood has been troubled with bad Negroes, and the neighbors were complaining to the Sixth Precinct police about them. But of late Pierce and Robinson had been camping on a door step on the street, and the people regarded their actions as suspicious. It got to such a point that some of the residents were afraid to go to bed, and last night this was told Sergeant Aucoin, who was rounding up his men. He had just picked up Officers Mora and Cantrell, on Washington Avenue and Dryades Street, and catching a glimpse of the blacks on the steps, he said he would go over and warn the men to get away from the street. So the patrolmen followed, and Sergeant Aucoin asked the smaller fellow, Pierce, if he lived there. The answer was short and impertinent, the black saying he did not, and with that both Pierce and Robinson drew up to their full height.

For the moment the sergeant did not think that the Negroes meant fight, and he was on the point of ordering them away when Robinson slipped his pistol from his pocket. Pierce had his revolver out, too, and he fired twice, point blank at the sergeant, and just then Robinson began shooting at the patrolmen. In a second or so the policemen and blacks were fighting with their revolvers, the sergeant having a duel with Pierce, while Cantrell and Mora drew their line of fire on Robinson, who was working his revolver for all he was worth. One of his shots took Mora in the right hip, another caught his index finger on the right hand, and a third struck the small finger of the left hand. Poor Mora was done for; he could not fight any more, but Cantrell kept up his fire, being answered by the big black. Pierce's revolver broke down, the cartridges snapping, and he threw up his hands, begging for quarter.

The sergeant lowered his pistol and some citizens ran over to where the shooting was going on. One of the bullets that went at Robinson caught him in the breast and he began running, turning out Sixth Street, with Cantrell behind him, shooting every few steps. He was loading his revolver again, but did not use it after the start he took, and in a little while Officer Cantrell lost the man in the darkness.

Pierce was made a prisoner and hurried to the Sixth Precinct police station, where he was charged with shooting and wounding. The sergeant sent for an ambulance, and Mora was taken to the hospital, the wound in the hip being serious.

A search was made for Robinson, but he could not be found, and even at 2 o'clock this morning Captain Day, with Sergeant Aucoin and Corporals Perrier and Trenchard, with a good squad of men, were beating the weeds for the black.

The *New Orleans Picayune* of the same date described the occurrence, and from its account one would think it was an entirely different affair. Both of the two accounts cannot be true, and the unquestioned fact is that neither of them sets out the facts as they occurred. Both accounts attempt to fix the beginning of hostilities upon the colored men, but both were compelled to admit that the colored men were sitting on the doorsteps quietly conversing with one another when the three policemen went up and accosted them. The *Times-Democrat* unguardedly states that one of the two colored men tried to run away; that Mora seized him and then drew his billy and struck him on the head; that Charles broke away from him and started to run, after which the shooting began. The *Picayune*, however, declares that Pierce began the firing and that his two shots point blank at Aucoin were the first shots of the fight. As a matter of fact, Pierce never fired a single shot before he was covered by Aucoin's revolver. Charles and the officers did all the shooting. The *Picayune's* account is as follows:

Patrolman Mora was shot in the right hip and dangerously wounded last night at 11:30 o'clock in Dryades Street, between Washington and Sixth, by two Negroes, who were sitting on a door step in the neighborhood.

The shooting of Patrolman Mora brings to memory the fact that he was one of the partners of Patrolman Trimp, who was shot by a Negro soldier of the United States government during the progress of the Spanish-American war. The shooting of Mora by the Negro last night is a very simple story. At the hour mentioned, three Negro women noticed two suspicious men sitting on a door step in the above locality. The women saw the two men making an apparent inspection of the building. As they told the story, they saw the men look over the fence and examine the window blinds, and they paid particular attention to the make-up of the building, which was a two-story affair. About that time Sergeant J.C. Aucoin and Officers Mora and J.D. Cantrell hove in sight. The women hailed them and described to them the suspicious actions of the two Negroes, who were still sitting on the step. The trio of bluecoats, on hearing the facts, at once crossed the street and accosted the men. The latter answered that they were waiting for a friend whom they were expecting. Not satisfied with this answer, the sergeant asked them where they lived, and they replied "down town," but could not designate the locality. To other questions put by the officers the larger of the two Negroes replied that they had been in town just three days.

As this reply was made, the larger man sprang to his feet, and Patrolman Mora, seeing that he was about to run away, seized him. The Negro took a firm hold on the officer, and a scuffle ensued. Mora, noting that he was not being assisted by his brother officers, drew his billy and struck the Negro on the head. The blow had but little effect upon the man, for he broke away and started down the street. When about ten feet away, the Negro drew his revolver and opened fire on the officer, firing three or four shots. The third shot struck Mora in the right hip, and was subsequently found to have taken an upward course. Although badly wounded, Mora drew his pistol and returned the fire. At his third shot the Negro was noticed to stagger, but he did not fall. He continued his flight. At this moment Sergeant Aucoin seized the other Negro, who proved to be a youth, Leon Pierce. As soon as Officer Mora was shot he sank to the sidewalk, and the other officer ran to the nearest telephone, and sent in a call for the ambulance. Upon its arrival the wounded officer was placed in it and conveyed to the hospital. An examination by the house surgeon revealed the fact that the bullet had taken an upward course. In the opinion of the surgeon the wound was a dangerous one.

But the best proof of the fact that the officers accosted the two colored men and without any warrant or other justification attempted to arrest them, and did actually seize and begin to club one of them, is shown by Officer Mora's own statement. The officer was wounded and had every reason in the world to make his side of the story as good as possible. His statement was made to a *Picayune* reporter and the same was published on the twenty-fifth inst., and is as follows:

I was in the neighborhood of Dryades and Washington Streets, with Sergeant Aucoin and Officer Cantrell, when three Negro women came up and told us that there were two suspicious-looking Negroes sitting on a step on Dryades Street, between Washington and Sixth. We went to the place indicated and found two Negroes. We interrogated them as to who they were, what they were doing and how long they had been here. They replied that they were working for some one and had been in town three days. At about this stage the larger of the two Negroes got up and I grabbed him. The Negro pulled, but I held fast, and he finally pulled me into the street. Here I began using my billet, and the Negro jerked from my grasp and ran. He then pulled a gun and fired. I pulled my gun and returned the fire, each of us firing about three shots. I saw the Negro stumble several times, and I thought I had shot him, but he ran away and I don't know whether any of my shots took effect. Sergeant Aucoin in the meantime held the other man fast. The man was about ten feet from me when he fired, and the three Negresses who told us about the men stood away about twenty-five feet from the shooting.

Thus far in the proceeding the Monday night episode results in Officer Mora lying in the station wounded in the hip; Leonard Pierce, one of the colored men, locked up in the station, and Robert Charles, the other colored man, a fugitive, wounded in the leg and sought for by the entire police force of New Orleans. Not sought for, however, to be placed under arrest and given a fair trial and punished if found guilty according to the law of the land, but sought for by a host of enraged, vindictive and fearless officers, who were coolly ordered to kill him on sight. This order is shown by the *Picayune* of the twenty-sixth inst., in which the following statement appears:

In talking to the sergeant about the case, the captain asked about the Negro's fighting ability, and the sergeant answered that Charles, though he called him Robinson then, was a desperate man, and it would be best to shoot him before he was given a chance to draw his pistol upon any of the officers.

This instruction was given before anybody had been killed, and the only evidence that Charles was a desperate man lay in the fact that he had refused to be beaten over the head by Officer Mora for sitting on a step quietly conversing with a friend. Charles resisted an absolutely unlawful attack, and a gun fight followed. Both Mora and Charles were shot, but because Mora was white and Charles was black, Charles was at once declared to be a desperado, made an outlaw, and subsequently a price put upon his head and the mob authorized to shoot him like a dog, on sight...

Legal sanction was given to the mob or any man of the mob to kill Charles at sight by the Mayor of New Orleans, who publically proclaimed a reward of two hundred and fifty dollars, not for the arrest of Charles, not at all, but the reward was offered for Charles's body, "dead or alive." The advertisement was as follows:

$250 Reward

Under the authority vested in me by law, I hereby offer, in the name of the city of New Orleans, $250 reward for the capture and delivery, dead or alive, to the authorities of the city, the body of the Negro murderer,

Robert Charles,

who, on Tuesday morning, July 24, shot and killed
Police Captain John T. Day and Patrolman Peter J. Lamb, and wounded
Patrolman August T. Mora.
PAUL CAPDEVIELLE, Mayor

This authority, given by the sergeant to kill Charles on sight, would have been no news to Charles, nor to any colored man in New Orleans, who, for any purpose whatever, even to save his life, raised his hand against a white man. It is now, even as it was in the days of slavery, an unpardonable sin for a Negro to resist a white man, no matter how unjust or unprovoked the white man's attack may be. Charles knew this, and knowing to be captured meant to be killed, he resolved to sell his life as dearly as possible.

SOURCE

Ida B. Wells-Barnett, *Mob Rule in New Orleans: Robert Charles and his Fight to Death, The Story of his Life, Burning Human Beings Alive, Other Lynching Statistics.* Project Gutenburg,1900. February 8, 2005. http://www.gutenberg.org/files/14976/14976-h/14976-h.htm (accessed March 21, 2016).

Ida B. Wells-Barnett, *The Arkansas Race Riot*, 1920

Headnote:

In this selection, focusing on the beginning and ending of her essay, Wells-Barnett examines the causes and consequences of the race riot. She begins by describing the sharecropping system and its inherent inequity, moving into the court proceedings and quoting them verbatim, drawing attention to the witnesses called, cross-examinations, and re-directs. In the end, she discusses the motion for a new trial, using the words of the defendant's representation to demonstrate the inherent unfairness in the legal system. Her mature, focused, and measured prose is interrupted less by her own points of view and instead is intended to stand on its own. The contrast between this later writing and her earlier pamphlets in both style and focus demonstrate her ability to develop new approaches for new audiences and her growing emphasis on the inequities in the legal system.

Excerpt:

Chapter ii.

Their Crime

The terrible crime these men had committed was to organize their members into a union for the purpose of getting the market price for their cotton, to buy land of their own and to employ a lawyer to get settlements of their accounts with their white landlords. Cotton was selling for more than ever before in their lives. These Negroes believed their chance had come to make some money for themselves and get out from under the white landlord's thumb.

Phillips County got plenty Negro labor to till the land and they toiled with a will to raise the cotton crops of 1919, which would make them independent at last. Most of these men and their families had worked for years "on shares" and had come out every year in debt or just barely out. The price of cotton had been low, and the landlord who furnished the land and supplies saw to it that the Negro laborer remained in his clutches from years to year. Always the owner or agent who rents the land owns a general store or opens an account for the tenant where he must trade and pay the prices charged or get no food and supplies for himself family or hired hands. The season begins in March and lasts till the cotton is picked and ginned in October and November. So that for the period of nine months the cropper is dependent on the landlord for supplies. He receives no money until cotton is sold and settlements are made.

When cotton is ready to be marketed, the landlord simply tells the cropper what his bill for the year is and what he will allow him for his crop. As a rule the bill for supplies is almost always greater than the amount due the hardworking Negro and his family, and he has not been able to help himself. He must stay on the farm another year or be turned adrift to go to work on another farm under the same conditions. If he leaves in debt the laws of the state make it a penal offense.

Thousands of Negro farmers have worked under this economic slavery for years...

The colored men who went to war for this democracy returned home determined to emancipate themselves from the slavery which took all a man and his family could earn, left him in debt, gave him no freedom of action, no protection for his life or property, no education for his children, but did give him Jim Crow cars, lynching and disfranchisement. If they could get all the farmers in that neighborhood to join an organization they could employ a lawyer to look after settlements at the end of the year; they could create a treasury and buy a tract of land for themselves; they could get all the farmers to hold their cotton for higher prices.

Is it any wonder the idea spread like wild-fire? The Progressive Farmers and Household Union of America had been revived the year before, and when Robert L. Hill came among them with the plan the meetings were crowded with men and women bringing their money to join. There is not a word in the constitution and by-laws of this order about conspiracy to murder white people, as will be seen by the reader of this book...

Motion For a New Trial

It was on this testimony that Frank Hicks, Ed Ware and the other ten men were sentenced to die in the electric chair. After agitation by lovers of justice against this unjust finding, able counsel in Little Rock was engaged to make motion for a new trial and the following is the exact wording of that motion:

Defendant, Frank Hicks, moves and prays the Court to set aside the verdict of the jury therein, and grant and give him a new trial herein, for the following reasons:

He is a Negro of the African race, and was at the time of the trial, and for a long time previous thereto a citizen of the United States and the State of Arkansas, and a resident of Phillips County;

That the deceased Clinton Lee, whom defendant is charged by the indictment with murdering, was killed on the 1st of October, 1919, by some person unknown to defendant, in a deadly conflict following a disturbance between the white and black races of said county, on the night previous; for which he was in no way responsible;

That the excitement of the white residents and citizens of said county was intense, and their feelings against the blacks including the defendant, bitter, active and persistent;

That in the course of it, some four or five white men and a large number of Negroes were killed, from 50 to 100.

That on or about the said first day of October, 1919, defendant was, along with many other Negroes, 200 or more, taken into custody by said whites, carried to the county jail and there kept in close custody and confinement until he was indicted and put upon trial;

That at the time of the returning of said indictment and trial, said excitement and bitterness of feeling among the whites of said county, against the Negroes, especially against the defendant, was unabated and still at the height of intensity;

That this feeling among the whites was coextensive with the county; that during his confinement he was frequently subjected to torture for the purpose of extracting from him admission of guilt—as were others then also in custody, to force them to testify against the defendant;

That he was given no opportunity to consult with friends, or to seek assistance for defense or relief, nor was he even informed of the charges against him until after his indictment;

That while he was thus confined, several hundred white men of said county, assembled at or near the court house and jail for the purpose of mobbing him, and were only prevented from doing so, as defendant is informed and believes, by the presence of United States soldiers;

That the indictment was returned on the 20th of October, 1919, by the grand jury composed wholly of white man; That on the 30th of the same month subpoenas for the State's witnesses were issued, to appear and testify in his case on the 3rd of November following;

That on the said 3rd day of November, without ever having been permitted to see or talk with any attorney, or any person in reference to his defense, he was carried from the jail to the court room and put upon trial—the court appointed an attorney for him, before a jury composed of white men;

That the excitement and feeling against the defendant among the whites of the said county was such that it was impossible to obtain an unprejudiced jury of white men to try him—and that no white jury, being fairly disposed, would have had the courage to acquit him regardless of the testimony;

That the trial proceeded without consultation on his part, with any attorney, without witnesses in his behalf, and without an opportunity on his part to obtain witnesses or prepare for defense;

That no evidence was offered in his behalf;

That he had no knowledge or familiarity with Court procedure, had never been at a trial in Court before, and had no definite idea of his rights therein, and had no conception of what steps should be taken for his protection;

That the whole course of trial, from beginning to end, occupied about three-fourths of an hour;

That the jury after hearing the State's evidence and the Court's charge retired and returned immediately; that is, within about from three to six minutes with a verdict of guilty against the defendant.

Defendant, Frank Hicks, further says that no copy of the indictment was ever served upon him nor upon any attorney for him, and he says that he never consented to waive such service, nor requested nor consented to the trial without same. Defendant, therefore, says that he was convicted and sentenced to death without due process of law.

That under the law as it has existed for many years, the Circuit Courts of the state at each term appoint jury commissioners to select grand and petit jurors to serve at the succeeding term; and for more than thirty years it has been the unbroken practice of said courts to appoint only white men on such commissions, and of such commissions to select only white men for grand and petit jurors for the succeeding terms—constituting a discrimination in the administration of the law against the Negroes, on account of their color and of their being members of the African race; and that if in the course of the Court's proceedings it became or becomes necessary to issue a venire for talesmen, to the sheriff, the invariable course is, and has been, to summon only white men; this practice, with reference to the selection of grand and petit jurors, and the summoning of talesmen, prevails and has prevailed in the Circuit Court of Phillips County, with unbroken uniformity, to the extent that no Negro has been appointed on a jury commission, or selected to serve as a juror, either grand or petit, for more than thirty years, and that no Negro has been appointed to or has sat upon any jury in said Court at any time during such period; that the Negro population of said county exceeds the whites at least five to one and that among them are a great many men, possessed of the intellectual, moral and legal qualification for jury commissioner, and for grand and petit jurors; and that they are excluded therefrom solely on account of their race and color.

That defendant has thus been, by said discriminating practices, and by said trial, deprived of his rights under the Constitution of the United States, and especially the Fourteenth Amendment thereto; and was in and by said trial and proceedings and still is, denied equal protection of the law.

Defendant further says, that while it is true, as he is now advised, that the proper and regular place and time to have objected to the grand jury, and to the indictment returned by it, would have been before the trial yet as before stated, he knew nothing about such proceeding or the proper order thereof; and was given no opportunity to object to the grand jury, or any member thereof, and knew nothing of his rights to raise any objections to either grand or petit jury; and nothing about how to challenge or object to either of them, and was not advised in that regard...

Chapter xi

The six men who were sent back to Phillips County by the Supreme Courts decision have been tried again in the Circuit Court and again sentenced to death—the faulty wording of the indictment this time having been corrected. In sending out the report of the same the Associated Press dispatch made again the charge that those Negroes were organized to kill white people and *seize their property*.

The dispatch reads as follows:

TRY SIX COLORED MEN

Second Trial of Accused Rioters in Arkansas.

Helena Ark., May 3.—Six Negroes sentenced to death for alleged participation in the Phillips County race disturbance last October, faced retrial here today. Ben Helm, Negro recently arrested, also will be tried on a first degree murder charge. The retrial was ordered because of faulty wording of the verdict.

Seventy five Negroes have been convicted of participation in the disorder, which resulted in the death of five white persons and unknown number of Negroes, and which were not controlled until Federal troops were sent into the district.

Of those convicted, 12 received sentence of death and 53 prison terms ranging from one to 21 years.

The disturbance according to evidence adduced at the original trials, was the premature outbreak of an insurrection followed by the Progressive Farmers and Household Union of of [sic] America, a Negro organization, the purpose of which it is said was the annihilation of all whites and the seizure of their property.

The American thinking public cannot bring back the dead but it can open the prison doors and let these poor defenseless men go tree. There must be enough justice in Arkansas to rest until this great wrong is righted. Not until this is done and the peonage system ended can Arkansas take her place among the brave and the free.

Governor Brough has started the movement. Let the Christian, moral and legal forces "carry on" until these black men are given their lives and their freedom and Arkansas cleans her skirts of this awful disgrace. When black men can receive protection to life and liberty and property, they will gladly give their labor for the prosperity of the South. As long as this dastardly crime is condoned, shielded and encouraged by white men, black men whose labor is needed for its development will avoid the state and leave the South to ruin and desolation as they are doing every day.

Meanwhile this booklet goes into the greatest court in the world and before the bar of public opinion pleads the cases of these helpless men. Every reader a member of that bar and the white people of Arkansas—the honest, law-abiding christian men and women of that state—are the judges and jury to whom this appeal is made. They are urged for the honor of the state and its material welfare to investigate the facts given in this book in an unprejudiced and impartial manner and if they are found to be true—these people will know what steps to take to right the great wrong done to these innocent hardworking men. If they are given freedom and opportunity, protection of the law for life and liberty—they will prove the greatest economic asset of the state. If not and this outrage is approved by the great Court of white public opinion in Arkansas, it will mean the lost [sic] of millions of dollars to the state, because Negroes will not remain in the state unless this great wrong is righted.

This is the answer to those who are honestly seeking a plan to stop Negro emigration from the farms of Arkansas. Put a stop to the plan of taking the fruit of the Negro's labor as was done at Elaine and Hoop Spur last October and is being done all over Arkansas where Negroes work the farms of white men.

SOURCE

Ida B. Wells Barnett, *The Arkansas Race Riot* (Chicago: Mrs. Ida B. Wells-Barnett, 1920). Excerpts.

BIBLIOGRAPHY

ARCHIVES

Department of Special Collections, Joseph Regenstein Library, University of Chicago, Illinois Ida B. Wells Papers

Library of Congress, Washington, D.C. National Association for the Advancement of Colored People Papers

National Museum of American History, Smithsonian Institute, Washington, D.C. Warshaw Collection of Business Americana

PRIMARY SOURCES

"15th Amendment to the Constitution." *The Library of Congress*, 1870. loc.gov/rr/program/bib/ourdocs/15thamendment.html (accessed March 21, 2016).

Acts of the State of Tennessee Passed at the General Assembly (Nashville: Albert B. Tavel, Printer to the State, 1891), chapter 52 (March 27), pp. 135–36.

Addams, Jane. "Respect for Law," in *Lynching and Rape: An Exchange of Views*, edited by Bettina Aptheker. New York: American Institute for Marxist Studies, 1977.

Allen, James. *Without Sanctuary: Lynching Photography in America*. Santa Fe: Twin Palms, 2000.

Bruce, Philip Alexander. *The Plantation Negro as a Freeman; Observations on His Character, Condition, and Prospects in Virginia*. New York: G. P. Putnam's Sons, 1889.

Chesapeake, O. & S.W. R.R. v. Wells. 1885a. Trial Record. No. 312, Circuit Court of Shelby County.

Chesapeake, O. & S.W. R.R. v. Wells. 1885b. Trial Record. No. 319, Circuit Court of Shelby County.

Chesapeake, O. & S.W. R.R. v. Wells. 1887. 4 S.W. 5 (Tenn.).

Civil Rights Act of 1875, 18 Stat. 335 (March 1, 1875).

Clanahan, W. L. "Will James, 'the Froggie,' Lynched in Cairo." *New York Age*, November 14, 1909. November 11, 2009. http://www.executedtoday.com/2009/11/11/1909-will-james-the-froggie-lynched-cairo-illinois/ (accessed March 21, 2016).

Cooper, Anna J. *A Voice from the South*. Xenia: The Aldine Printing House, 1892.

Corporation Laws of Tennessee: Including Counties and Municipalities, Also Federal Corporation Income Tax Law, Revised and Annotated, James L. Watts, ed. (Nashville: Marshall & Bruce Co. Publishers, 1910), chapter 155 (April 7, 1881), pp. 400–1.

Cutler, James. *Lynch-Law: An Investigation into the History of Lynching in the United States*. New York: Negro Universities Press, 1969.

Douglass, Frederick. *Narrative of the Life of Frederick Douglass, an American Slave. Written by Himself*. Boston: The Anti-Slavery Office, 1845.

———. "Lynch Law in the South." *The North American Review* 155 (July 1892): 17–24.

Du Bois, William Edward Burghardt. *The Souls of Black Folk*. Chicago: Project Bartleby, 1903.

———. *Efforts for Social Betterment among Negro Americans*. Atlanta: The Atlanta University Press, 1909.

———. "The Horizon." *The Crisis: A Record of the Darker Races* 15, no. 4 (1918): 157–208.

———. "Returning Soldiers." *The Crisis: A Record of the Darker Races* 18, no. 1 (1919): 13–14.

Duster, Alfreda, and Marcia McAdoo Greenlee. "Black Women Oral History Project. Interviews of The Black Women Oral History Project, 1976–1981." Schlesinger Library, Radcliffe Institute, March 8 and 9, 1978.

Editorial. "The Freedmen's Bureau The Bills Before Congress To-Day." *The New York Times*, February 9, 1865. http://www.nytimes.com/1865/02/09/news/the-freedmen-s-bureau-th (accessed March 21, 2016).

Editorial. "Illinois Women Participate in Suffrage Parade. This State Was Well Represented in Washington." *The Chicago Daily Tribune*, March 5, 1913.

Fortune, Timothy Thomas. *Black and White: Land, Labor, and Politics in the South*. New York: Fords, Howard, & Hulbert, 1884.

"Fortune and His Echo." *Freeman*, April 19, 1890.

Harper, Ida Husted. *The Life and Work of Susan B. Anthony: Including Public Addresses, Her Own Letters and Many from Her Contemporaries During Fifty Years, Volume III*. Indianapolis: Bowen-Merrill Company, 1908.

The Huffington Post, "Chicago Most Segregated City In America, Despite Significant Improvements In Last Decade." *The Huffington Post*. January 21, 2012, http://www.huffingtonpost.com/2012/01/31/chicago-most-segregated-c_n_1244098.html (accessed March 30, 2016).

"Miss Ida B. Wells, A Lecture." *Washington Bee*, October 22, 1892.

Moore et al. v. Dempsey, Keeper of Arkansas State Penitentiary. (1923) 261 U. S. 86.

Page, Thomas Nelson. *Among the Camps, or Young People's Stories of the War*. New York: Charles Scribner's Sons, 1891.

———. "A Southerner on the Negro Question." *The North American Review* 154 (April 1892): 401–13.

———. *Two Little Confederates*. New York: Charles Scribner's Sons, 1932.

"Sharecropper Contract, 1867." *The Gilder Lehrman Institute of American History*. n.d. http://www.gilderlehrman.org/history-by-era/reconstruction/resources/sharecropper-contract-1867 (accessed March 21, 2016).

St. Pierre Ruffin, Josephine. "Address to the First National Conference of Colored Women." *Woman's Era* 2 (August 1895): 13–15.

Terrell, Mary Church. "The Progress of Colored Women." Address to the National American Women's Suffrage Association, Washington, D.C. February 18, 1898.

———. "Lynching from a Negro's Point of View." *North American Review* 178 (1904): 853–68.

———. *A Colored Woman in a White World*. Amherst: Humanity Books, 1940.

"The Race Problem: Miss Willard on the Political Puzzle of the South." *The Voice* (New York), October 23, 1890.

Tillinghast, Joseph Alexander. "The Negro in Africa and America." *Publications of the American Economic Association* 3 (1902): 407–636.

Washington, Booker T. *Up from Slavery: An Autobiography*. Garden City: Doubleday & Company, Inc., 1901.

Wells, Ida B. *Southern Horrors: Lynch Law in All Its Phases*. 2013 edition. CreateSpace Independent Publishing Platform, 1892. February 8, 2005. http://www.gutenberg.org/files/14975/14975-h/14975-h.htm (accessed March 21, 2016).

———. *Crusade for Justice: The Autobiography of Ida B. Wells*, edited by Alfreda M. Duster. Chicago: The University Press of Chicago, 1970.

Wells, Ida B. *The Red Record: Tabulated Statistics and Alleged Causes of Lynching in the United States*. Chicago: Donohue & Henneberry, 1895.

Wells, Ida B., Frederick Douglass, Irvine Garland Penn, and Ferdinand Lee Barnett. *The Reason Why the Colored American is Not in the World's Columbian Exposition.* 1999 edition. Urbana: University of Illinois Press, 1893.

Wells-Barnett, Ida B. "Lynch Law in America." *The Arena* 23, no. 1 (January 1900): 15–24.

———. *Mob Rule in New Orleans: Robert Charles and His Fight to Death, the Story of His Life, Burning Human Beings Alive, Other Lynching Statistics.* Project Gutenburg, 1900. February 8, 2005. http://www.gutenberg.org/files/14976/14976-h/14976-h.htm (accessed March 21, 2016).

———. *The East St. Louis Massacre: The Greatest Outrage of the Century.* Chicago: The Negro Fellowship Herald Press, 1917.

———. *The Arkansas Race Riot.* Chicago: Mrs. Ida B. Wells-Barnett, 1920.

Wells-Barnett, Ida B., and Jacqueline Jones Royster. *Southern Horrors and Other Writings: The Anti-Lynching Campaign of Ida B. Wells, 1892–1900.* Boston: Bedford Books, 1997.

White, Walter. *A Man Called White: The Autobiography of Walter White.* Bloomington: Indiana University Press, 1948.

———. *Rope & Faggot: A Biography of Judge Lynch.* Notre Dame: University of Notre Dame Press, 2002.

Woolley, Celia Parker. *Practical Work among the Colored People.* Chicago: Frederick Douglass Center, 1906.

SECONDARY SOURCES

Abdullah, Melina A. "The Emergence of a Black Feminist Leadership Model: African-American Women and Political Activism in the Nineteenth Century." In *Black Women's Intellectual Traditions: Speaking Their Minds,* edited by Kristin Waters and Carol B. Conaway. Lebanon: University of Vermont Press, 2007, 328–45.

Anderson, Linda. *Autobiography.* New York: Routledge, 2001.

Ayers, Edward. *Promise of the New South: Life after Reconstruction.* New York: Oxford University Press, 1993.

———. "An American Nightmare: A Heartbreaking History of Segregation and Its Target Population." *The New York Times on the Web,* May 3, 1998. https://www.nytimes.com/books/98/05/03/reviews/980503.03ayrest.html (accessed March 21, 2016).

Barbeau, Arthur E. and Henri Florette. *The Unknown Soldiers: Black American Troops in World War I.* Philadelphia: Temple University Press, 1974.

Bardaglio, Peter. "Rape and Law in the Old South: 'Calculated to Excite Indignation in Every Heart.'" *The Journal of Southern History* 60 (1994): 749–72.

Barnard, Amii Larkin. "The Application of Critical Race Feminism to the Anti-Lynching Movement: Black Women's Fight against Race and Gender Ideology, 1892–1920." *UCLA Women's Law Journal* 3, no. 27 (1993): 1–38.

Bates, Beth Tompkins. "A New Crowd Challenges the Agenda of the Old Guard in the NAACP, 1933–1941." *The American Historical Review* 102, no. 2 (1997): 340–77.

———. *Pullman Porters and the Rise of Protest Politics in Black America, 1925–1945.* Chapel Hill: University of North Carolina Press, 2001.

Bay, Mia. "The Improbable Ida B. Wells." *Reviews in American History* 30, no. 3 (2002): 439–44.

———. *To Tell the Truth Freely: The Life of Ida B. Wells.* New York: Hill and Wang, 2009.

Beales, Marcia. "Premiere at the Chicago Historical Society: To Save a Kinsman: Ida B. Wells in the Case of Steve Green." *Chicago History* 8, no. 2 (1979): 111.

Beard, Charles A. and Mary R. *History of the United States.* New York: Macmillan Company, 1921.

Beck, E. M., and Stewart E. Tolnay. "When Race Didn't Matter: Black and White Mob Violence against Their Own Color." In *Under Sentence of Death, Lynching in the South,* edited by William Fitzhugh Brundage. Chapel Hill: University of North Carolina Press, 1997, 132–54.

Bederman, Gail. "'Civilization,' the Decline of Middle-Class Manliness, and Ida B. Wells's Anti-lynching Campaign (1892–94)." *Radical History Review* 52 (1992): 5–30.

———. *Manliness & Civilization: A Cultural History of Gender and Race in the United States, 1880–1917*. Chicago: University of Chicago Press, 1995.

Bergman, Jill. "'They Say': Ida B. Wells and the Reconstruction of Race (Review)." *Legacy: A Journal of American Women Writers* 27, no. 1 (2010): 222–23.

Blumenthal, Henry. "Woodrow Wilson and the Race Question." *The Journal of Negro History* 48, no. 1 (1963): 1–21.

Bogen, David S. "Why the Supreme Court Lied in Plessy." *Villanova Law Review* 52, no. 3 (2007): 411–470.

Bogira, Steve. "Separate, Unequal, and Ignored: Racial Segregation Remains Chicago's Most Fundamental Problem. Why Isn't It an Issue in the Mayor's Race?" *Reader*, February 10, 2011. http://www.chicagoreader.com/chicago/chicago-politics-segregation-african-american-black-white-hispanic-latino-population-census-community/Content?oid=3221712 (accessed March 21, 2016).

Bolotin, Norm, and Christine Laing. *The World's Columbian Exposition: The Chicago World's Fair of 1893*. Urbana: University of Illinois Press, 2002.

Braden, Anne. *The Wall Between*. New York: Monthly Review Press, 1958.

Brown, Elsa Barkley. "Negotiating and Transforming the Public Sphere: African American Political Life in the Transition from Slavery to Freedom." *Public Culture* 7 (1994): 107–46.

Brown, Mary Jane. *Eradicating This Evil: Women in the American Anti-lynching Movement, 1892–1940*. New York: Garland Publishing, 2000.

Brundage, William Fitzhugh. *Lynching in the New South: Georgia and Virginia, 1880–1930*. Urbana: University of Illinois Press, 1993.

Butler, Cheryl Nelson. "Blackness as Delinquency." *Washington University Law Review* 90 (2013): 1,335–97.

Campbell, Cory. "Revels, Hiram Rhoades." *The Online Reference Guide to African American History*. 2007–15. http://www.blackpast.org/aah/revels-hiram-rhoades-1827-1901 (accessed March 21, 2016).

Carby, Hazel V. "'On the Threshold of Woman's Era': Lynching, Empire, and Sexuality in Black Feminist Theory." *Critical Inquiry* 12, no. 1 (1985): 262–77.

Cartwright, Joseph H. *The Triumph of Jim Crow: Tennessee Race Relations in the 1880s*. Knoxville: University of Tennessee Press, 1976.

Cash, W. J. *The Mind of the South*. New York: Houghton Mifflin, 1941.

Cell, John W. *The Highest Stage of White Supremacy: The Origins of Segregation in South Africa and the American South*. Cambridge: Cambridge University Press, 1982.

Chandler, Susan. "Addie Hunton and the Construction of an African American Female Peace Perspective." *Affilia* 20 (Fall 2005): 270–83.

Chestnut, Trichita M. "Lynching: Ida B. Wells-Barnett and the Outrage over the Frazier Baker Murder." *Prologue* (Fall 2008): 21–29.

Clinton, Catherine. "Bloody Terrain: Freedwomen, Sexuality and Violence during Reconstruction." *The Georgia Historical Quarterly* 76, no. 2 (1992): 313–32.

Committee, Ida B. Wells Commemorative Art. "Ida B. Wells Monument," 2015. http://www.idabwellsmonument.org (accessed March 3, 2016).

Cooper, Brittney. "A'n't I a Lady?: Race Women, Michelle Obama, and the Ever-Expanding Democratic Imagination." *MELUS (Multi-Ethnic Literatures of the U.S.)* 35, no. 4 (2010): 39–57.

Corliss, Richard. "D.W. Griffith's The Birth of a Nation 100 Years Later: Still Great, Still Shameful." *Time*, 2015. http://time.com/3729807/d-w-griffiths-the-birth-of-a-nation-10 (accessed March 21, 2016).

Cronon, E. David. *Black Moses: The Story of Marcus Garvey and the Universal Negro Improvement Association*. Madison: University of Wisconsin Press, 1969.

Curry, Tommy J. "The Fortune of Wells: Ida B. Wells-Barnett's Use of T. Thomas Fortune's Philosophy of Social Agitation as a Prolegomenon to Militant Civil Rights Activism." *Transactions of the Charles S. Peirce Society* 48, no. 4 (2012): 456–82.

Darian-Smith, Eve. "Re-Reading W. E. B. Du Bois: The Global Dimensions of the US Civil Rights Struggle." *Journal of Global History* 7, no. 3 (2012): 483–505.

Davidson, James West. *"They Say": Ida B. Wells and the Reconstruction of Race*. New York: Oxford University Press, 2007.

Davis, Olga Idriss. "'I Rose and Found My Voice': Claiming 'Voice' in the Rhetoric of Ida B. Wells." In *Black Women's Intellectual Traditions: Speaking Their Minds*, edited by Kristin Waters and Carol B. Conaway. Lebanon: University of Vermont Press, 2007, 309–27.

Davis, Simone W. "The 'Weak Race' and the Winchester: Political Voices in the Pamphlets of Ida B. Wells-Barnett." *Legacy* 12, no. 2 (1995): 77–97.

D'Emilio, John, and Estelle B. Freedman. *Intimate Matters: A History of Sexuality in America*. Second edition. Chicago: University of Chicago Press, 1998.

D'ooge, Craig. "'The Birth of a Nation' Symposium on Classic Film Discusses Inaccuracies and Virtues." *Library of Congress Information Bulletin*, June 27, 1994. http://www.loc.gov/loc/lcib/94/9413/nation.html (accessed March 21, 2016).

Dray, Phillip. *At the Hands of Persons Unknown: The Lynching of Black America*. New York: Random House, 2002.

Dudden, Faye E. *Fighting Chance: The Struggle over Woman Suffrage and Black Suffrage in Reconstruction America*. New York: Oxford University Press, 2011.

DuRocher, Kristina. *Raising Racists: The Socialization of White Children in the Jim Crow South*. Lexington: The University Press of Kentucky, 2011.

Eagleton, Mary. "Ethical Reading: The Problem of Alice Walker's 'Advancing Luna- and Ida B. Wells' and J.M. Coetzee's Disgrace." *Feminist Theory* 2, no. 2 (2001): 189–203.

Eakin, Paul John. *How Our Lives Become Stories: Making Selves*. New York: Cornell University Press, 2001.

Eburne, Jonathan P. "Garveyism and Its Involutions." *African American Review* 47, no. 1 (2004): 1–19.

Edwards, Laura. *Gendered Strife and Confusion: The Political Culture of Reconstruction*. Urbana: University of Illinois Press, 1997.

Elliott, Mark. *Color Blind Justice: Albion Tourgée and the Quest for Racial Equality from the Civil War to Plessy v. Ferguson*. New York: Oxford University Press, 2008.

Ellis, Mark. *Race, War, and Surveillance: African Americans and the United States Government during World War I*. Bloomington: Indiana University Press, 2001.

Fairclough, Adam. *Better Day Coming: Blacks and Equality, 1890–2000*. New York: Penguin Books, 2002.

Feimster, Crystal N. *Southern Horrors: Women and the Politics of Rape and Lynching*. Cambridge, MA: Harvard University Press, 2009.

Ferrell, Claudine L. *Nightmare and Dream: Antilynching in Congress, 1917–1922*. New York: Garland Publishing, Inc., 1986.

Fields, Barbara. *Slavery and Freedom on the Middle Ground: Maryland during the Nineteenth Century*. New Haven: Yale University Press, 1985.

Finkelman, Paul. "Thomas R.R. Cobb and the Law of Negro Slavery." *Roger Williams University Law Review* 5, no. 1 (1999): 75–115.

Foner, Eric. *Reconstruction: America's Unfinished Revolution, 1863–1877*. New York: HarperCollins, 1988.

Ford III, James Edward. "Mob Rule in New Orleans: Anarchy, Governance, and Media Representation." *Biography* 33, no. 1 (2010): 185–208.

Foreman, P. Gabrielle. "The Memphis Diary of Ida B. Wells by Miriam DeCosta-Willis (review)." *African American Review* 31, no. 2 (1997): 363–65.

Foucault, Michel. *Discipline and Punish: The Birth of the Prison*. New York: Second Vintage Books Edition, 1995.

Fox-Genovese, Elizabeth. *Within the Plantation Household: Black and White Woman of the Old South*. Chapel Hill: University of North Carolina Press, 1988.

Franklin, John Hope. "The Enforcement of the Civil Rights Act of 1875." *Prologue Magazine* 6, no. 4 (1974): 225–35.

Frederickson, George M. *The Black Image in the White Mind: The Debate on Afro-American Character and Destiny, 1817–1914.* Middleport: Wesleyan University Press, 1971.

Friedman, Jean E. *The Enclosed Garden: Women and Community in the Evangelical South 1830–1900.* Chapel Hill: University of North Carolina Press, 1985.

Garnier, Katja von. *Iron Jawed Angels.* HBO Films, 2004.

Giddings, Paula J. *When and Where I Enter...: The Impact of Black Women on Race and Sex in America.* New York: William Morrow, 1984.

———. "Missing in Action Ida B. Wells, the NAACP, and the Historical Record." *Meridians* 1, no. 2 (2001): 1–17.

———. *Ida: A Sword among Lions, Ida B. Wells and the Campaign against Lynching.* New York: HarperColling Publishers, 2008.

Gilmore, Glenda. *Gender and Jim Crow: Women and the Politics of White Supremacy in North Carolina, 1896–1920.* Chapel Hill: University of North Carolina Press, 1996.

———. "Which Southerners? Which Southern Historians? A Century of Teaching Southern History at Yale." *The Yale Review,* January (2011): 56–69.

Ginzburg, Ralph. *100 Years of Lynchings.* Baltimore: Black Classic Press, 1988.

Gordon, Linda. "Black and White Visions of Welfare: Women's Welfare Activism, 1890–1945." *The Journal of American History* 78, no. 2 (1991): 559–90.

Gossett, Thomas F. *Race: The History of an Idea in America.* New York: Oxford University Press, 1997.

Hair, William Ivy. *Carnival of Fury: Robert Charles and the New Orleans Race Riot of 1900.* Baton Rouge: Louisana State University Press, 1976.

Hale, Grace. *Making Whiteness: The Culture of Segregation in the South 1890–1940.* New York: Pantheon Books, 1998.

Hall, Jacquelyn Dowd. "'The Mind That Burns in Each Body': Women, Rape, and Racial Violence." In *Powers of Desire: The Politics of Sexuality,* edited by Ann Snitow, Christine Stansell, and Sharon Thompson. New York: Monthly Review Press, 1983, 328–49.

———. *Revolt against Chivalry: Jessie Daniel Ames and the Women's Campaign against Lynching.* New York: Columbia University Press, 1993.

———. "'You Must Remember This': Autobiography as Social Critique." *Journal of American History* 85, no. 2 (September 1998): 439–65.

———. "'To Widen the Reach of Our Love:' Autobiography, History, and Desire." *Feminist Studies* 26, no. 1 (Spring 2000): 231–47.

Haller, Mark H. "Policy Gambling, Entertainment, and the Emergence of Black Politics: Chicago from 1900 to 1940." *Journal of Social History* 24, no. 4 (1991): 719–39.

Hamer, Fritz. "Wade Hampton: Conflicted Leader of the Conservative Democracy?", *Wade Hampton III—A Symposium.* Columbia: University of South Carolina, 2008.

Hamington, Maurice. "Public Pragmatism: Jane Addams and Ida B. Wells on Lynching." *The Journal of Speculative Philosophy* 19, no. 2 (2005): 167–74.

Hanson, Joyce Ann. *Mary McLeod Bethune and Black Women's Political Activism.* Columbia: University of Missouri Press, 2003.

Hardin, Robin, and Marcie Hinton. "The Squelching of Free Speech in Memphis: The Life of a Black Post-Reconstuction Newspaper." *Race, Gender & Class* 8, no. 4 (2001): 78–95.

Harris, J. William. "Etiquette, Lynching, and Racial Boundaries in Southern History: A Mississippi Example." *The American Historical Review* 100, no. 2 (April 1995): 387–410.

Harris, Sharon M. "'A New Era in Female History': Nineteenth-Century U.S. Women Writers." *American Literature* 74, no. 3 (2002): 603–18.

Hartman, Saidiya. *Scenes of Subjection: Terror, Slavery, and Self-Making in Nineteenth Century America.* New York: Oxford University Press, 1997.

Hatt, Michael. "Sculpting and Lynching: The Making and Unmaking of the Black Citizen in Late Nineteenth-Century America." *Oxford Art Journal* 24, no. 1 (2001): 3–22.

Hendricks, Wanda A. "'Vote for the Advantage of Ourselves and Our Race': The Election of the First Black Alderman in Chicago." *Illinois Historical Journal*, 87, no. 3 (1994): 171–84.

Higginbotham, Evelyn Brooks. *Righteous Discontent: The Women's Movement in the Black Baptist Church, 1880–1920*. Cambridge, MA: Harvard University Press, 1993.

Hixson, William B. Jr., *Moorfield Storey and the Abolitionist Tradition*. New York: Oxford University Press, 1972.

Hodes, Martha. *White Women Black Men: Illicit Sex in the Nineteenth-Century South*. New Haven: Yale University Press, 1997.

Hoganson, Kristin L. *Fighting for American Manhood: How Gender Politics Provoked the Spanish-American and Philippine-American Wars*. New Haven: Yale University Press, 1998.

Hunter, Tera W. *To 'Joy My Freedom: Southern Black Women's Lives and Labors after the Civil War*. Cambridge, MA: Harvard University Press, 1997.

James, Joy. "Shadowboxing: Liberation Limbos—Ida B. Wells." In *Black Women's Intellectual Traditions: Speaking Their Minds*, edited by Kristin Waters and Carol B. Conaway. Lebanon: University of Vermont Press, 2007, 346–64.

Jane Addams Hull-House Museum. "Jane Addams and Hull-House Museum: About Jane Addams," n.d., http://www.hullhousemuseum.org/about-jane-addams (accessed March, 21 2016).

Janken, Kenneth Robert. *White: The Biography of Walter White, Mr. NAACP*. New York: The New Press, 2003.

Jones, Jacqueline. *Labor of Love, Labor of Sorrow: Black Women, Work, and the Family from Slavery to the Present*. New York: Basic Books, 1985.

Karcher, C. L. "Ida B. Wells and Her Allies against Lynching: A Transnational Perspective." *Comparative American Studies* 3, no. 2 (2005): 131–51.

Keedy, Edwin R. "The Third Degree and Legal Interrogation of Suspects." *University of Pennsylvania Law Review* 85 (1937): 761–77.

Kern-Foxworth, Marilyn. *Aunt Jemima, Uncle Ben, and Rastus: Blacks in Advertising, Yesterday, Today, and Tomorrow*. Westport: Praeger, 1994.

Kimmel, Michael. *Manhood in America: A Cultural History*. New York: Free Press, 1996.

King, Nicole. "'A Colored Woman in Another Country Pleading for Justice in Her Own:' Ida B Wells in Great Britain." In *Black Victorians/Black Victoriana*, edited by Gretchen Holbrook Gerzina. New Jersey: Rutgers University Press, 2003, 88–109.

King, Preston. "Ida B. Wells and the Management of Violence." *Critical Review of International Social and Political Philosophy* 7, no. 4 (2004): 111–46.

Knupfer, Anne Meis. *"Toward a Tenderer Humanity and a Nobler Womanhood": African-American Women's Clubs in Chicago, 1890 to 1920*. New York: New York University Press, 1996.

———. "'To Become Good, Self-Supporting Women': The State Industrial School for Delinquent Girls at Geneva, Illinois, 1900–1935." *Journal of the History of Sexuality* 9, no. 4 (2000): 420–46.

Larson, Magali Sarfatti. *The Rise of Professionalism: A Sociological Analysis*. Berkeley: University of California Press, 1977.

Litwack, Leon F. *Trouble in Mind: Black Southerners in the Age of Jim Crow*. New York: Knopf, 1998.

Lowen, James. *Sundown Towns: A Hidden Dimension of American Racism*. New York: New Press, 2005.

Lumpkin, Katharine Du Pre. *The Making of a Southerner*. Athens: University of Georgia Press, 1991.

Lutes, Jean Marie. *Front-Page Girls: Women Journalists in American Culture and Fiction, 1880–1930*. Ithaca: Cornell University Press, 2006.

Mack, Kenneth W. "Law, Society, Identity, and the Making of the Jim Crow South: Travel and Segregation on Tennessee Railroads, 1875–1905." *Law and Social Inquiry* 24 (Spring 1999): 377–410.

MacLean, Nancy. *Behind the Mask of Chivalry: The Making of the Second Ku Klux Klan*. New York: Oxford University Press, 1994.

Manring, M. M. *Slave in a Box: The Strange Career of Aunt Jemima*. Charlottesville: University Press of Virginia, 1998.

Mathews, Donald G. "The Southern Rite of Human Sacrifice." *Journal of Southern Religion* v, no. III (August 2000). http://jsr.fsu.edu/mathews.htm (accessed March 21, 2016).

McMurry, Linda O. *To Keep the Waters Troubled: The Life of Ida B. Wells*. New York: Oxford University Press, 1998.

Miller, Kristie. "Ruth Hanna McCormick and the Senatorial Election of 1930." *Illinois Historical Journal* 81, no. 3 (1988): 191–210.

Mostern, Kenneth. "Three Theories of the Race of W. E. B. Du Bois." *Cultural Critique* 34 (1996): 27–63.

Murray, Gail. *American Children's Literature and the Construction of Childhood*. London: Twayne Publishers, 1998.

Nelson, Keith L. "The 'Black Horror on the Rhine': Race as a Factor in Post-World War I Diplomacy." *The Journal of Modern History* 42, no. 4 (1970): 606–27.

Newkirk, Pamela. "Ida B. Wells-Barnett: Journalism as a Weapon against Racial Bigotry." *Media Studies Journal* 14, no. 2 (2000). http://www.hartford-hwp.com/archives/45a/317.html (accessed March 21, 2016).

Nichols, Caroline C. "The 'Adventuress' Becomes a 'Lady': Ida B. Wells' British Tours." *Modern Language Studies* 38, no. 2 (2009): 46–63.

Olney, James. "Autobiographical Traditions Black and White." In *Located Lives: Place and Idea in Southern Autobiography*, edited by Bill J. Berry. Athens: University of Georgia Press, 1990, 66–77.

———. *Memory and Narrative: The Weave of Life Writing*. Chicago: University of Chicago Press, 2001.

Paddon, Anna R., and Sally Turner. "African Americans and the World's Columbian Exposition." *Illinois Historical Journal* 88, no. 1 (1995): 19–36.

Pascoe, Peggy. "Miscegenation, Court Cases, and Ideologies of 'Race' in Twentieth-Century America." *Journal of American History* 83, no. 1 (June 1996): 44–69.

Patrick, James. "The Horror of the East St. Louis Massacre." *Exodus*, February 22, 2000. http://www.usd116.org/profdev/ahtc/lessons/PollockFel10/4chorrorESL.pdf (accessed March 30, 2016).

Perkins, Linda M. "The Impact of the 'Cult of True Womanhood' on the Education of Black Women." *Journal of Social Issues* 39, no. 3 (1983): 17–28.

Pfeifer, Michael J. *Rough Justice: Lynching and American Society, 1874–1947*. Urbana: University of Illinois Press, 2004.

Phillips, Wendell. *Speeches, Lectures, and Letters*. Ann Arbor: University of Michigan Library, 2005.

Pilgrim, David. "'Who Was Jim Crow?'" Ferris State University, September 2010. http://www.ferris.edu/jimcrow/who.htm (accessed March 21, 2016).

———. "The Tom Caricature." *Ferris State University Jim Crow Museum of Racist Memorabilia*, December 2012. http://www.ferris.edu/jimcrow/tom/ (accessed March 21, 2016).

Rabinowitz, Howard N. *Race Relations in the Urban South, 1865–1890*. New York: Oxford University Press, 1978.

Rable, George C. "The South and the Politics of Antilynching Legislation, 1920–1940." *The Journal of Southern History* 51, no. 2 (1985): 201–20.

Raper, Arthur Franklin. *The Tragedy of Lynching*. Baltimore: Black Classic Press, 1933.

Reddick, Lawrence D. "Racial Attitudes in American History Textbooks of the South." *The Journal of Negro History* 19, no. 3 (1934): 225–65.

Reed, Touré F. *Not Alms but Opportunity: The Urban League & the Politics of Racial Uplift, 1910–1950*. Chapel Hill: University of North Carolina Press, 2008.

Richardson, Heather Cox. *The Death of Reconstruction: Race, Labor, and Politics in the Post-Civil War North, 1865–1901*. Cambridge, MA: Harvard University Press, 2001.

Roche, Roberta Senechal de la. *In Lincoln's Shadow: The 1908 Race Riot in Springfield, Illinois*. Carbondale: Southern Illinois University Press, 2008.

Rogin, Michael. "'The Sword became a Flashing Vision': D. W. Griffith's The Birth of a Nation." *Representations* 9 (Winter 1985): 150–95.

Rudwick, Elliott M., and August Meier. "Black Man in the 'White City': Negroes and the Columbian Exposition, 1893." *Phylon* 26, no. 4 (1965): 354–61.

Russo, Gus. *The Outfit: The Role of Chicago's Underworld in the Shaping of Modern America*. New York: Bloomsbury Press, 2002.

Rymph, Catherine E. *Republican Women: Feminism and Conservatism from Suffrage through the Rise of the New Right*. Chapel Hill: University of North Carolina Press, 2006.

Schechter, Patricia A. " 'All the Intensity of My Nature': Ida B. Wells, Anger, and Politics." *Radical History Review* 70 (1998): 48–77.

———. *Ida B. Wells-Barnett and American Reform, 1880–1930*. Chapel Hill: The University of North Carolina Press, 2001.

Schlesinger, Arthur. *The Crisis of the Old Order: 1919–1933 (The Age of Roosevelt, Vol. I)*. Boston: Houghton Mifflin, 1957.

Schuler, Edgar A. "The Houston Race Riot, 1917." *The Journal of Negro History* 29, no. 3 (1944): 300–38.

Schwalm, Leslie A. *A Hard Fight for We: Women's Transition from Slavery to Freedom in South Carolina*. Urbana: University of Illinois Press, 1997.

Senate Historical Office. "Former Slave Presides over Senate." *United States Senate: Senate History*. https://www.senate.gov/artandhistory/history/minute/Former_Slave_Presides_Over_Senate.htm (accessed March 21, 2016).

Shapiro, Herbert. *White Violence and Black Response: From Reconstruction to Montgomery*. Amherst: University of Massachusetts Press, 1988.

Sharp, Alan. *The Versailles Settlement: Peacemaking after the First World War, 1919–1923*. Second edition. New York: Palgrave Macmillan, 2008.

Simkins, Francis B. "Tolerating the South's Past." *Journal of Southern History* 21, no. 1 (1955): 3–16.

Smith, John David, and J. Vincent Lowery, eds, *The Dunning School: Historians, Race, and the Meaning of Reconstruction*. Lexington: University Press of Kentucky, 2013.

Smith, Sidonie, and Julia Watson. *Reading Autobiography: A Guide for Interpreting Life Narratives*. Minneapolis: University of Minnesota Press, 2002.

Sommerville, Diane Miller. "The Rape Myth in the Old South Reconsidered." *The Journal of Southern History* 61 (1995): 481–518.

———. *Rape and Race in the Nineteenth-Century South*. Chapel Hill: The University of North Carolina Press, 2004.

Spencer, Robyn. "Contested Terrain: The Mississippi Flood of 1927 and the Struggle to Control Black Labor." *The Journal of Negro History* 79, no. 2 (1994): 170–81.

Straughan, Dulcie. " 'Lifting as We Climb': The Role of The National Association Notes in Furthering the Issues Agenda of the National Association of Colored Women, 1897–1920." *Media History Monographs* 8, no. 2 (2006): 1–19.

Tambiah, Stanley J. "A Performance Approach to Ritual." In *Readings in Ritual Studies*, edited by Ronald Grimes. New Jersey: Prentice Hall, 1996, 495–510.

Thornbrough, Emma Lou. "The National Afro-American League, 1887–1908." *The Journal of Southern History* 27, no. 4 (1961): 494–512.

Tom, Brittany. "The Descendants: Ida B. Wells' Great Grandchildren Say She Was a 'Crusader' for All Injustices." *The Grio*, February 20, 2013. http://thegrio.com/2013/02/20/the-descendants-ida-b-wells-great-grandchildren-says-she-was-a-crusader-for-all-injustices/ (accessed March 21, 2016).

Totten, Gary. "Ida B. Wells and the Segregation: Embodying Cultural Work of Travel." *African American Review* 42, no. 1 (2008): 47–60.

Tourgée, Albion. *A Fool's Errand. By One of the Fools*. New York: Fords, Howard & Hulbert, 1879.

Townes, Emilie M. "Black Women and Social Evil: Ida B. Wells-Barnett's Social and Moral Perspectives as Resources for a Contemporary Afro-Feminist Social Ethic." *NWSA Journal* 1, no. 3 (1989): 568–69.

Tucker, David M. "Miss Ida B. Wells and Memphis Lynching." *Phylon* 32, no. 2 (1971): 112–22.

Tushnet, Mark V. *The NAACP's Legal Strategy against Segregated Education, 1925–1950*. Chapel Hill: University of North Carolina Press, 2005.

Tye, Larry. *Rising from the Rails: Pullman Porters and the Making of the Black Middle Class.* New York: Henry Holt & Company, Inc., 2004.

University of Alabama. "Genesis & Apocalypse of the 'Old South' Myth: Two Virginia Writers at the Turn of the Century." *Publisher's Bindings Online, 1815-1930: The Art of Books,* 2005. http://bindings.lib.ua.edu/gallery/nelson_page.html (accessed March 21, 2016).

University of Tennessee, School of Journalism & Electronic Media. "The Ida Initiative." *Ida B. & Beyond Conference,* September 16, 2013. https://theidainitiative.wordpress.com/ (accessed March 21, 2016).

Wade, Wyn Craig. *The Fiery Cross: The Ku Klux Klan in America.* New York: Simon and Schuster, 2005.

Waldrep, Christopher. *African Americans Confront Lynching: Strategies of Resistance from the Civil War to the Civil Rights Era.* New York: Rowman & Littlefield Publishers, 2009.

Washington, Reginald. "Sealing the Sacred Bonds of Holy Matrimony Freedmen's Bureau Marriage Records." *Prologue Magazine,* spring 2005. https://www.archives.gov/publications/prologue/2005/spring/freedman-marriage-recs.html (accessed March 21, 2016).

Waterman, John S., and Overton, Edward E. "The Aftermath of Moore v. Dempsey." *Washington University Law Review* 18, no. 2 (1993): 117–26.

Waters, Kristin. "Some Core Themes of Nineteenth-Century Black Feminism." In *Black Women's Intellectual Traditions: Speaking Their Minds,* edited by Kristin Waters and Carol B. Conaway. Lebanon: University of Vermont Press, 2007, 365–92.

Watkins, Ruth. "Reconstruction in Marshall County." *Publications of the Mississippi Historical Society* 12 (1912): 155–213.

Watkins, Rychetta N. "The Southern Roots of Ida B. Wells-Barnett's Revolutionary Activism." *Southern Quarterly* 45, no. 3 (2008): 108–27.

Wells, Ida B., *The Memphis Diary of Ida B. Wells: An Intimate Portrait of the Activist as a Young Woman,* ed. Miriam DeCosta-Willis. Boston: Beacon Press, 1995.

Welter, Barbara. "The Cult of True Womanhood: 1820–1860." *American Quarterly* 18, no. 2 (1966): 151–74.

White, Deborah Grey. *Too Heavy a Load: Black Women in Defense of Themselves, 1894–1994.* New York: W. W. Norton & Company, 1999.

Whites, LeeAnn. *The Civil War as a Crisis in Gender: Augusta, Georgia, 1860–1890.* Athens: University of Georgia Press, 2000.

Williams, Erma Brooks. *Political Empowerment of Illinois' African-American State Lawmakers from 1877 to 2005.* Lanham: University Press of America, 2008.

Williams, Joy Weatherley. "John Mitchell, Jr., and the Richmond Planet." *The Library of Virginia,* n.d. http://www.lva.virginia.gov/exhibits/mitchell/ (accessed March 21, 2016).

Williams, Joy Weatherley. "Lynch Law Must Go!" *The Library of Virginia,* n.d.

Williamson, Joel. *The Crucible of Race: Black/White Relations in the American South since Emancipation.* New York: Oxford University Press, 1984.

Wolgemuth, K. L. "Woodrow Wilson and Federal Segregation." *The Journal of Negro History* 44, no. 2 (1959): 158–73.

Wood, Amy Louise. *Lynching and Spectacle: Witnessing Racial Violence in America, 1890–1940.* Chapel Hill: University of North Carolina Press, 2009.

Woodward, C. Vann. *Origins of the New South, 1877–1913.* Baton Rouge: Louisiana State University Press, 1951.

———. *The Strange Career of Jim Crow.* New York: Oxford University Press, 1955.

Wyatt-Brown, Bertram. "The Civil Rights Act of 1875." *Western Political Quarterly* 18 (1965): 763–75.

INDEX